THE BIBLE CAN BE

UNLOCKING ANCIENT MYSTERIES OF A DIVINE IMPRINT

VINCE LATORRE

The Bible Can Be Proven – Unlocking Ancient Mysteries of a Divine Imprint
By Vincent R. Latorre

Published by HigherLife Development Services, Inc.
400 Fontana Circle
Building 1—Suite 105
Oviedo, Florida 32765
(407) 563-4806
www.ahigherlife.com

Unless otherwise noted, Scripture quotations are from the King James Version.

Cover Design: David Whitlock, Principle Design group

First Edition

12 13 14 15 — 9 8 7 6 5 4 3 2 1

Printed in the United States of America

ENDORSEMENTS

The Bible Can Be Proven contains a lot of good material to help assure believers that the Word of God can be trusted and provides possible solutions to passages and subjects that often trouble new believers.

Donald L. Brake, Ph. D. Dean Emeritus,
Multnomah Biblical Seminary Award winning author.

In *The Bible Can Be Proven*, Vince Latorre reveals biblical and scientific realities so many of us do not know. He merges historical facts and scriptural commentary, letting faith and reason work together. This book unlocks mysteries that Christ's followers need to know and those, who question Scripture, are seeking to learn.

Chris Maxwell
Emmanuel College Spiritual Life Director, Pastor, Speaker, and author

How can I describe this book? It's absolutely amazing. I found it impacting, informative, enlightening, and refreshingly different from any apologetic book I've read. My recommendation is that you get out your marker and go to work. You'll be glad you did.

Larry Titus
President of Kingdom Global Ministries

When I first met Vince Latorre, I was immediately impressed by his humble, thoughtful presentation. As I thumbed through his manuscript, I was wowed by his brilliance. In fact, I used this book as a resource in my homeschool classroom with my two teenagers this year. I hope this book gets into the hands of other young adults, especially those who struggle to believe and stare at the ceiling at night and ask, "Is the Bible really true?"

C. Hope Flinchbaugh
Editor, journalist, and award winning author

So many Christians are hesitant to get into any meaningful discussion about the authority and divine inspiration of the Bible. It's not because they don't believe it...they just don't feel armed with enough data to support what they believe. *The Bible Can Be Proven* is a marvelous tool that any Christ-follower can use to not only be encouraged and built up in their faith, but be emboldened to share that faith with others.

David Welday
President, Next Generation Institute

The culture is filled with Bible-talk, much miss-understood, taken out of context and post-modern perspective. *The Bible Can Be Proven* gives rare insight into Bible truth and will be a useful resource to those seeking real truth. As an educator, I wholeheartedly endorse this manuscript as a key tool to equip the Body of Christ for ministry.

Ossie Mills
Vice President of Advancement Oral Roberts University
and Winner of 3 Emmys, 10 Telly Awards, and multiple Communicator Awards.

Vince Latorre is always biblically oriented as an athlete to run the race for Christ's kingdom. Therefore, I endorse wholeheartedly *The Bible Can Be Proven* and I wish that all would take an opportunity to read it. I pray the Holy Spirit will work through this book to inspire as many as possible. I wish Vince great success in this endeavor.

Pastor John J. Puthuparampil
Elder of the United Methodist Upper NY Conference
and former pastor of Onondaga Hill United Methodist Church

To my parents, Jim and Faustina Latorre, who always demonstrated to me what Christian love is all about, and to my friends Raymond and Sherry, whose child-like faith and trust in God inspires me to all the more vigorously contend for that faith.

ACKNOWLEDGMENTS

This book began almost ten years ago, with me lugging stacks of reference books to park benches, scribbling in notebooks, researching on the internet and spending countless hours in libraries. When I finished the manuscript, I was praying for guidance as to how and where to proceed next. I thank the Lord for having an invitation card to the Philadelphia Writer's Conference mysteriously appear unsolicited in the mail, which compelled me to go to that same conference in 2009 and meet up with many talented writers, speakers, and editors. An open door from the Lord!

Of all the people I made contact with at the Philly conference, one stood out with her enthusiasm for the idea behind my book and for her encouragement to me—Hope Flinchbaugh, who was representing HigherLife Publishing. We kept in touch, and once I finished the manuscript, she worked many months with me to help me get started with the publishing process, as well as acting as an agent to pitch my book to major publishers. In retrospect, I am glad I got to publish with HigherLife, as they all seem to have that same encouraging way about them (must be a prerequisite for working there!) and are as excited about this book as I am. Thanks also to Dave Welday for laying out a comprehensive publishing plan and contract for me, as well for his involvement in marketing the book. Thank you also to Kristin Hester for her expert managing of the whole team responsible for this plan. Her enthusiasm is contagious, and she has also put in much time and has juggled many different tasks to help this book get out. Thanks also to Chris Maxwell for editing the content and helping me to cut out redundant items and shorten the text. My sympathies to him and also to the copyeditor for having to wade through the 400-plus footnotes! Thanks also to Wes Harbour in advance for his work in developing a marketing plan and the website. Thank you also to Dave Whitlock for drawing up a marketing contract and working on the website. And thank you to the typesetter (who had to wade through all my headings and sub-headings and sub-sub-headings) and all who will be involved in the printing and distribution process.

And a special thank you to everyone else associated with HigherLife for your roles in helping to get this book into people's hands.

Finally, I am thankful for the joy of knowing my Lord and Saviour, Jesus Christ, who gave His life for me, and for the gift of His marvelous Word, which I feel honored and privileged to be called on to defend.

TABLE OF CONTENTS

There are eleven main topics covered relating to both the uniqueness and trustworthiness of the Bible and also the evidence for the divine inspiration of the Bible's text.

These topics are:

Some of these topics discussed cover evidences of the trustworthiness of the Bible as a historical document but do not prove its divine inspiration. Rather, they are better classified as pointers to divine inspiration. The other sections contain definitive proof of divine inspiration and design of the Bible's text by one mind, the mind of God.

So, with all these claims and challenges, let's get into the Bible!

INTRODUCTION

While many people in America today are familiar with the Bible, an increasing majority do not believe it is authoritative for their beliefs or conduct. They do not see it as the inspired Word of God. Instead, it is thought to be a purely human product, a collection of nice stories with good morals. If inspired at all, it is in the sense that a human poet is inspired, or moved, by his/her surroundings to compose great art, rather than inspired by God to communicate to humankind.

Surprisingly, a significant number of people who don't take the Bible seriously are professing Christians—even pastors, priests, and clergy.

Why? There are many reasons. There are those who disagree with what the Bible says because it conflicts with their lifestyle—so they are more than happy to dismiss it. But there are also those who desire to believe the authority of the Bible and trust its promises as the foundation of their faith. Sadly, many in this second group are told by some "scholars" in the media that this notion is foolish.

I am writing this book to set the record straight. I believe the Bible is the inspired Word of God, an anchor for the Christian faith. I argue that this view can be proven and will show those proofs on the ensuing pages.

As the reader, do not blindly believe what you read. Challenge the claims. Examine the evidence for yourself. This practice is vitally important. Eternal consequences are just too significant.

When Christians depart from God's Word their faith is eventually "shipwrecked." For those who hold to the Christian faith this work is written to help dispel doubts and defend the faith. For those who are presently not Christians but are seeking truth and struggle with intellectual obstacles to faith, this book is an encouragement to examine the facts with an open mind that they may know the joy of believing.

CHAPTER ONE

AN ATTENTION-GETTING RÉSUMÉ

If the Bible is the inspired Word of God, then certain distinct, unique characteristics set it apart from all other literature on this planet. If we believe God created this world and universe, then it would make sense that He would also have the ability to send a written message we would recognize as being from Him. This is exactly what the Bible claims to be. If the Bible's teachings about the existence and deceptive methods of Satan are true, then we would also expect many counterfeit "words of god" to be produced, with the intent of confusing people so much that they simply throw up their hands and declare: "These 'words' must all be equal. We just can't know for sure which is the real word of God, since they all claim to be. We therefore can't come to any conclusions about which one is true."

We can demonstrate that the Bible differs from any other book on earth. We can demonstrate that the Bible differs from any other book on earth. There are many ways in which the bible is unique:"

UNITY IN DIVERSITY

? In what ways does the Bible show diversity?

The Bible contains sixty-six books, written by more than forty authors over a period of about fifteen hundred years. Its authors came from diverse walks of life, not one group or class of people. The Bible writers included priests, fishermen, kings, a doctor, and a tax collector, to name a few. It was written in three different languages, Hebrew, Aramaic, and Greek. It was written on three different continents, Asia, Africa, and Europe. There are many different writing styles such as poetry, law, prophecy, history, sayings, and parables, and correspondence. The Bible addresses multiple topics regarding morals, the nature of God, God's relation to mankind, spiritual truths, God's plan of salvation, etc. But given all of its diversity there is something amazing about this collection of books called the Bible.

? **The Bible's approximately forty authors wrote on many different topics, about which some people have had vastly differing opinions. If we collected a random group of books by forty authors who wrote about a particular topic, would they all agree?**

Not likely. Imagine a group of authors writing on the nature of God and God's relationship to mankind. Even if they were all from the same church, you would get some diverse concepts if they were just writing from their own human speculations. Even if they had similar backgrounds and were from the same period in history, you would get a whole spectrum of views.

? **When the Bible writers talk about a particular topic, do they all agree?**

The biblical writers, though diverse, show amazing agreement on a given topic. For example, the Bible writers basically agree on what is right and wrong, the nature of God, the way mankind is made right with God through faith, God's forgiveness and grace, how people can pray to God, and how we are to relate to God. There is one consistent theme throughout: man's inability to save him/herself and the need for redemption through a Messiah, or Savior.

The Bible is not sixty-six stories but is in essence one story from start to finish—the story of God's plan of redemption for humankind. It is the story of one person, Jesus Christ. In fact, both Jesus and the apostles used the Old Testament many times to show that the whole Bible spoke of Jesus and His redemption. The whole Bible indeed speaks of Jesus in many ways, as we shall see throughout this book.

? But some people say the Bible has many contradictions. So how does this affect this so-called unity?

When you examine these supposed contradictions closely and with sound interpretative principles you will actually see the unity of the Bible more clearly with the discoveries made from researching these "contradictions." I have seen no "contradiction" that does not have one or more satisfactory resolutions which in no way compromise the integrity of the whole Bible and in fact in some cases reveal previously undiscovered ways the Bible is tied together as one book.

? What does the unity of the Bible prove?

Many of the books of the Bible seem to have been written to expand on or clarify one another. In fact, the Bible turns out to be its own best commentary for that reason. Could all this be said of any other set of books? The consistency of the Bible is not a proof of inspiration, but it is hard to explain this unique feature if the Bible consists of error. By nature, error is haphazard, and truth is consistent. Could we imagine that the remarkable consistency of the Bible could be achieved by men who were deceivers? Would they even bother trying to make so many items look consistent or even have the ability to achieve it if they wanted to?

The Koran and the Book of Mormon were each written by one man (Mohammed and Joseph Smith, respectively). Yet they both contain proven historical errors and unreconciled contradictions, as we shall see.

The remainder of this book includes many examples which provide evidence that the Bible was designed by one mind.

THE CIRCULATION AND TRANSLATION OF THE BIBLE

? What is the all-time bestselling book in the world?

In terms of total circulation no book even approaches the Bible, which has sold not millions, but billions of copies! Now if a book were actually inspired by God you would expect it to be powerful. Why would the Bible sell so much? Perhaps because it meets a need of mankind that only God could know about and provide, being our Creator. And people are inspired to give it out, even for free. Personally, one example of the ubiquitous presence of the Bible that hits home for me is the

Bibles the Gideons place in hotels and motels. Pull open the nightstand drawer in almost every hotel, and there is a Bible placed by the Gideons. Is there any other book you can find in practically every room in every hotel (other than the phone book, and even they differ by location!)?

[?] **What book has been translated into the most languages?**

No other book, especially ancient literature, has been translated into so many languages as the Bible. Again, if this is a book from God, we would expect this to happen so that as many people as possible would have access to it.

THE BIBLE'S SURVIVAL

[?] **What book has been persecuted more than any other in history and yet has survived?**

The Bible has been the most persecuted book in history. Yet it has survived all of this persecution to remain the bestselling book in history. This makes sense based on what the Bible itself teaches. If Satan exists, as the Bible claims, it would seem he and his followers would attack any book from God like no other book. And since God always prevails, then despite all the persecution God would see to it that the Bible survives, and indeed it has survived the most intense attempts to eradicate it.

THE BIBLE'S IMPACT

[?] **What book has had the greatest impact on world leaders throughout history?**

The Bible's influence has extended all around the world throughout history. As a result, many great leaders and statesmen throughout history have had the greatest respect for the Bible. There are too many quotes to reproduce them all here, but I will give you a sample, with reference site attached.

"It is impossible to rightly govern without God and the Bible" (George Washington, *thinkexist.com/quotes*).

"The Bible is the Book of faith, and a Book of doctrine, and a Book of morals, and a Book of religion, of special revelation from God; but it is also a Book which teaches man his responsibility, his own dignity, and his equality with his fellow man" (Daniel Webster, June 17, 1843, speech at Bunker Hill Monument, Charlestown, MA, Burton Stevenson, the *Home Book of Quotations, Classical and Modern,* NY, Dodd, Mead and Co., 1967).

"Hold fast to the Bible as the steel anchor of our liberties; write its precepts on your heart and practise (sic) them in your lives. To the influence of this book we are indebted for the progress made in true civilization, and to this we must look for our guide in the future" (Ulysses Grant, *www.brainyquote.com*).

"The Bible is no mere book, but a living creature, with a power that conquers all that oppose it" (Napoleon*, thinkexist.com).*

There are many such quotes throughout history and from many nations. Note that none of the above quotes is from clergymen or theologians.

? Has history shown that the above statements are valid?

Evidence actually does exist for the high-sounding statements above. Again there is too much evidence to do the subject justice here, but I will give you some examples.

"When Charles Darwin first visited Tierra del Fuego, he found the inhabitants in a state of misery and moral degradation, but when he returned some years later, after the Bible had been introduced by missionaries, 'The change for the better was so indescribable that he not only testified his astonishment but became a regular contributor to the missionary society.'"[1]

"Some years ago, *Reader's Digest* carried a story titled 'Shimabuku the Village That Lives by the Bible.' It told how an advance patrol of American troops liberating the island of Okinawa were approaching a particular village when they were confronted by two old men carrying a Bible. Suspicious of a trap, they called for the chaplain, who said he felt they could go on. Entering the village, they found it spotless, the fields tilled and fertile, and everything a model of neatness and cleanliness totally unlike the other run-down villages they had seen. They soon discovered the reason for this amazing contrast. Thirty years earlier an American missionary on his way to Japan had called at Shimabuku and stayed long enough to leave behind two men who had come to believe in God. He also left a Japanese Bible, which he urged them to study and live by. Without any other outside human

---

1   John Blanchard, *Does God Believe in Atheists?* Evangelical Press, Auburn, MA, 2000, 411.

help the community had gradually been transformed. There was no jail, no brothel, no drunkenness, no divorce, a high standard of health and a remarkable spirit of social unity and happiness. Clarence Hall, the war correspondent who wrote the story, quoted the words of his dumbfounded driver: 'So this is what comes out of a Bible ... Maybe we are using the wrong weapons to change the world!'"[2]

THE CHARACTER AND NATURE OF THE BIBLE'S TEACHINGS

? How do the teachings of the Bible make it unique?

Many things can be said about the unique character of the Bible's teachings. Lewis S. Chafer, founder and former president of Dallas Theological Seminary, said: "The Bible is not such a book a man would write if he could, or could write if he would."

The Bible shows a connectedness with the human soul and insight into the soul's weaknesses and self-deceptions, as well as its deepest needs. This accounts for the Bible having transformed so many lives and is a testimony that the one who wrote it was also the Creator of human souls. It reads like an owner's manual for people. The teachings of the Bible are frank about the sinfulness of mankind, including some of the Bible's heroes like David or Abraham, and the powerlessness of people to save themselves. This contrasts greatly to other religions and their books, which lift the human condition up and tell us we can save ourselves, suspiciously sounding like what we would expect from a purely human product. We like to think we can lift ourselves up without help.

? How about such parts of the Bible we can't relate to, such as the existence of slavery?

Of course there are some parts we may not relate to when first read, because they were written in another time and culture in history. For example, some may read the books of Exodus and Leviticus and not understand why slavery wasn't abolished instead of being allowed.

But not only were the biblical laws concerning slavery far more just than any of that time, but you see a progression toward the equal treatment of people as we

---

2   Ibid., 414.

get into the New Testament, as God progressively takes us farther along morally. In fact, the book of Philemon in the New Testament, which teaches the treatment of a slave as a brother, was used by Christian abolitionists to eventually end slavery. This is in fact God's ultimate ideal, as seen in the book of Galatians: **"There is neither Jew nor Greek, there is neither bond nor free, there is neither male nor female, for ye are all one in Christ Jesus" (Galatians 3:28).**

Yet God could take people only so far at a given time in history, because of what Jesus called **"the hardness of their hearts" (see Matthew 19:8).** Also, the practice of slavery was as built in to the ancient economy as credit cards are to the modern-day financial system and just as hard to remove without total disruption. But over time, as God led people to more and more equal treatment of one another as brothers and sisters, slavery was eventually and rightfully abolished.

? Are the Bible's teachings what we would expect if it was an invention of man?

The Bible's teachings are not what we would expect a person to invent. Lift oneself up by humbling oneself. Love one's enemies. We are too egotistical to invent these principles. The way to greatness is to become a servant of all, not by lording over people. We go at things by self-effort, while the God of the Bible requires us to let Him make us a new creation and give up self-effort. All these go so against our human nature it seems incredible that the Bible could be solely a human product.

One of the most unlikely to be invented teachings of all is also the main focus of the Bible. In order to save us God would become man and die on a cross to pay the penalty for our sins. Our salvation consists of trusting in the work of Jesus on the cross and abandoning our own good works as a way to achieve salvation. This teaching sounds so strange to the natural man that it seems incredible that a human would ever invent something like it.

SUMMARY

Any book can claim to be the "word of god." The real Word of God should show evidence of being set apart from other books. The Bible is indeed unique. Its unity, popularity, survival, impact, character and many other things make it stand out. Although uniqueness is not a proof for divine inspiration of the Bible, it is a strong indicator of such. If we are looking for the book of God, the Bible has the credentials we would expect from such a book.

CHAPTER TWO

INSIDE INFORMATION OR LUCKY GUESSES?

SCIENTIFIC FOREKNOWLEDGE

Even though the Bible is not written in the language of a science textbook, we can find a great degree of scientific foreknowledge in its pages. **Scientific foreknowledge contained in biblical verses reflects knowledge of scientific facts discovered centuries or even millennia after the Bible was written, with many of these facts not discovered until the twentieth century.**

Skeptics commonly charge that the Bible contains scientific mistakes. For example, the Bible is sometimes accused of teaching a flat earth or that the whole universe revolves around the earth. As we look at some specific verses dealing with various facts about our environment, we shall see that not only are these charges false, but the Bible contains scientific insight explainable only if it is a divinely inspired book.

EXAMPLES OF SCIENTIFIC INSIGHT IN THE BIBLE

> "Astronomers have found proof that the universe sprang into existence abruptly, in a sudden moment of creation, as the Bible said it did."
>
> *NASA astronomer Robert Jastrow*

? Does the Bible teach that time, space, and matter have always existed? What does twentieth century science say about this?

Genesis 1:1 says, "In the beginning God created the heaven and the earth." Until the twentieth century it was believed that the universe had always existed, and there was not much known about what it consisted of. In the last century we determined that the universe consists of space, time, and matter as a "continuum." What was even more startling and disturbing to some was that scientists such as Einstein and later Stephen Hawking and others found evidence that the universe had not always existed but came into existence at a finite point in time in the past. They also found evidence that matter, space, and time all began simultaneously, called "space-time." They concluded that prior to this beginning space and time did not exist.

Look at Genesis 1:1 again. "In the beginning (time) God created the heaven (space) and the earth (matter)." The Bible is the only book that says matter, time, and space all began simultaneously at a finite time in the past. All other ancient cosmologies start with eternal matter or chaos. It appears that the Bible shows remarkable scientific insight on the beginning of the universe. Some scientists have taken note of this. Robert Jastrow, a NASA astronomer, commented: "Most remarkable of all, astronomers have found proof that the universe sprang into existence abruptly, in a sudden moment of creation, **as the Bible said it did**" (emphasis theirs).[1]

There is also a relevant verse in the New Testament, **Titus 1:2: "In hope of eternal life, which God, that cannot lie, promised before the world began."** The word for "world" is the Greek word *aionios*, which is where we get the word "eons." The idea is that of a space/time continuum. Again time is portrayed as having a beginning, with something/someone transcendent to it.

---

1   As quoted in *The Creator Beyond Time and Space,* Chuck Missler and Dr. Mark Eastman, The Word for Today, Costa Mesa, CA, 1996, 7.

Many fine books address this subject and demonstrate the true facts of science, as opposed to theories and speculations. *The Genesis Record* by Dr. Henry Morris, *The Biblical Basis for Modern Science*, also by Morris, *Earth's Catastrophic Past* by Dr. Andrew Snelling, and *The Creator Beyond Time and Space* by Dr. Mark Eastman and Chuck Missler are just a few good examples.

Our purpose is to demonstrate that there are no known natural explanations for the scientific foreknowledge revealed in the Bible verses we are discussing, but rather that this knowledge was supernaturally imparted. **How do we explain how the ancient authors of the Bible knew that time had a beginning, simultaneous with matter and space, when the science of that time thought matter was eternal and so was time?**

? What do the first and second laws of thermodynamics say about matter and energy?

The first law of thermodynamics, simply put, states that matter and energy can neither be created nor destroyed, only transformed one into the other. No new matter appears without a corresponding decrease in energy, or vice-versa. The second law states that things break down and wear out over time, as the matter and energy in the universe go from order to disorder. The energy available to perform work decreases over time, which is called the law of entropy. The result of the second law is what is called the "heat death" of the universe, when all energy is evenly spread out and no more is available to perform work.

? Are the first law and second law of thermodynamics in the Bible?

The first law: Genesis 2:2 says, "And on the seventh day God ended his work which he had made; and he rested on the seventh day from all his work which he had made." The word "rested" simply means "ceased," and it implies that the work of creation was finished from that time on and no new space, time, or matter is now being created. This is exactly what we observe in the first law of thermodynamics—no matter or energy can be created. **Hebrews 1:3 says that God is "upholding all things by the word of his power."** Nothing can be annihilated.

The second law: The second law of thermodynamics is also in the Bible. For example, the Bible says this about the universal property of decay in the universe: **"Lift up your eyes to the heavens, and look upon the earth beneath: for the heavens shall vanish away like smoke, and the earth shall wax old like a garment, and they that dwell therein shall die in like manner; but my salvation shall be forever, and my righteousness shall not be abolished"** **(Isaiah 51:6).** The heavens and the earth are "waxing old," according to the second thermodynamic law. Another passage that speaks of universal decay is **Romans 8:21–22: "Because the creature itself also shall be delivered from the bondage of corruption into the glorious liberty of the children of God. For we know that the whole creation groaneth and travaileth in pain together until now."**

? When the Bible was written, what did most cultures believe about the earth and the universe? How does the Bible teach differently?

It was unlikely that the ancients believed the earth and the universe, especially the stars, were not eternal. Yet **Matthew 24:35 says, "Heaven and earth shall pass away, but my words shall not pass away."** When the Bible was written, no evidence had been discovered that the universe was decaying. In that day they believed just the opposite. And they ridiculed the idea that the universe was finite and had a beginning. But some modern scientists have noticed how recent discoveries confirm the biblical perspective.

The idea that the universe was created from nothing was not in the thinking of the ancients. They always started with pre-existing materials.

"The atheist's model begins with an even more impressive miracle-the appearance of all the matter in the universe from nothing, by no one, and for no reason."

Chuck Missler and Dr. Mark Eastman, The Creator Beyond Time and Space, p. 17.

? So did the universe spring into existence from

nothing, without a creator, according to the scientific evidence?

It's a lot easier for us today to think of a finite universe with a beginning, since the big bang theory is currently the most widely accepted theory. But the big bang without a creator has some major difficulties. **Without a creator the big bang theory is essentially: "Nothing went 'bang!' and out came the universe."** The atheist, like the theist, believes that matter and energy came into existence without pre-existing materials and then was ordered against the known second law of thermodynamics, which says things naturally go from order to disorder. So either way this event was outside known natural laws and therefore was a supernatural event. The main difference is that the atheist has to believe in a supernatural event without a supernatural cause adequate to explain it. Missler and Eastman comment on this: **"The atheist's model begins with an even more impressive miracle—the appearance of all the matter in the universe from nothing, by no one, and for no reason."**[2]

Astronomer David Darling says, "Don't let the cosmologists try to kid you on this one. They have not got a clue either—despite the fact that they are doing a pretty good job of convincing themselves and others that this is really not a problem. 'In the beginning,' they will say … 'there was a quantum fluctuation from which....' Whoa! Stop right there. You see what I mean? First there is nothing, and then there is something. And the cosmologists try to bridge the two with a quantum flutter, a tremor of uncertainty that sparks it all off. They are away, and before you know it they have pulled a hundred billion galaxies out of their quantum hats.

"You cannot fudge this by appealing to quantum mechanics. Either there is nothing to begin with, in which case there is no quantum vacuum, no pre-geometric dust, no time in which anything can happen, no physical laws that can effect a change from nothingness into somethingness; or there is something, in which case that needs explaining."[3]

The fabric of the universe was "stretched," according to science ... and the Bible!

---

2   Chuck Missler and Dr. Mark Eastman, *The Creator Beyond Time and Space,* The Word for Today, Costa Mesa, CA, 1996, 17.

3   "On Creating Something from Nothing," *New Scientist,* vol. 151, September 14, 1996.

There's another fascinating insight in the Bible about the creation of the universe. One main feature of current cosmologies is that when the universe was formed, space itself was stretched out like a material being stretched, rather than matter exploding into empty space that was already there. **Space itself, according to current theory, was stretched out from a point of beginning. In the Bible we see an amazing correlation with this idea in over a dozen verses where it says the Lord "stretched out the heavens." In Isaiah 42:5 it says, "Thus saith God the Lord, he that created the heavens, and stretched them out." Psalm 104:2 says, "Who coverest thyself with light as with a garment; who stretchest out the heavens like a curtain."**

Other verses have this same phrasing. The idea that space was stretched during its creation is a modern scientific idea. Is it something ancient writers would have been able to deduce on their own? We can allow just so many lucky guesses!

? What did ancient cultures believe about the number of stars? What did the Bible teach about this?

When the Bible was written, only three thousand to four thousand stars were visible to the naked eye, and no telescopes had been invented yet. But listen to this verse in **Jeremiah 33:22: "As the host of heaven cannot be numbered, neither the sand of the sea measured, so will I multiply the seed of David my servant, and the Levites that minister unto me."** God was saying that David's spiritual descendants through Christ would be very numerous, and He used the figure of speech of the endless stars of heaven and the endless number of sand grains to illustrate a very great number. What is provocative about this illustration is that scientists currently estimate the number of known stars to be approximately equal to the estimated number of sand grains on the earth, both very large numbers.

If this passage was just a human insight, how did the writer know the stars were so many as to be innumerable? Many scientists before the invention of the telescope charted what they believed were all the known stars. Now we realize more than one hundred billion galaxies exist, each with at least one hundred billion stars. Could it be that the writer had inside information from the Creator Himself that yet undiscovered myriads of stars were in the sky?

? Does the Bible teach that the sun revolves around the earth, as the charge is often made?

Let's look at **Psalm 19:4b–6. "In them he set a tabernacle for the sun, which is as a bridegroom coming out of his chamber, and rejoiceth as a strong man to run a race. His (the sun's) going forth is from the end of the heaven, and his circuit unto the ends of it, and there is nothing hid from the heat thereof."** We have now found that the sun indeed moves through the galaxy, and the galaxy itself moves through intergalactic space. To say that the sun rises and sets is a term we use even today, using earth as a reference point, and it does not mean the sun orbits the earth.

? Does the Bible teach a flat earth?

The idea for this mistaken view might have been taken from **Revelation 7:1: "And after these things I saw four angels standing on the four corners of the earth."** This is one instance where the King James Version has a mistranslation. The original Greek word translated as "corners" actually means "quarters" and refers to the four directions (north, south, east, west) and so does not teach a flat, four-cornered earth at all.[4] Furthermore, the Bible actually teaches a round earth: **"It is he that sitteth upon the circle of the earth, and the inhabitants thereof are like grasshoppers; that stretcheth out the heavens as a curtain, and spreadeth them out as a tent to dwell in" (Isaiah 40:22).** The word "circle" in this verse actually means "sphere" in the Hebrew.[5]

A round, rotating earth: According to Missler and Eastman,[6] the ancient Greeks thought the earth was supported on the back of Atlas; the Hindus portrayed the earth on the back of a big elephant or turtle. The idea of a free-floating earth was unknown in most ancient cultures and myths. In contrast, the **Bible described the earth as it hangs unsupported in space: "He stretcheth out the north over the empty place, and hangeth the earth upon nothing" (Job 26:7). The Bible also describes the rotation of the earth: "it (the earth) is turned as clay to the seal" (Job 38:14).** According to Morris,[7] this passage refers to the earth as rotating as a clay cylinder being turned on a potter's wheel to receive the imprint of a seal or signet, as the earth turns and the sun shines upon it and reveals it.

---

4   Missler and Eastman, *The Creator Beyond Time and Space,* 90.

5   Ibid., 91.

6   Ibid., 91.

7   Dr. Henry Morris, *The Remarkable Record of Job,* Master Books, Green Forest, AR, 1988, 40.

Another passage which shows the roundness and rotation of the earth is found in **Luke 17:34–36**, referring to the day of the coming of the Lord: **"I tell you, in that night there shall be two men in one bed; the one shall be taken, and the other shall be left. Two women shall be grinding together, the one shall be taken, and the other left. Two men shall be in the field; the one shall be taken, and the other left."** This shows that when the Lord comes it will be night somewhere, morning in another place (when the women would do their grinding of meal) and midday somewhere else (when the men are in the field), at the same time. This shows the earth is rotating and is round, with one side only facing the sun at a time. So there is no flat-earth society in the Bible!

? **How did the Bible writers know about the earth's water cycle, when scientists didn't understand it until about three hundred years ago?**

The water cycle was not understood until recent centuries. **About three hundred years ago Pierre Perrault and Edme Marriote studied the Seine River and eventually came to a detailed understanding of the water cycle.**[8] In the Middle Ages the source of rain was a mystery. They may have figured out that when dark clouds formed rain came—but they didn't connect cloud formation with the ocean. Now we know rain clouds develop from evaporation of ocean water. Water is lifted against gravity and transported inland. To do that, we need air motion, and we have a specific circulation pattern of the winds, which are caused by the earth's rotation and jet streams. A global diagram of air circulation patterns reveals that the winds flow in a circular pattern from north to south and back again. Again none of this was officially "discovered" until about three hundred years ago.

But there are verses in the Bible that describe details of the water cycle. "The wind goeth toward the south, and turneth about unto the north; it whirleth about continually, and the wind returneth again according to his circuits" (Ecclesiastes 1:6). What a remarkable description of global air patterns! And remember, they didn't have the weather channel back then. The knowledge that water comes from the ocean and eventually runs off and returns to the ocean was only acquired in relatively modern times; yet listen to **Ecclesiastes 1:7: "All the rivers run into the sea; yet the sea is not full; unto the place**

---

8   Missler and Eastman, *The Creator Beyond Time and Space*, 94.

from whence the rivers come, thither they return again." How could the ancient author have known about these facts?

Consider the book of Job. **The book of Job alone is full of scientific foreknowledge. It contains no mythical embellishments and more than a dozen scientific facts not discovered until modern times.**[9]

Another biblical anticipation of scientific discovery, seen in the book of Job, is the process of rainfall. The process of rainfall from clouds, the coalescing of small drops of water vapor into larger drops of liquid water to eventually fall as rain, was not understood in ancient times as mentioned above. **Yet Job 36:27–28 says, "For he maketh small the drops of water; they pour down rain according to the vapor thereof; which the clouds do drop and distil upon man abundantly."** Henry Morris[10] describes how drops of rain are "made small" as they start off within the clouds too small to fall to earth and eventually coalesce into drops heavy enough to fall to earth despite the updrafts of air. How are clouds kept aloft? Modern science has discovered that small drops of water in the clouds are kept aloft by the updrafts of air. The downward force of gravity is balanced by the upward force of the air at this point. What does the Bible say? **"He bindeth up the waters in his thick clouds; and the cloud is not rent under them" (Job 26:8). "Dost thou know the balancings of the clouds?" (Job 37:16). Another verse in that same chapter says, "By watering he wearieth the thick cloud" (Job 37:11).**

"Centuries before Semmelweis, God had already detailed the most effective method of washing. To prevent the spread of disease, modern science has merely rediscovered the biblical method."

None of These Diseases

---

9   Ibid., 35.

10   Morris, *The Remarkable Record of Job*, 38.

? How did the Bible writers know the wind has weight?

Another scientific insight from the book of Job is this: **"For he looketh to the ends of the earth, and seeth under the whole heaven; to make the weight for the winds, and he weigheth the waters by measure" (Job 28:24–25).** As Morris explains,[11] it turns out that the relative global weights of air and water need to be in a certain critical proportion to each other to maintain life on this planet and that life could not exist if these weights were much different since they affect the atmosphere and what is called the hydrosphere. Indeed, the very idea that the winds have weight was only discovered about three hundred years ago and is not something ancient man would likely have even conceived of. Yet this concept is seen in the Bible. In fact, the weight of the winds controls worldwide air mass movements that transport water from the oceans inland to the continents. How did Job know this was such an important thing? Did he study modern meteorology?

Other scientific insights

Springs of the sea: The book of Job has many more scientific insights we don't have space for here. I will mention one more, however, relating to the ocean. **Job 38:16 says, "Hast thou entered into the springs of the sea?" It is only recently that springs have been discovered on the sea bottom.** Did Job take a trip with Jacques Cousteau? Or was he a recipient of some insight from the Creator of the oceans?

Life and blood: There are some insights into biology. For instance, **Leviticus 17:11 says that "the life of the flesh is in the blood."** Yet before modern times, blood-letting, where blood was let out of a patient thinking it would cure him, was practiced. The importance of blood to physical life was discovered only about five hundred years ago. Yet the Bible revealed this important fact thousands of years before.

Clotting of blood: The Bible exhibits advanced medical knowledge. **In Genesis 17:2 newborns are instructed to be circumcised on the eighth day.** Why? When an infant is born, the blood-clotting mechanism is immature. After several days, vitamin K in the infant's diet allows an important clotting factor, prothrombin, to form, and **this clotting factor peaks on the eighth day of the infant's life.**

---

11 Ibid., 37.

This is not a factor in modern times because injections of vitamin K are now given at birth.[12,13]

Could the right day have just been stumbled on by trial and error? Other cultures that performed this procedure settled on day 1, 4, 6, 7 or 20.[14] **How did Abraham know the eighth day was the safest time? Did he have inside information from the divine physician?**

[?] Did ancient cultures know about invisible germs? Did the Bible alone anticipate their discovery?

The Law of Moses, the Torah, comprises the first five books of the Bible. This law was written soon after Israel had been captive in Egypt, where they were exposed to Egyptian technology, including their medical methods. If you look at Egyptian medicine, they were very advanced in some ways, but primitive in others. The treatment methods they used were sometimes more deadly than the illness they were meant to treat. They did not seem to have an awareness of things such as invisible germs that could infect someone.[15]

Germs in cooking utensils: In Leviticus 6:28 there is a command to scour and rinse metal cooking vessels in water after using them, which would have disinfected them. How could Moses have known about dangerous germs in cooking pots?

Poor Dr. Semmelweis! All he wanted was for them to wash their hands!

In Leviticus 11:35 animal carcasses were declared unclean, and anything that touched them was unclean. This protected the Israelites from invisible, deadly germs. People had trouble believing in invisible germs even up to the late 1800s. Jeffrey describes how in 1845 a Hungarian doctor, Ignaz Semmelweis, was disturbed by the high death rate of women giving birth in Vienna hospitals, about 15 to 30 percent. The doctors in the hospital did not wash their hands between patients, a practice which to us now seems abhorrent. **But Dr. Semmelweis instructed the doctors who were now under his supervision to wash their hands well in water and chlorinated lime between expectant mothers they saw, and the death rate fell to less than 2 percent.**

---

12 Grant R. Jeffrey, *The Signature of God,* Frontier Research Publications, Toronto, Ont., 1996, 155–156.

13 Missler and Eastman, *The Creator Beyond Time and Space,* 95–96.

14 Ibid., 96.

15 Jeffrey, *The Signature of God,* 140–143.

Yet the Bible reveals knowledge of washings and other sanitary practices millennia earlier. Medical doctors McMillen and Stern comment: "Centuries before Semmelweis, God had already detailed the most effective method of washing. To prevent the spread of disease, modern science has merely rediscovered the biblical method."[16]

Running water: Leviticus 15:13 talks about using running water to wash when dealing with infectious diseases. Jeffrey[17] describes how until the last century most doctors, when they washed, washed their hands in a stagnant bowl of water, allowing the germs to remain.

Quarantine: If the rules for dealing with leprosy in Leviticus 14 are examined we can see that they are very similar to medical quarantine orders today. In the fourteenth century the Bubonic Plague, also known as the Black Death, killed more than sixty million people in Europe. Doctors had no knowledge of how to treat the patients. The plague was finally defeated when the church fathers in Vienna took a look at **Leviticus 13:46: "All the days wherein the plague shall be in him he shall be defiled; he is unclean; he shall dwell alone; without the camp shall his habitation be."** Those that were infected with the Black Death were placed outside the city in quarantine and buried outside the city when they died, and the progress of the Black Death was soon halted there.[18]

Other biblical practices preventing infection: According to Jeffrey,[19] instructions are given on the incineration of animal waste and decaying flesh in Leviticus 4:11–12, instructing them to burn these items outside the camp. **The water of purification used for the red heifer sacrifice in Numbers 19 contained ashes with cedar and hyssop. Hyssop happens to be a very effective antibacterial agent which is still used today in hyssop oil.**[20] In Numbers 31:23 materials were disinfected after being captured from an enemy. Then there was the problem of human waste. As cities grew, untreated waste became a huge problem and resulted in many diseases such as typhoid and cholera, due to unsanitary

---

16 S. I. McMillen, M.D., and David E. Stern, M.D., *None of These Diseases,* Fleming A. Revell, div. of Baker Book House, Grand Rapids, MI, revised and expanded edition, 2000, 25.

17 Jeffrey, *The Signature of God,* 147.

18 Ibid., 148–149.

19 Ibid., 156–158.

20 Ibid., 153.

conditions. Deuteronomy 23:12–13 instructed the Israelites to bury their waste, rather than leave it exposed.[21]

All of these instructions are truly amazing when we realize the discovery of invisible germs was more than 3,500 years in the future. It is unlikely that these advanced medical and sanitation practices would have been thought of by Moses as a result of his upbringing in Egyptian culture or even exposure to earlier cultures. Isn't it reasonable to conclude that the divine physician gave the Israelites "inside information" to ensure their protection and well-being?

SUPPOSED SCIENTIFIC ERRORS IN THE BIBLE

[?] Some of the commands in the Law of Moses sound strange. What was their purpose?

Some of the commands in the Law of Moses seem ridiculous to the modern man. But one purpose of many of these commands was to prevent the Jews, as God's chosen people, from mixing with other peoples who ate certain foods in association with practices of idolatry and worshipping false gods.

Unclean animals: Many types of animals are declared unclean in Leviticus 11. For example, animals who did not chew the cud were declared unclean. According to Jamieson, Fausset, and Brown, in those days livestock ate plants in the field and could sometimes eat poisonous plants. It turns out that a large part of these poisons passes out of the animal's system through the salivary glands when they chew the cud, and so their flesh would have been safer to eat than non-cud chewers as a rule. The same with animals who "part the hoof"—that is, much poison in plants eaten is also discharged from the parting between the hooves and toes. Verse 9 talks about fish without scales and fins being unclean. Again, fins and scales are used to excrete poisons by perspiration in fish. Those without fins and scales, especially in hot climates, cause many digestive disorders. These included frogs, eels, and shellfish. Many of the unclean birds listed fed on carrion and other noxious items.[22]

Other prohibitions concerning seeds and clothes: Some of the laws pertaining to leprosy in Leviticus 13–14 distinguished between contagious and

---

21 Ibid., 157.

22 Robert Jamieson, A. R. Fausset, and David Brown, *Commentary on the Whole Bible*, Zondervan Publishing House, Grand Rapids, MI, revised ed., 1961, 91–92.

non-contagious forms and so preserved the services to their society of those who weren't contagious. How about the prohibition in Leviticus 19 about mingling certain seeds? Now certain types of seeds were sown by idolatrous nations as they performed magical rites and invocations, which of course would be unfamiliar to us unless we studied history. But it also turns out that those who have studied diseases of vegetables and crops have found that when the pollen of two different genera of grains is sown in the same field it produces plants, called "chess" by the farmers, which are inferior to the two grains that produced it. Wearing two types of cloth such as wool and linen was also probably associated with some superstition, but wool combined with linen in hot climates is actually harmful and causes blisters and exhaustion and heat problems. So it seems that even the most ridiculous-sounding laws had a practical application of one sort or another.[23]

Furthermore, even if there are not any apparent practical applications in some of these laws, it must also be recognized that many of the laws forbid practices that were done by neighboring religions, and so there was a spiritual aspect to these laws as well. Israel was to be "set apart" from the practices of its pagan neighbors.

? Does the Bible give an inaccurate value for pi?

Another such "error" that is often charged to the Bible is in 1 Kings 7:23, where it is charged that the Bible gives an incorrect value for pi by saying the circumference of the "molten sea" basin was three times the diameter. But every math student knows the circumference of a circle is equal to pi times the diameter, where pi equals 3.141592 to six decimal places. Now what are the alternatives to the charge of "error"? First of all, there is such a thing as round numbers or "significant figures," so ten cubits and thirty cubits would be perfectly acceptable if so intended. Also it is mentioned that it is a handbreadth thick, and so the circumference measured may be on the inside of the basin, which could turn out to be about 3 times rather than 3.14 times the diameter. But neither of these two assumptions is necessary. **There is a marvelous little detail in the Hebrew that clears up this whole problem.**

As we shall talk more about in the next section, Hebrew letters have a numerical value assigned to each of them, called alphanumerics. Here is the text of **1 Kings 7:23: "And he made a molten sea, ten cubits from the one brim to the other; it was round all about, and his height was five cubits: and a line of thirty cubits did compass it round about."** According to Chuck Missler, in Hebrew

---

23 Ibid., 100–101.

there is a word for circumference, *qav* ("line" in the English). But here in the text it is used but seems to be misspelled: "*qaveh*," adding a "heh" (h). When the Jewish scribes copied a text it was their practice not to alter a text which they felt had been copied wrong. In the Hebrew Bible they noted in the margin what they thought the text should be. The written variation is called a *kethiv*, while the marginal note is called the *qere*. As Missler notes in his book *Cosmic Codes*: "To the ancient scribes, this was also regarded as a *remez*, a hint of something deeper. This appears to be a clue to treat the word as a mathematical formula."[24]

Missler notes that the numerical value of the correct spelling of the word in the margin is 106. The "misspelled" version of the word adds a "heh," which has a value of 5, and so increases the value of the word to 111. Using the word as a formula, the ratio of 111/106 multiplied by 30 cubits gives a circumference of 31.41509433962 cubits. If a cubit, as is thought, equaled 1.5 feet, **this results in a value for the circumference which is off by less than 15 thousandths of an inch! The ratio of the numerical values 111/106, multiplied by 3, gives a value for pi which is correct to four decimal places!**[25] Why was this "spelling error" in the text, possibly even in the original? Was it deliberately done by the inspiration of the Holy Spirit or the creation of men? How would these men even know the value of pi to do this? **They wrote several centuries before Archimedes (287–212 B.C.) defined pi.** What a coincidence that it equals pi so precisely, if simply an "error"! This shows not only the reliability of the Bible, but also how the numerical values of the letters can carry hidden significance. More about this subject will be covered in another chapter.

24 Chuck Missler, *Cosmic Codes,* Koinonia House, Coeur d'Alene, ID, revised ed., 2004, 289.
25 Ibid., 288–289, for complete discussion.

CHAPTER THREE

THE RIGHT PERSON,
THE RIGHT PLACE,
THE RIGHT TIME

PROPHECY OVERVIEW

Prophecy is history written in advance. Obviously this can only be done with 100 percent accuracy by someone who somehow knows what is going to happen before it happens. The person who predicts with perfect exactness would have to somehow have perfect knowledge of the outcome of future events.

? Why is prophecy so important?

God claims in the Bible that what sets Him apart is His unique and perfect knowledge of the future. A God who could create us is also obviously able to get a message to us. But how does God set His Word apart from counterfeit "words of god," so we know the message is genuinely from Him? One way is to show that the real Word of God has as its author the Creator, who is not confined to our created time and space domain called the universe. In the book of the prophet Isaiah we read: **"Behold, the former things are come to pass, and new things do I**

declare: before they spring forth I tell you of them" (Isaiah 42:9). And also: "I am God, and there is none like me. Declaring the end from the beginning and from ancient times the things that are not yet done" (Isaiah 46:9b–10).

? How accurate must a biblical prophet be?

The Bible is about 30 percent prophecy. And it can be shown that the Bible is 100 percent correct in what it predicts, with no proven false prophecies. In fact, the Bible itself states that to be a prophet of God **100 percent accuracy is required**: **"When a prophet speaketh in the name of the Lord, if the thing follow not, nor come to pass, that is the thing which the Lord hath not spoken, but the prophet hath spoken it presumptuously: thou shalt not be afraid of him" (Deuteronomy 18:22).** This makes obvious sense, since God by definition could not be wrong about the future, whereas someone else could.

? What kinds of prophecies are in the Bible?

We will look at several categories of prophecies in the Bible: messianic prophecies in this chapter, which are predictions relating to Jesus Christ, and in the next chapter prophecies of specific geographical locations, including Israel, and New Testament prophecy. We will also look at other supposed "prophets" such as Nostradamus and others, in order to show the clear qualitative distinctions between biblical prophecy and other so-called "prophecy." So let's jump in!

MESSIANIC PROPHECY

More than three hundred prophecies and allusions in the Old Testament speak of the Messiah. We shall show that one Person, Jesus Christ, best fits all these prophecies. One of the unique things about Jesus is that His birth, life, death, and resurrection were predicted centuries and even millennia in advance.

? What are some of the things predicted about Jesus?

- The place of His birth, as well as His virgin birth (Micah 5:2; Isaiah 7:14).
- His genealogy is progressively laid out, from Abraham, Isaac, Jacob, the tribe of Judah, David, etc. (Genesis 12:8, 49:10; 2 Samuel 7:12).
- He would be judge, king, and prophet.

THE BIBLE CAN BE PROVEN

- He would be preceded by a messenger to prepare His way (Isaiah 40:3).

- He would do miracles such as giving sight to the blind and making the lame walk (Isaiah 35:5–6).

Many details of His last twenty-four hours on earth were predicted, such as the whipping, mocking, betrayal price, gambling for His clothing, the details of His crucifixion (predicted seven hundred years before crucifixion was even invented) and His resurrection (Isaiah 53:5; Psalm 22:7–8; Zechariah 11:12; Psalm 22:14–18, 2:7, 16:10).

One of the ways Jesus authenticated Himself as the long-awaited Messiah was by being the one who fulfilled all three hundred of these messianic predictions and allusions. In fact, Jesus pointed to Himself as the fulfillment of prophecies given throughout the Old Testament: **"And beginning at Moses and all the prophets, he expounded unto them in all the scriptures the things concerning himself" (Luke 24:27);** and again in **Luke 24:44: "These are the words which I spake unto you, while I was yet with you, that all the things must be fulfilled, which were written in the law of Moses, and in the prophets, and in the psalms, concerning me."**

[?] Could messianic prophecy be fulfilled by chance?

A critic might say many persons could fulfill all of these just by chance, especially since so many people have been born into the world. Though one person might fulfill a few of these by chance, as the number of prophecies increases, it becomes increasingly harder for chance to explain it.

One of the things a person might ask is: How sure can we be that God exists and that the Bible demonstrates itself to be His Word? There are more than three hundred prophecies about Jesus. What if we took just four of them and figured out what the odds are that they all could be fulfilled by one person solely by chance? This exercise has already been done by several well-known authors, the most comprehensive original study by Peter Stoner in *Science Speaks.*[1] He picked several prophecies, assigned reasonable odds to their fulfillment by one particular person in history, and then calculated the composite probability that one person could fulfill all these prophecies by chance. Anyone can do this exercise. Here are four examples of how.

---

1   Peter Stoner, *Science Speaks,* Moody Bible Institute, Chicago, IL, 1958.

Birthplace of Jesus predicted

In Micah 5:2 the Messiah's birthplace, Bethlehem, is predicted: "But thou, Bethlehem Ephratah, though thou be little among the thousands of Judah, yet out of thee shall he come forth unto me that is to be ruler in Israel; whose goings forth have been from of old, from everlasting." In the Gospels that prediction is fulfilled in places like **Matthew 2:1: "Now when Jesus was born in Bethlehem of Judea."** What are the odds that a person born throughout history would be born in Bethlehem? Bible scholar Chuck Missler performed a probability analysis of various prophecies[2] and set these odds by figuring the average world population for known history and dividing the average population of the city of Bethlehem for all of history. Without exact figures he estimated that the average population of Bethlehem has been about ten thousand, and the average world population has been two billion. **Then the odds that a particular person would be born in Bethlehem would be 10,000/2,000,000,000, or 1/200,000.** Get the idea?

The Messiah would be presented as king on a donkey

The Messiah was predicted to be presented as king while riding on a donkey: **"Rejoice greatly, O daughter of Zion; shout, O daughter of Jerusalem: behold, thy King cometh unto thee: he is just, and having salvation; lowly, and riding upon an ass, and upon a colt the foal of an ass" (Zechariah 9:9).**

The fulfillment: **Matthew 21:7–9: "And brought the ass, and the colt, and put on them their clothes, and they set him thereon. And a very great multitude spread their garments in the way; others cut down branches from the trees, and strewed them in the way. And the multitudes that went before, and that followed, cried, saying, Hosanna to the son of David: Blessed is he that cometh in the name of the Lord; Hosanna in the highest."**

We will assign Missler's figure of 1/100 odds for this prediction.

Jesus was betrayed for thirty pieces of silver

3. When we read **Zechariah 11:12**, at first it may be hard to even see that it is a prophecy: **"And I said unto them, if ye think good, give me my price; and if not, forbear. So they weighed for my price thirty pieces of silver."** In this scripture, a messianic object lesson in Zechariah, the shepherd/servant is

---

2   Chuck Missler, *Footprints of the Messiah,* tape commentary, Koinonia House, Coeur d'Alene, ID, 1992, his material adapted in turn from *Science Speaks* by Peter Stoner.

speaking, whose flock has not been grateful for his care, and he is asking his flock for the amount they thought he was worth. As Missler comments, they gave him the price of a gored slave, thirty pieces of silver (see Exodus 21:32). But we see in Jesus' betrayal the amount His betrayers thought the Good Shepherd Himself was worth: **"Then one of the twelve, called Judas Iscariot, went unto the chief priests, and said unto them, What will ye give me, and I will deliver him unto you? And they covenanted with him for thirty pieces of silver" (Matthew 26:14–15).**

What a coincidence! **How many people in history have been betrayed for exactly thirty pieces of silver, as opposed to twenty-nine, fifty, etc.?** Missler gives **odds of one over one thousand (1/1000)**, and that is probably being very generous.

Jesus' hands and feet pierced

Consider **Psalm 22:16: "They pierced my hands and my feet." Many scholars see this psalm as a prophecy of Christ's crucifixion. The hands and feet were pierced with nails. And, remarkably, this psalm was written seven hundred years before crucifixion was invented. Missler gives odds of about one in ten thousand that a given criminal executed throughout history would have died by crucifixion.**[3]

? So how sure can we be that chance fulfillment can be ruled out?

We have sampled four prophecies and assigned conservative odds to them. To get the composite probability of just these four we would multiply the individual probabilities together. **So the odds that one person in history would fulfill just four of the above prophecies would be:**

1/200,000 (Micah 5:2)

X 1/100 (Zechariah 9:9)

X 1/1000 (Zechariah 11:12)

X 1/10,000 (Psalm 22:16)

= 1/2x10 to the 14th power!

---

3 *Footprints of the Messiah*, tape commentary by Chuck Missler, Koinonia House, Coeur d'Alene, ID, 1992.

We have selected four of the three hundred prophecies and picked four of the more simple ones. Many of the others are much more technical and so have more remote probabilities of being fulfilled by chance. **Missler did a similar exercise with eight of the simpler prophecies and came up with a probability of one in ten to the seventeenth power.**[4]

To get a feel for how big a number one in ten to the seventeenth power is, let's look at an illustration that several authors have used.[5] Imagine the state of Texas covered in silver dollars two feet deep. Mark one of the silver dollars, mix them up so that the marked silver dollar somehow has an equal probability to the others of being selected and then blindfold someone and send them out into this sea of silver dollars in Texas to randomly select one silver dollar. The likelihood that they would randomly pick the one marked silver dollar is equal to one in ten to the seventeenth power.

We can see that the probability that one person could fulfill these prophecies by chance is so remote that we can have absolute certainty that Jesus Christ is who He claimed to be: the One that was the fulfillment of these three hundred prophecies. If we reject Jesus' claim to be the Messiah, we are rejecting a fact proven more absolutely than we could possibly ask for.

Messianic prophecy fulfilled deliberately?

[?] Were the Old Testament prophecies written after the time of Christ?

Hold on, says the skeptic! Maybe these Old Testament prophecies were written after the fact, after the life of Christ had already taken place. This is a pretty difficult objection to sustain for several reasons. **Most scholars date the closing of the Old Testament to be around 450 B.C. Furthermore, the entire Old Testament was translated into Greek, called the Septuagint, around 250 B.C.** So whatever theory as to who wrote different books of the Old Testament is held, the Old Testament was definitely written down almost three centuries before Christ was born. Not many try to explain messianic prophecy by postdating. If they try, they are going against available evidence.

---

4   Ibid.

5   Ibid. Also see D. James Kennedy, *Evangelism Explosion,* Tyndale House Publishers, Wheaton, IL, fourth edition, 1996, 151.

? Did Jesus read the Old Testament and then deliberately fulfill prophecy?

Many doubters say Jesus really lived but that He knew about the prophecies and simply deliberately arranged to fulfill them all to proclaim Himself Messiah. Indeed, we see in several cases that Jesus knew He was fulfilling prophecy, or the Gospel writer indicates that something Jesus did fulfilled a specific messianic prophecy. **But there are two main problems with this theory. One is that it makes Jesus into a deceiver, pretending to be someone He wasn't.** Imagine Him trying to hoodwink people with sleight-of-hand fake miracles because it was prophesied the Messiah would heal people and do miracles. **Could anyone by trickery or sleight of hand convince devout Jews to change their tightly held beliefs, causing them to be persecuted?**

? Could Jesus have been deluded or dishonest?

Imagine Him saying: "Man, if I ride this donkey into Jerusalem, people will think I am the Messiah and make me king and I'll be rich!" And He would have to do something like this three hundred times, one for each prophecy! **Why would He need to bother with trying to fulfill all three hundred of them if His intent was to deceive? Also, this would mean a deceiver would have given the world its highest moral code, taught honesty and love of both neighbor and enemies, and given the most self-sacrificing example the world has ever known.** And finally this deceiver's ploy would have ended in death. If someone wants to believe the incredible and the ridiculous, this is a good theory.

What if you say He was deluded but sincere? **Do deluded fanatics inspire the transformation of the moral structure of society, save people from sin, and speak such sober, practical material as the Sermon on the Mount?** Again it takes more faith to believe this than that He was sane and honest.

? Could all the prophecies be fulfilled deliberately?

The second problem is that many of the prophecies are beyond the control of a mere human being to fulfill.

- A person can't decide in what city they are going to be born. In Jesus' case it was the decree of a pagan king that God used to cause Him to be born in Bethlehem.

- The time in history of His birth is predicted. **A person can't arrange to be born in a certain decade or year.**

- **You can't decide who your parents and grandparents will be**; yet all this was prophesied of the Messiah. His lineage was one of the proofs of Messiahship.

- If Jesus was faking, He couldn't control things such as: His betrayal; the mocking; the beatings; or the soldiers on duty that day who just happened not to break Jesus' legs after being crucified, as was their normal practice, but instead pierced His side in exact fulfillment of prophecy (see Zechariah 12:10 and John 19:34).

- How could He control the fact that **He had to be born into the world at the time when crucifixion was being used by the Romans and then control the manner of His execution?**

- **How could He control the reactions of His enemies,** which were predicted, even down to their very words in some cases, as well as their rejecting Him and His message or casting lots for His clothing (Psalm 22)?

- And imagine, as we said before, **Jesus convincing His disciples that He had died and then risen, with all power in heaven and earth given to Him, and then faking an ascension! All this would be a greater miracle than if Jesus is really who He claimed to be.**

Fulfilled prophecy invented?

? Could the New Testament writers have invented Jesus or details of His life to have someone fulfill the messianic prophecies?

The only other alternative for skeptics who want to avoid the validity of the messianic prophecies is to say that Jesus was a mythical character invented by an author or authors who were familiar with the Old Testament prophecies and wanted to make up a character and a story to fit them. Or, if they conceded that Jesus was a real person, to say that these conjuring authors embellished Jesus' life, inventing miracles and events to exactly match the messianic prophecies, in order to create a larger-than-life fictitious portrayal of Jesus. Presumably these authors were very clever, and they found some worldly gain or prestige by doing this, in order to control people for their own ends.

? Was there a motive for the writers to invent? Did they profit as a result?

We have already mentioned some difficulties with this idea. **Instead of getting them fame and fortune, promoting the Christian message got people persecuted and killed. So much for motivation to invent! Unlike other religious leaders who gained power, spoil, and followers, the New Testament writers usually lost all of the above by becoming Christians.**

? What difficulties were involved with a supposed collaboration to invent a Messiah character?

- **First, these inventors would have to be writing in the correct time period.** Presumably they may have had deceased predecessors who studied the prophecies and left messages saying, "Don't try this at home, at least until after 32–33 A.D.!" But let's say they invented their character at the right time period.

- **We need to point out that there would have to be at least eight New Testament writers, who would have to be shown by historical investigation to have written in widely scattered times, places, and circumstances.** These writers would have to have somehow collaborated to make sure the basic story and doctrine were the same and yet somehow include genuine-looking discrepancies.

- **Would deceivers bother with this or with having to write an intricate story that takes in all three hundred prophecies and allusions?** Remember that scholars conclude John wrote his Gospels about forty years after Paul wrote his letters!

- **All of Luke's "faking" in the book of Acts would have to stand up to archaeological investigation!**

But let's ignore these major difficulties for now and imagine we are one of these inventors, reading the Old Testament and conjuring up our story. And let's ask some honest questions about this scenario as we go.

? Could there have been just one writer/inventor?

How could just one writer invent all the other New Testament writers, including their unique styles, and have the characters and events be consistent with each other, with added coincidences (such as the events in Paul's letters coinciding with events in the book of Acts)?

Would he also be able to convince the rest of the church that all the writings were authoritative?

Would deceivers be this diligent or patient? Why bother? And if the other writers were not invented, but there really were eight or more, would they also be such diligent deceivers?

But let's say one or more inventors still pulled all this off (although remember that improbability piled on top of improbability heads toward impossibility) and were therefore the most unlikely and clever deceivers in the history of the world. And so here they are, writers inventing or re-inventing Jesus.

Hmm, they say! Why bother with three hundred of these? All we need is five or ten maybe to build this Messiah character.

A virgin birth?

So the inventors read **Isaiah 7:14: "A virgin shall conceive, and bear a son, and shall call his name Immanuel." Now, would they from this want to manufacture a virgin birth, such as in the Gospels?** Why even touch this one? Wouldn't that make this created character a little too incredible for everyone to believe in? Or why wouldn't they portray it as the mythologies do, like the Greek gods who consorted with earthly women to produce offspring?

The Messiah character must fit a real genealogy to be credible:

Remember that this person must fit a real genealogy, namely, be a proven descendant of Abraham, Isaac, Jacob, from the tribe of Judah, Jesse, the son of David, etc. Furthermore, they would have to make sure that the legal rights to the throne of David descended from David to Joseph and then somehow convince everyone that Joseph had a son named Jesus (but still maintain a virgin birth). And the blood line would have to descend from David by a different son down to Mary, since in the line leading to Joseph a blood curse was placed on Jeconiah (see Jeremiah 23) so his blood descendants would not sit on the throne of David. (More insurmountable problems with a fictitious genealogy will be pointed out later.)

Why make their character a prophet if there is no such thing?

They would have to make their created character a prophet (see Deuteronomy 18:18), a priest (Psalm 110:4), and a king (Psalm 2:6; Zechariah 9:9), and yet also have the bizarre result of making a king that ruled no nation and offered himself as a sacrifice! As for Jesus being a prophet, **if our inventors did not believe in real prophecy, why make up a character to appear to fit prophecies or who could prophesy himself?**

Great selling point for a Messiah character—his own people reject him!

Why have their own people, especially if the inventors are Jewish writers manufacturing a Messiah, reject that Messiah? And why do this in response to reading a verse like **Psalm 118:22: "The stone which the builders refused is become the head stone of the corner."** And if they are non-Jewish, would they even bother with this idea or be familiar with these passages in the Jewish scriptures?

A king on a donkey?!

Why not ignore the prophecy about the Messiah coming as a king on a donkey (Zechariah 9:9)? Not a great selling point for their created character! Why not on a fine horse or even an elephant or camel? The story just seems too strange and humble-sounding to be the product of a deceiver.

Twenty-nine prophecies fulfilled in twenty-four hours?

Here's a good challenge. **Why have twenty-nine prophecies fulfilled in your fictitious character's life in only his last twenty-four hours?** In reference to the Gospels, twenty-nine prophecies that were written from about 1000–500 B.C., a five-hundred-year span, were fulfilled in twenty-four hours in Jesus' life.[6] Some examples of these: betrayed by a friend, sold for thirty pieces of silver, silent before accusers, smitten and spat upon, the exact words of people who mocked, hands and feet pierced, side pierced, people shook their heads, given vinegar to drink, lots cast for garments, etc. **Would they as deceivers be this clever or go to this much trouble?**

---

6   Josh McDowell, *Evidence That Demands a Verdict,* Thomas Nelson/Here's Life Publishers, San Bernadino, CA, 1972, 158.

Thirty pieces of silver?

Why would anyone think Zechariah 11:12–13, relating to the thirty pieces of silver being cast to the potter in the house of the Lord, was a prophecy? (See Matthew 27:3–7 for the fulfillment.) And as we shall see below, many obscure, almost bizarre prophecies and allusions wouldn't be taken for prophecies until discerned after the fact. When they are discerned there is amazing underlying design. **Why would a deceiver bother with or even perceive these strange and intricate prophecies?**

An innocent man makes no defense?!

Look at **Isaiah 53**. Then read **verse 7: "He was oppressed, and he was afflicted, yet he opened not his mouth: he is brought as a lamb to the slaughter, and as a sheep before her shearers is dumb, so he openeth not his mouth." Why make up a trial based on this, especially when the defendant is innocent, accused of a capital crime, yet does not speak in his defense?** If they are looking for people to buy their story, this is definitely not the direction to take to be credible. Again, if the inventors were Jews, why have Jews putting him to death, and if they were not Jewish, would they even be familiar with Isaiah 53 or care about what it says?

The inventors found an Old Testament prophecy that fits crucifixion, and they just happened to be born at the right time in history to exploit it?

And it just so happens that crucifixion has now been invented and at the right time. Maybe some predecessors left notes saying, "Don't try this deception until a fitting method of punishment is invented at the right time." As we shall see, the time of the Messiah's first coming is pinpointed by several prophecies, so one would have to arrange to be around to write this story at the right time.

In fact, when one reads Psalm 22, especially verses 17–18, it sounds as if whoever inspired the writer knew the details of crucifixion intimately, including its effects on the body. And would the Old Testament prophecy writer himself have been able to guess that a method of execution fitting this psalm so closely would happen to be there seven hundred years later, in time to fulfill other prophecies that pinpoint the time of His first coming at the same time)

Now the faker, reading this psalm, would most likely assume the writer was talking about David, wouldn't he? Yet the first words of Jesus on the cross—"My God, my God, why have you forsaken me?"—are the first words of this psalm. And the last words of this psalm are "he hath done this." They are essentially the same as the last words of Jesus from the cross: "It is finished." Would you think of such details as a deceiver? **And there is no debating that crucifixion was not invented until about seven hundred years after Psalm 22 was written.** Remarkable.

Would you have the Roman soldiers break their normal execution routine?

Psalm 34:20 says, "He keepeth all his bones: not one of them is broken." Why invent something saying Roman soldiers deliberately disobeyed their protocol and refrained from breaking the legs of your character after he was dead? Too strange and uncontrived to be an invention. (We shall see an even more remarkable allusion to this in the feast of the Passover, a prophecy in itself.) And why have them thrust him through with a spear? Would you create this event from **Zechariah 12:10**, where it says, **"They shall look upon me whom they have pierced"**? ("Pierced" in this passage means "thrust through.") **Why bother incorporating all of these prophecies at all, much less having them all fulfilled within hours of each other?**

Buried with the wicked and the rich? Why make the fulfillment so complicated?

And how about **Isaiah 53:9? "And he made his grave with the wicked, and with the rich in his death." Why make up the idea of the two thieves crucified along with Jesus and the burial in the tomb of the wealthy Joseph of Arimathea? Why not simply say your character was buried with some wicked rich men?**

I think the point has been thoroughly made. **All of the fulfillments of the messianic prophecies we read in the Gospels are not at all what we would expect if contrived. So the invention theory does not fit the evidence at all.**

Messianic prophecy time-restricted prophecies

? Are there prophecies that predicted when the Messiah would come?

A few prophecies forecast the time in history when the Messiah came for the first time. One of these is **Genesis 49:10: "The scepter shall not depart from Judah, nor a lawgiver from between his feet, until Shiloh come, and unto him shall the gathering of the people be."** *The scepter spoken of refers to the right of the Jews to administer law and capital punishment. According to Smith and Eastman,*[7] *they had this right, even during their captivity in Babylon, right up until 7 A.D., when a Roman procurator named Caponius restricted the legal power of the Sanhedrin so they could no longer administer capital punishment. This is why they had to appeal to Rome to have Jesus put to death. Josephus the historian spoke of this transfer of power in his writings.*[8]

[?] Was the interpretation of this prophecy a Christian invention?

The above interpretation of Genesis 49:10 is not a Christian invention, for, according to Smith and Eastman, **in the writings of the Jews themselves, we can see that they believed this passage spoke of the Messiah** and that the departure of the scepter from Judah was this transfer of power in 7 A.D. They write in the Targum of Onkelos: "The transmission of dominion shall not cease from the house of Judah, nor the scribe from his children's children, forever, until the Messiah comes." In the Babylonian Talmud it states: "The world was created for the sake of the Messiah, what is this Messiah's name? **The school of Rabbi Shila said 'his name is Shiloh, for it is written; until Shiloh come.'"**[9]

[?] Was Genesis 49:10 fulfilled?

According to Smith and Eastman, the Babylonian Talmud[10] records that the Jews were grieved because they believed this prophecy had not come to pass. "When the members of the Sanhedrin found themselves deprived of their right over life and death, a general consternation took possession of them: they covered their heads with ashes, and their bodies with sackcloth, exclaiming: **'Woe unto us for the scepter has departed from Judah and the Messiah has not come.'"** But while they were grieving, a young boy was growing up in the city of Nazareth who

---

7   Chuck Smith and Mark Eastman, *Search for Messiah,* Joy Publishing Company/The Word for Today, (co-publishers), Fountain Valley/Costa Mesa, CA, revised and expanded ed., 1996, 101–102.

8   Ibid., 99.

9   Ibid., 100.

10 Ibid., 102.

was indeed Shiloh, the Messiah! So the timing of Jesus' arrival had to be before 6–7 A.D., and it was.

So a deceiver would have to make up a character at the right time period (and have to be born after this time period himself) and somehow have this fictitious character stand up to historical investigation and have secular sources mention him at the right time.

[?] What is one of the most amazing prophecies in the Bible?

An even more remarkable prophecy pinpoints the time of the Messiah: **Daniel 9:25–26: "Know therefore and understand, that from the going forth of the commandment to restore and to build Jerusalem unto the Messiah the Prince shall be seven weeks, and threescore and two weeks: … And after threescore and two weeks shall Messiah be cut off, but not for himself."** Most scholars believe the book of Daniel was written around 530 B.C. Some scholars try to late-date Daniel to around 160 A.D.; but not only is there much evidence to refute these late-dating attempts, **no scholars date Daniel after the time of Christ.**

[?] When is the starting point of this prophecy?

It is the decree to rebuild Jerusalem. The only decree that fits is in *Nehemiah 2:1*, where King Artaxerxes Longimanus grants the request of Nehemiah to have the city rebuilt. **The time period is given in verse 1: "In the month Nisan, in the twentieth year of Artaxerxes the king."**

A book in which some very important research seems to have been done about this prophecy is *The Coming Prince* by Sir Robert Anderson. According to Anderson,[11] Artaxerxes Longimanus ascended his throne in the Medo-Persian Empire in July 465 B.C. According to Smith and Eastman,[12] the Hebrew tradition says that if the day of the month is not specifically given, then it means the first day of that month or, in this case, the first day of Nisan. **This date of the decree of Artaxerxes corresponds to March 14, 445 B.C.** The date indicated for the decree to rebuild Jerusalem above has been verified by astronomical calculations at the British Royal Observatory.[13]

11 Sir Robert Anderson, *The Coming Prince,* Kregel Classics, Grand Rapids, MI, reprinted 1957, 66.

12 Smith and Eastman, *Search for Messiah,* 105–106.

13 Sir Robert Anderson, *The Coming Prince,* 124.

? How long between prediction and fulfillment according to Daniel 9? How long is the "seven and threescore weeks"?

Seven and threescore weeks add up to sixty-nine weeks, the endpoint of the prophecy being at sixty-nine weeks. (There is a seventieth week also, which points to end-time prophecy, which we will not discuss here.) In Jewish usage the "weeks" here implied are weeks of years, much as we would say a "decade" for a period of ten years.[14] Many ancient calendar years were 360 days in length,[15] including the biblical calendar years. According to Anderson,[16] the length of the biblical year was 360 days, as was the prophetic year. Therefore, for the prophetic calendar Jews used 360-day years. So how long would sixty-nine weeks of years be? **It would be 69 x 7 years x 360 days = 483 years, or 173,880 days. This is the duration of the prophecy, the time between prediction and fulfillment.**

? Where is the endpoint of this prophecy in history?

The endpoint is the coming of the **"Messiah the Prince."** The Hebrew word for "prince" is nagid, which actually means "king." Now in the Gospels, on many occasions, people tried to take Jesus and make Him king by force. He did not allow that to happen until on a particular day, during His triumphal entry into Jerusalem (called Palm Sunday), four days before His crucifixion.

Can scriptural clues help us determine this date? In the Gospel of Luke, Luke informs us of the start of John the Baptist's ministry: **"Now in the fifteenth year of the reign of Tiberius Caesar … the word of God came unto John the son of Zacharias in the wilderness" (Luke 3:1, 2).** In the fifteenth year of Tiberius Caesar, John the Baptist began his ministry. According to Anderson,[17] Tiberius Caesar began to reign in August of 14 A.D. So the fifteenth year of Tiberius Caesar would have been 28 A.D. (the year Tiberius's fifteenth year began, his first year beginning August of 14 A.D.), with Jesus beginning His ministry in the fall of that year. Most scholars agree there were four Passovers and three and a half years in Jesus' ministry and that He was crucified on the last of those four Passovers. This would correspond to the year 32 A.D., on the fourteenth of Nisan. This was

---

14 For example, see in Genesis 29:27–28, where Jacob completes a "week" by working for Laban for seven years.

15 One example would be ancient Babylon

16 Anderson, *The Coming Prince,* 67–75. Anderson refers to many places in the Bible, especially the books of Daniel and Revelation, in demonstrating this.

17 Ibid., 96.

equivalent to April 10, 32 A.D., **and the triumphal entry into Jerusalem would therefore be dated April 6, 32 A.D. (the tenth of Nisan).**[18]

? Luke said Jesus was "about thirty" when He began His ministry. But wasn't Jesus actually born about 4 B.C.? Wouldn't that make Him thirty-two years old when He began His ministry?

One objection that might be raised to the above dating is that Luke in his Gospel states that Jesus was "about thirty" when He began His ministry (Luke 3:23). This would seem to be a problem if Jesus was around thirty in 28 A.D., because many believe Jesus to have been born around 4 B.C. There are two ways to answer this difficulty. Sir Robert Anderson in his book assumes the traditional 4 B.C. date, and he notes that the fifteenth year of Tiberius Caesar actually began in August of 28 A.D. and went until August of 29 A.D. Anderson also noted that the word for "about" in the Greek implies the time up to the end of Jesus' thirty-first year, which would fit the date of Jesus beginning His ministry in the fall of 28 A.D., when Tiberius Caesar's fifteenth year was already under way. (Remember: there is no year 0.)[19]

? Was Jesus born in 4 B.C.?

Several lines of compelling evidence indicate a birth date of 2 B.C. rather than 4 B.C. for Jesus and allow for the "about thirty" to be more precisely thirty. Josephus mentioned but did not date an eclipse that was thought to have occurred in 4 B.C.; it had been traditionally used to pinpoint King Herod's death at 4 B.C. This tradition also assumed Jesus could have been up to two years old before Herod's death (which could push Jesus' birth date back to almost 6 B.C.) since Herod had all the babies two and under killed when he heard about Jesus' birth and Herod died about a month later. But the Greek word for young child, paidon, used in Matthew 2:9 can also mean an infant and is in fact so used of Jesus when He was only eight days old in Luke 2:21.

? What evidence is there for a 2 B.C. birthdate for Jesus?

There was also a similar eclipse that occurred in January of 1 B.C., according to astronomical research.[20] It turns out that erroneous conclusions

---

18 Ibid., 106–118, 127–128.

19 Ibid., 97.

20 Chuck Missler, *The Christmas Story,* tape commentary, Koinonia House, Coeur d'Alene, ID, 1994.

about the 4 B.C. eclipse caused many to fix Herod's death in January of 4 B.C., when in fact there are several reasons to conclude that Herod died in 1 B.C., "shortly after" an eclipse; so the eclipse Josephus mentioned (Antiquities, Book XVII, vi, 4) was actually the 1 B.C. eclipse.[21] Magillath Ta'anith, an ancient Jewish scroll contemporary with Jesus, states that Herod died January 14, 1 B.C.[22] There would have been at least two or three months between the birth of Jesus and Herod's death, during which the family fled to Egypt after Herod's decree, putting Jesus' birth in 2 B.C.

Other historical evidence:

- Tertullian, born about 160 A.D., stated that Augustus began to rule forty-one years before the birth of Jesus and died fifteen years after that event. Augustus died on August 19, 14 A.D., putting Jesus' birth at 2 B.C. (no year 0 between B.C. and A.D.).

- Tertullian also noted that Jesus was born twenty-eight years after the death of Cleopatra in 30 B.C., again fitting the 2 B.C. date.

- Other writers such as Irenaeus and Eusebius state facts that confirm the 2 B.C. date as well.[23]

Missler discusses one more line of evidence. John the Baptist's father, Zacharias, was a priest who was of the "course of Abijah," one of twenty-four courses of priests who each officiated in the temple in succession, a week at a time. When the temple was destroyed by Titus on August 5, 70 A.D., the first course of priests had just taken office. The course of Abijah being the eighth course, it can be traced backward to Zacharias and determined that he ended his duties on July 13, 3 B.C. John the Baptist's birth would then have been April 19-20 of 2 B.C. and Jesus' birth in the fall of 2 B.C.[24]

? How accurate was the prophecy in Daniel 9?

What all this means is that we can accept the 32 A.D. endpoint for this prophecy. So how does the data compare? We determined above that the beginning date for

---

21 Ibid.

22 William Filmer, "The Chronology of the Reign of Herod the Great" published in Oxford's *Journal of Theological Studies*, Oct. 1966, as referenced in websites **www.walkinthelight.ca/year_of_herod.htm.** and **www.herald.org/1997/97nd_7.htm.** Both web articles titled "The Year of Herod's Death."

23 Missler, *The Christmas Story*.

24 Ibid.

the prophecy was March 14, 445 B.C., that the length of time was 173,880 days, and that the endpoint of the prophecy was April 6, 32 A.D. So how many days are actually between March 14, 445 B.C., and April 6, 32 A.D.?

According to Anderson,[25] from March 14, 445 B.C., to March 14, 32 A.D., is 476 years (remember: there is no year 0). That is **476 years x 365 days/year = 173,740 days**. Leap year days need to be added, and they don't occur in century years unless divisible by 400, so we must add 3 fewer leap year days in four centuries, which equals 116 total additional days. From March 14 to April 6 is an additional 24 days. **So the total days = 173,740 + 116 + 24 = 173,880 days!! The exact number of days!!** Coincidence?! Or an amazing demonstration that God is able to see the beginning from the end and that the inspirer of this prophecy indeed can see outside the time domain? Surely this has to be one of the most remarkable prophecies of the Bible.

? Were the numbers "made to fit"?

Before we leave this prophecy it must be pointed out that some have tried to charge that the numbers have been "made to fit." Some writers have assumed the crucifixion took place in 29 or 30 A.D. because they assume the 4 B.C. date or earlier date for Jesus' birth. This date would mean that the fifteenth year of Tiberius Caesar, when John the Baptist began his ministry, would have to be pushed back several years earlier from A.D. 28. To get around this problem, they claim there was a period of time where Augustus and Tiberius were joint rulers (Tiberius was not yet the official caesar during this time), making the fifteenth year of Tiberius several years earlier. But there is nowhere to be found on coins or monuments or other sources, that Tiberius's length of reign would be accounted for by including the time he may have been co-ruler with Augustus. And these scholars come to their conclusions with much less precision than what we looked at above, citing only the years they believe the prophecy began and ended, without calculating numbers of days.

Another author, Harold Hoehner,[26] comes up with the same time interval, 173,880 days, but with the starting and ending date a year later (444 B.C. and 33 A.D.). The precision of days matches Anderson's approach, but in the opinion of some scholars Hoehner changes Anderson's starting and ending points from Nisan 445 B.C. to Nisan 444 B.C. and Nisan 32 A.D. to Nisan 33 A.D., shifting the calculations

---

25 Anderson, *The Coming Prince,* 127–128.

26 Tim LaHaye and Thomas Ice, *The Endtimes Controversy,* Harvest House, Eugene, OR, 2003, 327–330.

of the starting and ending points of the prophecy by one year. (Note: 33 A.D. as the endpoint does not cause a problem with previous calculations regarding Jesus' birth year, since the fifteenth year of Tiberius Caesar, the year Jesus began His ministry, ran from August of 28 to August of 29 A.D.) Regardless, the fact that Hoehner got the same exact number of days can hardly be coincidence. Anderson and Hoehner seem to have done the most precise research pertaining to this prophecy in Daniel 9.

There are a couple of more remarkable things about this prophecy in Daniel 9. **It says the Messiah will be "cut off" after the sixty-nine weeks, but "not for himself." The Hebrew word for "cut off" is** *karat,* **which means to be "executed for a capital crime."**[27] So the Messiah was predicted to have been executed for a capital crime, after His presentation as king, and that He would do this not for Himself. But the New Testament states why He did it—it was for our sins! And this was all predicted in advance. **What inventor would want to have their Messiah executed for a capital crime?**

This passage from Daniel 9 also says the temple will be destroyed. The second temple was destroyed in 70 A.D., so the prophecy had to be fulfilled before then. Another time restriction![28]

We have seen that many amazing prophecies predict the details of the Messiah's life. **When one person arrives on earth and fulfills all of these three hundred prophecies, He authenticates them and the Old Testament as a whole as God's Word.** And that is just what happened. **And Jesus Himself, in Luke 19:42–44, held the Jews accountable for knowing this, the "time of thy visitation."**[29]

---

27 Smith and Eastman, *Search for Messiah,* 110.

28 Ibid., 110.

29 Ibid., 111.

CHAPTER FOUR

HISTORY IN ADVANCE

PROPHECIES ABOUT PEOPLE

? How specific and accurate are Bible prophecies?

In contrast to the non-biblical "prophecies" (which will be discussed below), the Bible contains many very specific prophecies about places and people. Many have straightforward, discernible predictions about people and places, including some that use specific names, unlike the vague predictions of Nostradamus and others.

? What are some examples of prophecies naming specific people or places?

Jesus' birthplace: Bethlehem was named as the Messiah's birthplace about seven hundred years beforehand (Micah 5:2). And this prophecy was fulfilled by the decree of a pagan king, who ordered Mary and Joseph back to Bethlehem for the census.

Cyrus the Persian King

Isaiah, writing in about 700–680 B.C., specifically named the Persian king who would conquer Babylon. Isaiah also predicted the Babylonian capture of the Jews (see Isaiah 13). Here are some of the verses concerning the king of Persia: **"That saith of Cyrus, He is my shepherd, and shall perform all my pleasure: even saying to Jerusalem, Thou shalt be built; and to the temple, Thy foundation shall be laid" (Isaiah 44:28). "Thus saith the Lord to his anointed, to Cyrus, whose right hand I have holden, to subdue nations before him ... For Jacob my servant's sake, and Israel mine elect, I have even called thee by thy name: I have surnamed thee, though thou hast not known me" (Isaiah 45:1a, 4).**

Not only did Isaiah name this Persian king, but he also predicted this king would end their captivity so they could rebuild the temple at Jerusalem. The prophecy was given in about 700 B.C. and was fulfilled when a Persian king named Cyrus indeed conquered Babylon in 538 B.C. This would be as astonishing as finding a writer naming former President George W. Bush in a document dating from the 1840s and President Bush picking up this old document and seeing his name there!

[?] Was the prophecy about Cyrus written after its fulfillment?

Although some critics have tried to date Isaiah later so as to be written after 538 B.C., **there is much evidence that the book of Isaiah was written by one author in the eighth–seventh centuries B.C.** After laying out two chapters putting forth the extensive internal and external evidence for one writer, namely Isaiah, writing in the eighth century B.C., well-known Old Testament scholar Gleason Archer states: "In view of all the foregoing evidence, it may fairly be said that it requires a far greater exercise of credulity to believe that Isaiah 40–66 was not written by the historical eighth-century Isaiah than to believe that it was. Judging from the internal evidence alone, even apart from the authority of the New Testament authors, *a fair handling of the evidence can only lead to the conclusion that the same author was responsible for both sections and that no part of it was composed as late as the Exile.*"[1]

---

1   Gleason Archer, *A Survey of Old Testament Introduction,* Moody Press, Chicago, IL, revised and expanded ed., 1994, 390.

The Naming of King Josiah

Another king, Josiah, was named by a prophet in about 920 B.C. in the days of King Jeroboam, in 1 Kings 13:2, about 350 years before Josiah actually became king as chronicled in 2 Kings 23. Both the time period and the names of the kings of Israel and Judah have been verified by historical data and archaeology, as mentioned in the sections above.

The Bible has hundreds of predictions about specific places in the world; not only are these predictions clear and unambiguous, but not one of them has been proven false. Someone might say, "I can make predictions too." But will you be always right, especially centuries later?

> "The span of time between the writing of these prophecies and their fulfillment is so great that the most severe critic cannot claim that the predictions were made after the events happened."
>
> *Science Speaks*

[?] **Before we look at more prophecies, what about the skeptic's solution that all the so-called prophecies were simply written after the events they claim to predict?**

The accusation that the prophets wrote after the fulfillments happened, called post-dating, is naturally the line skeptics will take, for that is the only way they can deny that prophecy can actually happen. But they run into a major problem, not only with messianic prophecies or the prophecies of people's names already mentioned, as we have shown, but also with other prophecies in the Old Testament of specific places.

Multiple biblical prophets make many predictions about places like Tyre, Samaria, Gaza, Ashkelon, Jerusalem, Edom, Nineveh, Babylon, and more. Peter Stoner, in his book *Science Speaks*, commented on the biblical prophecies concerning the places listed above and the idea of post-dating these prophecies: "The span of time between the writing of these prophecies and their fulfillment is so great that **the**

most severe critic cannot claim that the predictions were made after the events happened. One of these prophecies was completely filled before Christ. Two had small parts fulfilled before Christ and the remaining parts after Christ. All other prophecies considered were completely fulfilled after Christ. If we were to strike out all estimates given for parts of prophecies fulfilled before Christ, our probability number would still be so large that the strength of its argument could not be comprehended"[2] (emphasis mine).

Bernard Ramm comments on post-dating: "Furthermore, **in practically every case we have given the radical the benefit of the doubt in dating the prophecies, so that the examples of fulfilled predictions lie outside the dates of the passages set by the radical critic"**[3] (emphasis mine).

[?] Are the historical fulfillments of Bible prophecies contrived?

I saw a comment by an atheist on the internet concerning Bible prophecy, and it went something like this: "Prophecy is like throwing a lawn dart and, wherever it lands, drawing a bull's-eye." The inference was that historical details are contrived or creatively interpreted to fit a Bible prophecy, and then the prophecy's fulfillment is claimed. Keep this accusation in mind as we look at a few examples of prediction and fulfillment concerning specific places and nations. See for yourself how clear the Bible's predictions are spelled out, and then see what the historical facts really are. The important thing is, how do they match up?

THE CITY OF TYRE PROPHECIES

One dramatic example is the predictions concerning the city of Tyre, as seen in the book of Ezekiel. It is important to know that the book of Ezekiel is firmly dated by scholars from 590–570 B.C. As mentioned earlier, the Septuagint translation of the Old Testament was made in 280–250 B.C.

The ancient city of Tyre was located in what is now the country of Lebanon. In the book of Ezekiel several predictions are made about the city of Tyre. Here is the text of **Ezekiel 26:3–5, 7, 12–14: "Therefore thus saith the Lord God; Behold,**

---

2   Peter Stoner, *Science Speaks,* Moody Bible Institute, Chicago, IL, 1963, 96, as quoted in McDowell, *Evidence That Demands a Verdict, 272.*

3   Bernard Ramm, *Protestant Christian Evidences,* Moody Press, Chicago, IL, 1957, 96, as quoted in McDowell, *Evidence That Demands a Verdict, 273.*

I am against thee, O Tyrus, and will cause many nations to come up against thee, as the sea causeth his waves to come up. And they shall destroy the walls of Tyrus, and break down her towers; I will also scrape her dust from her, and make her like the top of a rock. It shall be a place for the spreading of nets in the midst of the sea; for I have spoken it, saith the Lord God; and it shall become a spoil to the nations ... ,Behold, I will bring upon Tyrus Nebuchadrezzar king of Babylon, a king of kings, from the north ... And they shall make a spoil of thy riches, and make a prey of thy merchandise, and they shall break down thy walls, and destroy thy pleasant houses; and they shall lay thy stones and thy timber and thy dust in the midst of the water. And I will cause the noise of thy songs to cease; and the sound of thy harps shall be no more heard. AndI will make thee like the top of a rock; thou shalt be a place to spread nets upon; thou shalt be built no more: for I the Lord have spoken it, saith the Lord God."

? What is predicted about Tyre?

God placed His reputation on the line, saying, "I have spoken it," as He has challenged us with all His prophecies. Let's look at some of the specific predictions:

- Nebuchadnezzar will come against the city of Tyre.
- Many nations will come against Tyre.
- Tyre will become like a bare rock, with fishnets spread over the site.
- Tyre will have its stones, timber and rubble thrown into the sea.
- A time would come when Tyre would be "built no more."

I think we can see that these are very clear predictions. Nothing vague about them. And we can also see these predictions are plainly contained in the verses of Ezekiel quoted above, and we determined these were written anywhere from 590–570 B.C. So all that remains is to compare them with actual historical data.

The siege of Nebuchadnezzar: Nebuchadnezzar indeed laid siege to Tyre from 585–573 B.C., a thirteen-year siege in all. Tyre was situated so there was a mainland city on the coast and an island part of the city. When Nebuchadnezzar entered and destroyed the mainland city he found that most of the people had moved to the island part of the city. Nebuchadnezzar stopped there and did not go on to conquer the island.

Tyre's stones and rubble cast into the sea: Two hundred forty years later Alexander the Great attacked the now heavily walled island city of Tyre. He encountered a well-fortified city indeed, and it was hard to get near it without being hit by weapons and objects thrown from behind its walls. So Alexander the Great devised a strategy to build a causeway from the mainland to the island. He did this by **casting the debris and stones of the ruins of the mainland city into the water. So just as predicted, many nations came against Tyre, and the city ruins were literally thrown into the water.** As he progressed by using the stones and debris as a causeway he encountered deeper water and more resistance closer to the island.

Many nations come against Tyre: Alexander needed a larger navy to conquer the city, and so he organized and used the navies of six or seven countries he had already conquered, to bring them against Tyre and blockade the city. He finally built up the causeway enough to use battering rams and other weapons to break down the city walls. Alexander conquered Tyre three years later. Notice how the verse in **Ezekiel 26:12 reads: *"They ... shall lay thy stones and thy timber and thy dust in the midst of the water."*** This was *after* Nebuchadnezzar, when Alexander and many other nations were attacking; therefore the term "they" was used.

Tyre as a bare rock with fishnets spread over the site: In a history book from 1889, author Philip Myers[4] states of Tyre: "Alexander the Great ... reduced it to ruins (332 B.C.). She recovered in a measure from this blow but never regained the place she had previously held in the world. The larger part of the site of the once great city is now **bare as the top of a rock**—a place where the fishermen that still frequent the spot **spread their nets to dry**" (emphasis mine). And listen to these observations in a book by Nina Nelson titled *Your Guide to Lebanon*: **"Pale turquoise fishing nets were drying on the shore ... The ruins of ancient Tyre are different from all the others—situated ... in the heart of the sea"** (emphasis mine).[5]

Tyre "built no more": What exactly does this last prediction mean? According to McDowell,[6] Tyre was rebuilt and besieged more than once over the following

---

4   Philip Myers, *General History for Colleges and High Schools,* Ginn and Co., Boston, MA, 1889, 55, as quoted in McDowell, *Evidence That Demands a Verdict,* 276.

5   Nina Nelson, *Your Guide to Lebanon,* Alvin Redman, Ltd., London, UK, 220, as quoted in McDowell, *Evidence That Demands a Verdict,* 278.

6   McDowell, *Evidence That Demands a Verdict,* 279

centuries, only to fall for the final time to the Moslems in 1291 A.D. The original island city is now under water. A small modern city called Sur now stands near the ruins of the ancient mainland city, **but the original large city with all its walls, splendor and trading commerce has never been restored, although in an ideal location for a large city. The current small city is geared more toward fishing—hence the nets spread on rocks. This is actually expected since it was predicted that nets would be spread on the rocks.**

> "I considered the proclamations of the prophets to be so general that almost anything could be predicted from them. However, it was not long before I was shown that this was not the case."
>
> *A. J. Monty White, physical chemist and former atheist*

Some will say that any city on this site falsifies the prediction of "built no more." The fortified island city, however, is now under the sea. The ruins of the original large mainland city are scattered over a large area of land with a few columns still standing.[7] Athough a small city is built near some of the ancient ruins, it is not on the same site, nor is it by any means the original powerful city of Tyre that used to exist.[8] So it was never rebuilt in terms of its power and influence, much like a large castle could not be said to have been rebuilt because a few small buildings now stand on its original site.

So we can see that each specific prediction was fulfilled in detail—and some of these over many centuries after the prophecy was written. **Here is proof the author was writing history in advance, something beyond human ability and done accurately 100 percent of the time only by God.**

---

7   David Padfield, "The Destruction of Tyre", internet article, retrieved 10/7/2011 from http://www.padfield.com/1994/tyre.html.

8   Internet article on Tyre, at http://www.middleeast.com/tyre.htm.

"In view of the many fulfilled Bible prophecies...I began to think that perhaps Bible prophecy could be trusted."

A. J. Monty White, former atheist

PREDICTIONS ABOUT SAMARIA

We will look briefly at another example of this type of biblical prophecy. There was a prophecy about Samaria, the capital city of the northern Hebrew kingdom of Israel when the Jews were split into two kingdoms. This prophecy is given in **Micah 1:6**, written in about 700 B.C.: **"Therefore I will make Samaria as a heap of the field, and as plantings of a vineyard: and I will pour down the stones thereof into the valley, and I will discover the foundations thereof."**

? What is predicted about Samaria?

- Samaria will become as a "heap of the field."
- Vineyards will be planted there.
- Samaria's stones will be poured down into a valley.
- Samaria's foundations will be "discovered."

? What does history say about Samaria?

According to McDowell,[9] Samaria was attacked by Sargon in 722 B.C., where it fell by the sword. It was attacked again in 331 B.C. by Alexander the Great, and a third time in 120 B.C. by John Hyrcanus. All these conquests caused great destruction in Samaria. Samaria's final destruction came later on, in 1265 A.D., by the Muslims who defeated the Crusaders protecting the city.

John Urquhart quotes Van Velde: **"Samaria has been destroyed, but her rubbish has been thrown down into the valley; her foundations stones, those grayish ancient quadrangular stones of the time of Omri and Ahab, are discovered, and lie scattered about on the slope of the hill"**[10] (emphasis mine).

---

9 McDowell, *Evidence That Demands a Verdict,* 282.

10 John Urquhart, *The Wonders of Prophecy,* C. C. Cook, New York, n.d., 128, as quoted in McDowell, *Evidence That Demands a Verdict,* 282–283.

A. J. Monty White, a physical chemist and former atheist, mentions the prophecy about Samaria as one of the things that convinced him the Bible can be trusted: "One of the reasons why I rejected Christianity was because of Bible prophecy. I considered the proclamations of the prophets to be so general that almost anything could be predicted from them. However, it was not long before I was shown that this was not the case. There are four specific predictions in this one verse of prophecy (Micah 1:6) that was uttered in the latter half of the eighth century B.C. The first is that Samaria's ruins would become a heap of rubble. The second is that the stones used to construct Samaria would be pushed into a valley. The third is that Samaria's foundations would be laid bare. And the fourth is that Samaria would eventually become a place where vineyards would be planted.

"Although this destruction of Samaria was predicted by the prophet Micah in c. 730 B.C., it was not until A.D. 1265, almost 2,000 years later, that the prophecy began to be fulfilled. No one can argue that the prophet Micah saw this happen and then wrote it down spuriously claiming that he lived decades before the event and so had successfully prophesied Samaria's destruction ... Arabs living in the vicinity cleared much of the ruins in order to use the site for agricultural purposes, and in doing so, **they dug up its foundations and dumped them into a valley nearby. Today grapevines can be seen growing on this ancient site, just as prophesied by Micah over 2,700 years ago.**

"In view of the many fulfilled Bible prophecies, including the prediction of the destruction of the city of Samaria with such incredible accuracy, I began to think that perhaps Bible prophecy could be trusted"[11] (emphasis mine).

Again we see **specific, unambiguous predictions, clearly observed to be fulfilled**, with the type of observation and facts which could be easily verified as true or false. If the descriptions were colored to make them fit the prophecy, this again could easily be checked out by simply visiting the site. Yet when people have visited these sites they are astonished by the accuracy of the biblical descriptions.

---

11 A. J. Monty White, as quoted in *On the Seventh Day,* edited by John F. Ashton, Master Books, Green Forest, AR, 2002, 34–35.

PREDICTIONS ABOUT EDOM

Let's next look at Edom. The kingdom of Edom was located southeast of the Dead Sea and was almost as large as the state of New Jersey.[12] The people of Edom were the descendants of Esau. Edom was a constant enemy of Israel, and six different prophets spoke against it, with some very detailed predictions. We will look at just a few of these. **Jeremiah 49:18 reads: "No man shall abide there; neither shall a son of man dwell in it."**

Isaiah 34:13–15 states: "And thorns shall come up in her palaces, nettles and brambles in the fortresses thereof; and it shall be a habitation of dragons, and a court for owls. The wild beasts of the desert shall also meet with the wild beasts of the island, and the satyr shall cry to his fellow; the screech owl also shall rest there, and find for herself a place of rest. There shall the great owl make her nest, and lay, and hatch, and gather under her shadow; there shall the vultures also be gathered, every one with her mate."

Isaiah 34:10 reads: "It shall not be quenched night nor day; the smoke thereof shall go up forever: from generation to generation it shall lie waste; none shall pass through it for ever and ever."

Ezekiel 35:7 says: "Thus will I make mount Seir most desolate, and cut off from it him that passeth out and him that returneth."

? What was predicted about Edom?

It is predicted that:

- Edom would be desolate.

- Edom would become a habitation of wild animals.

- No one would pass through there, which could also mean that commerce and trade would cease.

- There is a specific reference to Mount Seir being desolate.

Some objections concerning Edom prophecies

"Now wait a minute," the skeptic says. "Look at the verses above. Doesn't it also predict that there shall be smoke going up from Edom forever? And in **Isaiah 34:7**

---

12 McDowell, *Evidence That Demands a Verdict,* 293.

THE BIBLE CAN BE PROVEN

doesn't it also say that **'their land shall be soaked with blood, and their dust made fat with fatness'**? And doesn't Jeremiah 49:17, which you skipped, say that everyone who passes by it shall be astonished and hiss? If you go there, you better make sure and watch out for the smoke, and, of course, don't forget to hiss or the prophecy won't be fulfilled!"

[?] Are these false prophecies or just figurative language?

These are typical of the kinds of rebuttals and ridicule skeptics put forth against this type of Bible prophecy. **They choose to ignore the fact that in Hebrew writing poetic and figurative language is used along with straightforward literal language.** The idioms of "smoke going up from them forever" are used throughout the Old Testament as a word picture of the aftermath of violent destruction and desolation. And "hissing" simply meant that people would be making exclamations of astonishment that such an impregnable-looking kingdom could fall. The use of "everyone" is obviously not intended to be literal, but in general that will be people's reaction, which is how we would use it today. And "land soaked with blood" is often used in and out of the Bible to describe a bloody war in the land, not every bit of land being covered with blood!

The use of these word pictures and figures of speech in no way negates the verses that make literal predictions such as "no man shall abide there" or "from generation to generation it shall be desolate," or describing it as the habitation of wild animals, which could also be used as a metaphor. As we shall see, nonetheless, this was literally fulfilled.

[?] What are the literal fulfillments about Edom?

Edom "disappears": All the prophecies about Edom were completed around 570 B.C., the lower range for the dating of Ezekiel. Isaiah wrote in the 700s and Jeremiah from about 620–580 B.C.[13] Sometime around 312 B.C. the Nabataeans conquered Edom and Petra, its fortified rock city.[14] According to McDowell,[15] the Jews also conquered Edom as related in the first book of Maccabees. Then Edom was attacked by John Hyrcanus. They became incorporated into the Jewish nation at the time of Christ and were known as Idumaea: "The Edomites were now

---

13 "Fulfilled Bible Prophecy Dealing with Nations," internet article, www.clarifyingchristianity.com.

14 Ibid.

15 McDowell, *Evidence That Demands a Verdict*, 290.

incorporated with the Jewish nation, and the whole province was often termed by Greek and Roman writers Idumaea. Immediately before the siege of Jerusalem by Titus, 20,000 Idumaeans were admitted to the Holy City, which they filled with robbery and bloodshed. **From this time, the Edomites, as separate people, disappear from the page of history."**[16]

Edom made desolate: Petra, located in the land of Edom, which was a highly fortified rock city, existed for many centuries following. It was practically impregnable from the assault of an army, a city not very likely to become desolate or the habitation of only wild animals. Because it was located next to the mountains called Mount Seir, Petra was often referred to as "Mount Seir" by other nations and people, referring to its strength and high-up position. **The city of Petra flourished until the Romans conquered Petra in 106 A.D. From that time it declined, becoming almost uninhabited from the seventh to twelfth centuries A.D. when it revived slightly. Afterward it declined again and has been basically desolate since then.**[17]

Edom a habitation for wild animals: In 1865 George Smith quoted various writers to describe what Petra was like in his day: "Captain Mangles, who visited these ruins, says that when surveying the scenery of Petra, 'the screaming of the eagles, hawks, and owls, who were soaring over our heads in considerable numbers, seemingly annoyed at anyone approaching their lonely habitation, added much to the singularity of the scene.' ... And Volney relates that the 'Arabs, in general, avoid the ruins of the cities of Idumaea, on account of the enormous scorpions with which they swarm.' ... As the **term 'satyr'** is known to be applied to a fabulous animal, the use of the name in the Scriptures has occasioned some surprise and inquiry. **The word signifies 'a rough hairy one' and may well have been used to designate the wild goat, large herds of which are found on these mountains."**[18]

Herbert Stewart describes it further: "The stone on which the traveler may sit is **surrounded by nettles and thistles in what had been in the precincts of noble temples or palaces."**[19]

---

16 Merrill F. Unger, *Unger's Bible Dictionary,* Moody Press, Chicago, IL, rev. ed., 1966, 286, as quoted in McDowell, *Evidence That Demands a Verdict,* 290.

17 "Fulfilled Bible Prophecy Dealing with Nations."

18 George Smith, *The Book of Prophecy*, London, Longmain, Green, Reader and Dyer, 1865, 221-222, as quoted in McDowell, *Evidence That Demands a Verdict,* 291.

19 Herbert Stewart, *The Stronghold of Prophecy,* Marshall, Morgan and Scott Publications, London, 1941, 71-72, as quoted in McDowell, *Evidence That Demands a Verdict,* 291.

So Petra and Edom were laid waste and were indeed a habitation for the kinds of animals described in the prophecies.

And Petra today? It was the site where *Indiana Jones and the Last Crusade* **was filmed, the "temple" being a large tomb cut in the cliff. The area is still desolate.**[20]

No one to pass through Edom anymore: The Edomites themselves are gone as a people. Furthermore, the traffic and commerce that used to pass through that region is so reduced as to be almost negligible, as talked about by William G. Blaikie in his 1904 book *A Manual of Bible History*: "The objection that the prophecy has not been literally fulfilled, inasmuch as travelers have passed through Edom, is evidently frivolous. When the vast streams of traffic that used to pass through Edom have been so withdrawn that not a single caravan is ever seen on the route, the prophecy has surely been abundantly verified."[21]

It seems when Bible prophecy says a city will be desolate forever it happens. And in other cases cities are prophesied of as having sieges and wars; yet if the Bible says they will not pass away or will be re-inhabited they survive or are rebuilt after being destroyed and are still around today. For example, the sister city of Tyre was Sidon. It was prophesied to have much bloodshed and war; yet there was no mention of its destruction. And, sure enough, Tyre is destroyed, but Sidon, even though destroyed several times, has always been rebuilt and exists today.[22] Why was one destroyed and not the other?

OTHER PREDICTIONS ABOUT SPECIFIC PLACES

The manner of the destruction of Nineveh predicted

Other cities like Nineveh are mentioned as being destroyed, as are some of the specifics of the destruction. The destruction of Nineveh was prophesied by the prophet Nahum.

Nineveh was prophesied to be destroyed in a state of drunkenness (Nahum 1:10), by fire (Nahum 3:13), and also by flood (Nahum 1:8; 2:6). Pretty specific. So what does history show?

---

20 "Fulfilled Bible Prophecy."

21 William G. Blaikie, *A Manual of Bible History,* Thomas Nelson and Sons, London, UK, 1904, 141, as quoted in McDowell, *Evidence That Demands a Verdict,* 293.

22 McDowell, *Evidence That Demands a Verdict,* 281.

As McDowell notes,[23] there was **drunkenness among the Assyrian army** which was a significant factor in their being conquered, **the king set fire to his own palace** when defeated, and **flood conditions were also a major factor in Nineveh's rapid defeat.** Nineveh fell in 612 B.C., and the date of Nahum's prophecy has been dated as early as 654 B.C., for which there is a good deal of evidence, and some scholars prefer a date of 625 to about 620 B.C.[24]

Of course, skeptics and rationalists, who presuppose there is no such thing as prophecy, date it to after 612. But they try to do this with all prophecies, because their faith must be that all the Jewish writers made up prophecies and faked fulfillments of prophecy. Some of these critics must even believe the Jews invented their own history and were therefore liars! **If that is what they want to believe, then that is their faith; but it is question-begging at best, as well as being very insulting to the Jews.**

There are many more examples of prophecies of specific places and quotes from historians and other observers about their historical fulfillment. **For much more extensive information, Josh McDowell's** *Evidence That Demands a Verdict* from which I have drawn many of these quotes, is an excellent reference.

❓ Is Isaiah 17:1-2 a false prophecy, as skeptics charge?

Some have tried to find some false prophecies concerning cities, as mentioned above. For example, the charge has been made that **Isaiah 17:1–2** is a false prophecy, because in some modern Bible translations, such as the Revised Standard Version, the verses read as follows: **"Damascus will cease to be a city, and will become a heap of ruins. Her cities will be deserted forever."** Since Damascus is still here, is this a false prophecy, as they charge?

When we examine the Hebrew and more reliable translations such as the King James or the NIV, we see that Isaiah says in verse 2 of chapter 17 that the "**cities of Aroer are forsaken," not Damascus. Damascus is simply spoken of as being a "ruinous heap," but the idea of Damascus being "deserted forever" is not found.** The cities of Aroer were on the banks of the Arnon River, in the land of Moab near Israel, whereas Damascus was Syria's capital, much farther to the

---

23 Ibid., 299.

24 Archer, *A Survey of Old Testament Introduction,* 392.

north. This can be verified on any good Bible lands map. This is also referenced in the text of the Bible in 2 Kings 10:33.

So these verses do not actually say Damascus was going to be a heap of ruins forever, or, for that matter, the cities of Aroer. Damascus was attacked by Assyria, Persia, the Greeks, the Romans, and the Byzantines and is described in historical references as having suffered "disaster and destruction" and "neglect" and "deterioration" but was not destroyed forever. It revived again and again.

> "This restoration of a nation after twenty-five centuries is utterly astonishing, a phenomenon without parallel in the history of any other peoples ... "
>
> *Dave Hunt, A Cup of Trembling*

Many cities were destroyed and rebuilt, as described above. And even the skeptics would have to allow for the description that Damascus would "become a heap of ruins" as possibly figurative for a loss of their power. So the charge of a proven "false prophecy" itself is false.

[?] What precautions need to be taken when discerning Bible prophecy?

This kind of case shows that **it is important in citing these prophecies to check as closely as possible the meaning of the Hebrew in the few cases where some significant differences may exist between different popular Bible translations.** Sometimes, but not always, figurative and poetic language is used. It is important to make all these distinctions when evaluating Bible prophecy concerning specific places.

We have seen that many specific predictions about cities and nations have come to pass. Each of these predictions can be given odds on their fulfillment. There are so many of them that even if each is given very conservative odds, when they are taken collectively, **the odds are so great against their being fulfilled by chance as to be impossible in practical, scientific terms. Here then is another proof for the divine inspiration of the Bible.**

We have saved talking about prophecy concerning one specific nation for the next section. This is the unique Bible prophecy concerning the nation Israel.

PROPHECY ABOUT THE NATION ISRAEL

Author and lecturer Dave Hunt has said a person can't look honestly at the Bible prophecies about Israel and their historical fulfillments and credibly remain an atheist or agnostic. Hunt calls prophecy about Israel "The Overlooked, Irrefutable Proof" in the title of a chapter of his latest book.[25] Hunt also wrote *A Cup of Trembling,* which deals with Israel and prophecy. Some of his research will be noted below. Let's examine what the Bible says about Israel, as well as the historical record.

? **What are the specific predictions and fulfillments concerning the nation Israel in the Bible?**

A promised land

Loss of this promised land through disobedience

Many nations could have picked out a "promised land" for themselves and later been driven from that land. But from the Babylonian exile forward, the predicted history of Israel becomes unique.

Jews scattered around the world: God said His people would be scattered all over the world, **"among all people, from the one end of the earth even unto the other" (Deuteronomy 28:64; also see Nehemiah 1:8; Zechariah 7:14).** The expression "wandering Jew" came about because this is exactly what happened, the Jews having no country of their own from about the time of the Babylonian captivity until just before 1948, when the Jews reentered their land as a nation.

Irrational anti-Semitism: Furthermore, God warned the Jews that wherever they went they would be **"an astonishment, a proverb, and a byword, among all nations" (Deuteronomy 28:37), "a curse ... and a reproach, among all the nations whither I have driven them" (Jeremiah 29:18; also see 44:8).** Even after the Holocaust anti-Semitism is still around, and everyone seems to speak against the Jew, even the news media (for some disturbing information about this,

---

25 Dave Hunt, *Cosmos, Creator, and Human Destiny,* The Berean Call, Bend, OR, 2010, 447–471.

see the recent book *Philistine* by Ramon Bennett[26]). No other nation or people have been the object of such hatred and reproach.

Persecuted and killed like no other nation: God also foretold that the Jews would be persecuted and killed like no other nation on earth. (See Deuteronomy 28:65–66, Jeremiah 29:18, and many others.) As Hunt describes, this is exactly what has happened to the Jews century after century, no matter where they have lived. With Hitler, some Roman Catholic popes' and among Protestant groups also the Jews have been physically persecuted and killed.[27]

Even with all this persecution God said He would preserve the Jews as a nation and a people separated. (See Jeremiah 30:11; 31:35-37; Exodus 33:16; Leviticus 20:26.)[28] It is not the purpose or within the scope of this book to go into all the spiritual dynamics behind God's allowing Israel to be persecuted by their enemies, His reasons for their judgment' or His plan to preserve Israel as a nation with His promises for their blessed future. Rather, what is being shown here is that what God said would happen to Israel has indeed happened, and natural/coincidental explanations for the fulfillment of these prophecies fail.

Preservation of Israel as a nation despite centuries without a homeland

As Hunt describes: **"The Jews had every reason to intermarry, to change their names and hide their despised identity by any possible means in order to escape persecution. Why preserve their bloodline when they had no land of their own, when most of them didn't take the Bible literally and when racial identification imposed only the cruelest disadvantages?"**[29] Could "tradition" without real faith in God's biblical promises be that strong? In some situations it was even against the law for them to intermarry, such as when the popes forbid Jews to marry Christians. So in these cases forces outside their control prevented them from losing their identity.[30] Could it be that God had providentially preserved them as a nation, just as He foretold they would be? According to Hunt, **no other nation has ever survived more than a few centuries as an identifiable people once they lost their land. Yet the Jewish nation has retained their identity over**

---

26 Ramon Bennett, *Philistine,* Shekinah Books Ltd., Citrus Heights, CA, 1995.

27 Hunt, *A Cup of Trembling,* Harvest House, Eugene, OR, 1995, 100–101.

28 Ibid.

29 Ibid.

30 Ibid.

2500 years. This is absolutely unprecedented in history and yet was the prediction of the God of the Bible concerning His people.[31]

Israel brought back into their own land

God preserved them because He promised to bring them back into their land as a nation (see Jeremiah 30:10; 31:8-12; Ezekiel 36:24, 35–38, etc.) Here is the text of Ezekiel 36:24: "For I will take you from among the heathen, and gather you out of all the countries, and *will bring you into your own land*" (emphasis mine). This and many other prophecies clearly predict the restoration of the nation Israel to their own land. But for centuries people must have thought this was impossible and therefore thought the Bible contained a false prophecy. But then, in 1948, Israel was indeed restored as a nation into their own land. According to Hunt, "this restoration of a nation after twenty-five centuries is utterly astonishing, a phenomenon without parallel in the history of any other peoples and inexplicable by any natural means, much less by chance."[32]

> [?] Did the Jews return to their own land deliberately just to fulfill prophecy?

The skeptic may object that the Jews returned to their own land to deliberately fulfill prophecy. Let's see how this objection holds up. There indeed was a small group of people called Zionists who had hopes of recovery of the land. But very few actually believed the Bible prophecies would come to pass. Furthermore, there was no real support from any world powers for the idea that the Jews had any special claim to their own land.[33]

The Balfour Declaration

As Hunt describes, in 1917 President Woodrow Wilson laid down requirements for peace that included the establishment of an international organization of nations to guarantee that independent states could have security in their lands from takeover as the result of war. And also in 1917 the British foreign secretary Arthur James Balfour issued a statement that came to be known as the Balfour Declaration, which

---

31 Ibid.
32 Ibid., 102.
33 Ibid., 109.

favored the establishment of a Jewish homeland in what was called Palestine. The Supreme Council of Allied and Associated Powers gave approval in 1920 for the provisions of the Balfour Declaration to be put in place, and Jewish immigration into Palestine was encouraged. From 1922 to 1935 the number of Jews there went from about 85,000 to 250,000.[34]

Britain goes back on their declaration

According to Hunt, the large Arab population (about 650,000) at the time was not able to compete educationally and technologically with the incoming Jews, this competition built resentment, and finally riots occurred. In 1939 Britain yielded to the Arabs and decided to put tight limits on all Jewish immigration into Palestine, going back on their former declaration. They issued a decree called the White Paper that even denied the original British intention in the Balfour Declaration to establish an independent Jewish state, instead promising a Palestinian state that would be governed by both Jews and Arabs. Neither side was happy, the Jews feeling let down and the Arabs not wanting to share the land.[35]

The Holocaust: Who would deliberately go through this?

Then came the Holocaust of World War II and all the associated murders and atrocities against the Jews. Even after the Holocaust, when the Jewish people tried to return to their homes, they were killed by townspeople who did not want to give up their homes.[36] Yet, amazingly, little world sympathy was aroused, Britain still severely limiting immigration of Jews. The Jews then began organized smuggling of Holocaust survivors into Palestine, and despite British blockades the Jewish population there was about 600,000 by 1947. Finally Britain decided policing this was too great a burden, and they capitulated, stating they would remove restrictions by May 15, 1948. In late 1947 the United Nations voted to divide up Palestine west of the Jordan River, with about 18 percent for the Jews' homeland, the rest to the Arabs.[37] The United Nations did this because of the desperate situation of the many homeless Holocaust survivors.

---

34   Ibid., 109–110.

35   Ibid., 110–111.

36   Ibid., 111.

37   Ibid., 112.

Author Dave Hunt comments on this: "Volumes have been written in an attempt to explain how a loving God could have allowed the Holocaust. We will make no such attempt. One thing is certain, however: Without that slaughter, the State of Israel would not exist today. That was the catalyst which moved complacent Jews to desperation and momentarily aroused the conscience of the world. **The Holocaust and the spectacle of its homeless survivors awakened sufficient public shame and sympathy for the world powers to take the necessary and long-delayed action to provide a national Jewish homeland. That action could not have taken place at any other time in history either before or since"**[38] (emphasis mine).

But the Arabs did not want to share Palestine, and they attacked the Jewish settlement and transports. **With no help from the U.N. or the British, the heavily outgunned and outnumbered Jews themselves eventually gained victory overall, and on May 14, 1948, the nation of Israel was officially born.**

One further note: according to Hunt,[39] the land of Israel had never been divided before the present day, even when held by other empires in the past. Only in modern times has the land been "parted" by many nations, as the prophet Joel describes: **"I will also gather all nations … and will plead with them there for my people and for my heritage Israel, whom they have scattered among the nations, and parted my land" (Joel 3:2).**

[?] What does Israel's history show about prophecy?

What the history of Israel shows is that many circumstances outside Israel's control, and undesirable to them, contributed to the fulfillment of this prophecy. Furthermore, a large percentage of today's Israelis do not claim to believe the Bible prophecies or that God is the reason they are back in their land. The Bible predicts that God would bring Israel back into the land first, while they were still unbelievers (see Ezekiel 36 and 37). **Even if they did believe the Bible, would they have thought it was worth being persecuted and killed to be back in their land? And would it have been predicted that so many Jews would be brought in from places like the Soviet Union, which had to be broken up to accomplish this? Who would have expected the breakup of the USSR?**

---

38 Ibid.

39 Hunt, *Cosmos, Creator, and Human Destiny,* 463.

THE BIBLE CAN BE PROVEN

All these things are so unlikely to have been fulfilled either by chance or deliberately fulfilled by the Israelis themselves that atheism or agnosticism indeed seems impossible to maintain intelligently.

> **[?]** Is there any prophecy that foretells the time period when Israel would be restored as a nation?

As if all this wasn't enough, the Bible also holds some clues regarding the timing of the restoration of Israel. This is similar to the prophecy of Daniel's seventy weeks but quite a bit more obscure. Nevertheless, it is worth looking at to see what clues the Holy Spirit may have left us in Scripture.

Ezekiel 4:4–6 reads: "Lie thou also upon thy left side, and lay the iniquity of the house of Israel upon it: according to the number of days that thou shalt lie upon it thou shall bear their iniquity. For I have laid upon thee the years of their iniquity, according to the number of the days, three hundred and ninety days: so shall thou bear the iniquity of the house of Israel. And when thou hast accomplished them, lie again on thy right side, and thou shalt bear the iniquity of the house of Judah forty days: I have appointed thee each day for a year."

This is an object lesson the Lord is teaching through Ezekiel (who perhaps performed this action at a set time in the center of town), equating the number of days he lies on his side with the number of years Israel was to be punished for their iniquity. The things we are going to look at in these verses are the numbers: **390 + 40 years = 430 years.** Thus this verse seems to say that Israel would be punished for 430 years for their iniquities. But they were only in captivity in Babylon for 70 years, from 606 B.C. to 536 B.C., so 360 years would have still remained.

According to Grant Jeffrey,[40] when we look at Jewish history we see there was no return to their country at the end of either 360 or 430 years. Why didn't anything significant occur for Israel at those times, especially 430 years after the beginning of their captivity in 536 B.C.? At first we would be inclined to dismiss the verse as symbolic, or a skeptic might say it was a false prophecy if someone were to assert that it was indeed a prophecy.

---

40   Jeffrey, *The Signature of God,* 167.

Now the Bible states that Israel did not repent of their sins at the end of their seventy-year captivity. Looking in Leviticus 26, we see that the Lord sets out punishments and rewards based on Israel's obedience or disobedience.

Jeffrey points out that four times in this passage in Leviticus God declares to Israel that if after being punished for her sins she still did not repent, the punishment already decreed by God would be multiplied seven times. If we apply this principle, then after the 70 years of captivity, since Israel did not repent, the 360 remaining years of further punishment would be multiplied seven times, to equal **360 x 7 = 2,520 years.**[41]

As we saw earlier, there is plenty of external and internal evidence that a biblical year was 360 days. So **2,520 years x 360 days = 907,200 days.** Following Jeffrey's calculations, to convert this into our current calendar years, divide 907,200 by 365.25 days which equals 2,483.8 years. The end of the Babylonian captivity occurred in spring of 536 B.C. When we add 2,483.8 years to 536.4 B.C., taking into account that there is no year 0, we come to 1948.4 A.D., or about May of 1948!![42] Contrived? What a coincidence then! The odds seem too great, and the fit to how the Lord has designed other parts of Scripture too close, to dismiss this one to chance.

Even without considering the above possible prediction in Ezekiel of the date of the birth of the nation Israel, which some consider to be a bit too obscure, the other prophecies of the nation Israel already mentioned above are so precise as to be impossible to be fulfilled by chance. It is also totally unreasonable to believe they have been deliberately fulfilled. **They thus prove the existence of God, that the Bible is the inspired Word of God and that the Jews are indeed His people chosen by Him to reveal Himself to the world.**

Present-day Israel

A further note: there are many prophecies concerning the nation Israel whose fulfillments are yet future. But some further possible fulfillments in modern times should be mentioned. Although these are not as concrete fulfillments as what we have already talked about and could be thought of as somewhat subjective, the author presents them here for consideration.

---

41 Ibid., 167–168.

42 Ibid., 168–170.

The present state of the nation of Israel: We have already talked about the rebirth of the nation Israel in 1948, a remarkable fulfillment of prophecy. How about what is going on in Israel today? How does that fit in? First, let's check what the Bible says about Israel, and Jerusalem in particular, in **Zechariah 12:2, 3 and 6: "Behold, I will make Jerusalem a cup of trembling unto all the people round about, when they shall be in the siege both against Judah and Jerusalem. And in that day will I make Jerusalem a burdensome stone for all people: all that burden themselves with it shall be cut in pieces, though all the peoples of the earth be gathered together against it … In that day will I make the governors of Judah like a hearth of fire among the wood, and like a torch of fire in a sheaf; and they shall devour all the people round about, on the right hand and on the left, and Jerusalem shall be inhabited again in her own place, even in Jerusalem."**

? Do events in present-day Jerusalem fit prophecy?

Jerusalem is a focal point: As Dave Hunt describes,[43] at the time these words were written, it must have seemed difficult to imagine that many nations would be very concerned over Jerusalem. **When Zechariah penned this prophecy, the city of Jerusalem lay in barrenness and desolation.** Furthermore, Jerusalem doesn't have anything special to offer in terms of location or natural resources; yet **many experts today see Jerusalem as a contention point for a major war. Much of the tension is surrounding the Temple Mount in Jerusalem, considered a holy site by both Jews and Muslims; the experts agree it is a focal point for peace or war.** How are we to explain all this? **Has Jerusalem indeed become a "burdensome stone"?**

Israel's victories in war despite seeming superior opposition: The tiny nation of Israel has repeatedly turned back larger armies of Islamic attackers, even when those attackers have been backed by the former Soviet Union. **Israel has one of the most powerful militaries in the world, after the USA, Russia, and China, even though they are such a tiny country. Has Israel indeed become a "cup of trembling" and a "fire among the wood"?**[44]

---

43 Hunt, *A Cup of Trembling,* 307.

44 Ibid., 307–309.

NEW TESTAMENT PROPHECY BY JESUS CHRIST

? What happened when Christ pronounced judgment on specific cities?

So far we have been dealing with Old Testament prophecy. There is also prophecy in the New Testament. An example of this involves four ancient cities mentioned in the New Testament: Capernaum, Chorazin, Bethsaida, and Tiberias. **In Matthew 11 Jesus rebukes the inhabitants of Capernaum, Chorazin and Bethsaida for not repenting after all the miracles that were done in their cities. He pronounced "woe" on all three of these cities, but no such judgment was pronounced on Tiberias.** All of these cities were situated near or on the shores of the Sea of Galilee.

Today only the city of Tiberias stands. The other three cities perished in an earthquake around 400 A.D. Josh McDowell brings together some provocative quotes on these cities: "Ancient **Bethsaida's** situation on the shore of the Sea of Galilee had been so beautiful that about 700 A.D. King Albalid I of Damascus decided to build a magnificent winter palace on the site of the ruined city. For fifteen years his workmen labored erecting the palace. Then **King Albalid died, and the great palace was never completed. As the centuries rolled by, the palace became mere ruins."**[45]

Concerning **Capernaum,** Davis writes: "For long centuries the synagogue lay buried under the earth like the rest of the destroyed city ... **A man conceived the idea of restoring the ancient synagogue from its ruins.** At length parts of the walls of the building were re-erected, and a number of the pillars were put in their places. Then the unexpected happened. **The architect of the partly restored synagogue suddenly died—just as King Albalid had died centuries ago before his palace in Bethsaida was completed."**[46]

Davis comments on Tiberias: **"Not one word of judgment was pronounced on the city of Tiberias by our Lord. It has been partly destroyed several times, but it has always been rebuilt."**[47] He concludes: **"Each time we have visited**

---

45 George Davis, *Bible Prophecies Fulfilled Today,* The Million Testaments Campaigns, Inc., Philadelphia, PA, 1955, 36–37, as quoted in McDowell, *Evidence That Demands a Verdict,* 310–311.

46 Ibid., 38, as quoted in McDowell, *Evidence That Demands a Verdict,* 310–311.

47 Ibid., 40, as quoted in McDowell, *Evidence That Demands a Verdict,* 311.

Tiberias and the area around the Sea of Galilee we have been impressed anew with the truthfulness and the supernatural inspiration of the Word of God. There are the ruins of three cities, destroyed exactly as foretold by our Lord, and one city, Tiberias, upon which no word of judgment was uttered, still standing and flourishing after nineteen long centuries."[48]

Just another coincidence? The occurrence of so many "coincidences" is becoming quite incredible.

[?] Were Jesus' predictions fulfilled in history?

Jesus made several statements, predictions which have been fulfilled in history, but which seemed very unlikely at the time He made them. Here are a few examples.

Matthew 24:35 declares, "Heaven and earth shall pass away, but my words shall not pass away." Even though the Bible has been persecuted throughout history like no other book, it remains the best-selling book through to today. When Jesus spoke these words, He was an obscure carpenter who did very limited traveling, so one would think only His followers would care about His words. But those words have been read, obeyed, and loved in more nations than any other person's words ever written. They indeed have not passed away.

The thriving of the Christian church: In Matthew 16:18 Jesus said, "Upon this rock I will build my church; and the gates of hell shall not prevail against it." This small band of disciples, uneducated fishermen and other ordinary people, multiplied and thrived despite horrible opposition, and all this founded simply on the belief that Jesus is the Son of God!

The gospel carried to the remotest parts of the earth: Acts 1:8 states, "Ye shall be witnesses unto me ... unto the uttermost part of the earth." Again, who would think the message carried by this obscure preacher and His band of disciples would reach the ends of the earth? **Yet with radio, TV, air travel and the like there are very few areas on the globe where the gospel hasn't gone.**

More problems for the invention theory: These prophecies are another powerful evidence for the authenticity of the Gospels. It doesn't help to say the New Testament writer misquoted or exaggerated what Jesus said or even invented what He said. The New Testament writers can hardly be charged with manufacturing the

---

48 Ibid., 41, as quoted in McDowell, *Evidence That Demands a Verdict,* 311.

prophecy's fulfillments. This in itself would be a greater miracle than if Jesus actually made these statements and was who He said He was.

NON-BIBLICAL "PROPHETS": THE DIFFERENCE IS OBVIOUS!

? Are there true prophets outside the Bible? Can these "prophets" accurately predict the future?

We need to answer a question often heard when biblical prophecy is mentioned: "What about Nostradamus, Jean Dixon, etc.? Aren't they prophets too? What's so special about biblical prophets? After all, lots of people are out there making predictions!"

Deuteronomy 13 discusses how a false prophet may sometimes (but not a hundred percent of the time) be able to predict something accurately. Some of these false prophets may just be good guessers, but some others may actually be in contact with various spiritual entities (demonic) which can supply them with information.

Remember that, according to the Bible, a false prophet is one who either makes a wrong prediction (one strike and you're out!) and/or leads you to follow other gods.

? Allowances for genuine predictions aside. what about the track record of some of these non-biblical "prophets"?

Many psychics and "prophets" claim to be able to predict the future. When they "predict," they seem to be very general in many cases, sometimes attaching contingencies to their forecasts. Then they can always reinterpret if their original prediction doesn't come to pass. And here is the first difference. As we saw in Deuteronomy 18 above, if a Bible prophet predicts something it always comes to pass. This makes sense since he/she is getting information from God, who cannot be mistaken.

We mentioned above that Deuteronomy 13 says God sometimes allows even false prophets to predict correctly. Now if a non-biblical "prophet" has a "spirit guide" who is supplying information, this demonic spirit can supply the person with information and even visions of places and people and facts the spirit knows and impart that knowledge to the "prophet" or psychic who is contacting them. Thus, the psychic "knows" facts about a person he or she has never met or sees places he/she has never been and so amazes his/her listeners. **All this is supernatural, but not from God.**

? **But what about those famous "prophets" like Nostradamus or Jean Dixon? Didn't they have great track records? Didn't they get everything mostly right? Why aren't they like the biblical prophets?**

Nostradamus was probably the most famous astrological predictor, who lived in France in the 1500s. He wrote about four thousand verses, called "quatrains," supposed predictions of the future. Some believe Nostradamus correctly predicted the rise of Hitler. Here is the text that is supposed to predict Hitler's rise: "In the year that is to come soon, and not far from Venus, The two greatest ones of Asia and Africa, Shall be said to come from the Rhine and Ister, Crying and tears shall be at Malta and on the Italian Shore."[49] Nostradamus's followers tell us that "Ister" means Hitler.

But, according to Irwin Lutzer, instead it is very likely that "Ister" is a river, because another version of this same prophecy says: "From the Rhine and the Lower Danube they will be said to have come."[50]

Then they say Nostradamus predicted the death of Hitler in this translation of his prophecy: "Beasts ferocious with hunger will swim across rivers. The greater part of the army will be against Hister" (literally *hister sera*"). The great one shall cause him to be dragged into a cage of iron, when the German infant (literally *"enfant de Germain"*) observes no law."[51] But, according to Norman Geisler, "Hister" (another version of "Ister") can be shown to mean the Lower Danube (a river). So the translation should not be "Hitler," but "Danube." Furthermore, "de Germain"

---

49 Ray Comfort, *The Secrets of Nostradamus Exposed,* Living Waters, Bellflower, CA, 1996, 47, as quoted in Irwin Lutzer, *Seven Reasons Why You Can Trust the Bible,* Moody Press, Chicago, IL, 1998, 88.

50 Lutzer, *Seven Reasons Why You Can Trust the Bible,* 89.

51 Quatrain 2–24, Nostradamus, as quoted on web site for the Nostradamus Society of America, www.nostradamususa.com.

does not mean Germany but means near relative or brother. So "child of Germany" should read "child brother" or "child relative."[52]

So an incorrect translation makes a river into Hitler and a relative into Germany. If this type of translating were used to prove a prophecy in the Bible, it would have been ripped to shreds by critics a long time ago.

? Did Nostradamus predict the Kennedy assassinations?

Another Nostradamus "prophecy" is supposed to have predicted the assassination of President John Kennedy and Senator Robert Kennedy. He wrote: "The great man will be struck down in the day by a thunderbolt, the evil deed predicted by the bearer of a petition. According to the prediction another falls at night time. Conflict in Reims, London, and pestilence at Tuscany."[53] As Lutzer comments, how would we pick out these specific assassinations? Who is the bearer of the petition? And why the mention of Reims, London and Tuscany? Furthermore, other Nostradamus scholars give this prophecy a completely different interpretation, saying it refers to the taking over of Czechoslovakia by Hitler, the resignation of President Benes and dissension between France and England.[54] *What we see is that not only are Nostradamus's "predictions" vague, but scholars disagree among themselves on the interpretations of his "predictions."*

? Did Nostradamus accurately predict dates?

Nostradamus very seldom gave dates for his prophecies. His defense for this was to say that he could give dates but didn't want to. This is not surprising, **because in the few cases where he did try to set dates he was wrong.** For example, one of these is that he predicted Venice would become a great power and influence in the world by 1792. He also predicted the downfall of the Catholic clergy in 1609. He also predicted China would "subdue the whole northern section" of the world.[55] None of these events happened.

---

52 Norman Geisler, *Nostradamus,* web excerpt from *Baker Encyclopedia of Christian Apologetics,* Baker Book House, 1999, p. 1 of article.

53 Comfort, *The Secrets of Nostradamus Exposed,* 55, as quoted in Lutzer, *Seven Reasons Why You Can Trust the Bible,* 89.

54 Lutzer, *Seven Reasons Why You Can Trust the Bible,* 90.

55 Robert A. Morey, *Horoscopes and the Christian,* Bethany House Publishers, Minneapolis, MN, 1981, 20–21.

If Nostradamus had claimed to be a prophet of God in biblical times, he would have been stoned to death (see Deuteronomy 18:20).

? How about Jean Dixon? Wasn't she a genuine prophet?

Astrologer Jean Dixon is said to have made some very specific predictions. She is said to have predicted that a Democrat would win the 1960 election and then be assassinated in office. John F. Kennedy was indeed elected and then assassinated. **Now, as we said above, sometimes a false prophet can get it right, but a prophet of God is always right.** It turns out that Jean Dixon said the president elected would either be assassinated or die in office. And it turns out that three presidents in the twentieth century had died in office and two others were critically ill; so her odds were pretty good of getting that one.

Jean Dixon made many false predictions. She said World War III would begin in 1954. She said the Vietnam War would end in 1966, and it didn't end until 1975. She predicted that Fidel Castro would be overthrown in Cuba in 1970, which he was not. She predicted on October 19, 1968, that Jaqueline Kennedy would not remarry, and the next day Kennedy wed Aristotle Onassis![56]

? How about Edgar Cayce?

He was one "prophet" who used to go into trances and diagnose illnesses for patients hundreds of miles away (these phenomena could be explained by the presence of a "spirit guide"). Once in a while he would try to make predictions. **Just as the others he made wrong predictions**, such as that California would fall into the Pacific Ocean in the early 1970s, and then he had the audacity to say God does not know the future.[57] Cayce made many other false predictions, and in general his predictions, like Nostradamus's, were quite vague.

It should also be mentioned that even if these non-biblical prophets got most of their predictions right, which they did not, **they were using occultic techniques and astrology which are condemned by the Bible (see Isaiah 47:13–14, Deuteronomy 18:9-12 and other places), and they advocated unbiblical teachings, so they absolutely could not and would not have been Bible prophets.**

---

56 www.greatcom.org, A Ready Defense—False Prophets.

57 Ibid.

SUMMARY: BIBLICAL PROPHECY PROVES DIVINE INSPIRATION

No other author of any "holy book" bases His reputation on His ability to predict things with 100 percent accuracy before they happen. No other book but the Bible takes that risk. And when it is put to the test the proof is clear. Whether it is prophecies of Christ, of places in the world, of Israel or anything else, the Bible proves its authenticity as God's Word. We could end the discussion right here and go home. But, believe it or not, there is much more. This is where it gets even more exciting.

CHAPTER FIVE

HOW CLOSE ARE WE TO THE ORIGINAL BIBLE?

When evaluating an ancient text, one of the most important things to examine is the textual evidence. This will help us to answer the following important questions.

? How sure are we that the copy of the Bible we have now represents what was originally written? How can we know this if the original Bible manuscripts are lost? How sure can we be that the Bible as we have it now was not corrupted significantly from the original?

THE TEXTUAL EVIDENCE FOR THE NEW TESTAMENT

To answer the above questions, we need to ask and answer two more. **How many manuscripts of the document do we have, and how long is the time interval between the earliest of these manuscripts and the composition of the original?**

We will look at the New Testament first. Lightfoot[1] tells us the general definition of a biblical manuscript is a document written by hand in the original language—therefore the Greek language for the New Testament. There are almost 5,800 manuscripts in Greek, divided into four main types.

- **Papyrii**—118 in number, written on paper-like material made from the papyrus plant. These are generally dated from the second to sixth century A.D.[2]

- **Uncials**—317 in number, written in all capital letters, dating from the fourth to tenth centuries A.D. These are written on sheepskins or goatskins, called parchment, or on specially prepared calfskins, called vellum.[3]

- **Miniscules** or "cursives"—written in connected letters in small script. According to Price, there are 2,877 of these to date, from the ninth to sixteenth centuries A.D.

- **Lectionaries**—2,433 to date, which were used for daily reading in the early church and specially arranged for that purpose.[4]

No other ancient document comes close to having this many. The nearest one, Homer's *Iliad*, has 643 manuscripts. **And the Bible also has, in addition to the Greek manuscripts, at least 15,000 to 20,000 copies that are in other languages**, called "versions" (see below).

Many scholars say that with this many copies of the New Testament it is possible to reconstruct the original with almost complete accuracy. One of the leading authorities on textual criticism today, Dr. Daniel Wallace, comments in an interview with author Lee Strobel: **"Essentially, scholars**

> "Scholars do not have to come up with conjecture about what the wording of the original text might be. We have the wording of the original in the manuscripts *somewhere*."
>
> *Dr. Daniel Wallace, textual criticism expert*

1   Neil R. Lightfoot, *How We Got the Bible*, ACU Press, Abilene Christian University, 1986.

2   Randall Price, *Searching for the Original Bible*, Harvest House, Eugene, OR, 2007, 77.

3   Ibid., 77–78.

4   Ibid., 77–78.

do not have to come up with conjecture about what the wording of the original text might be. We have the wording of the original in the manuscripts somewhere. Pragmatically, we could say that the wording of the original can be found in the text of our published Greek New Testaments or in their footnotes"[5] (emphasis mine).

As far as the time interval goes, again the New Testament leaves its competitors in ancient literature way behind. The earliest **complete** manuscripts of the New Testament go back to about 325 A.D., about 225 years after the time of the originals, but there are also major fragments that go back much further. In fact, there were very few early complete manuscripts because they were very bulky to use, being written by hand. Many manuscripts contained just a part of the New Testament on purpose, some the Gospels only, others only Paul's letters.[6] Here is a short listing of the most important early New Testament manuscripts:

- The **John Ryland's MS**, discovered in 1920, dated from about 100–125 A.D.,[7] is a portion of the Gospel of John. Discovery of this one manuscript overturned a popular theory of German skeptics that John's Gospel wasn't composed until at least 160 A.D.—too late to be useful for historical research.[8]

- The manuscript group known as the **Bodmer Papyri** (P 66, 72, 74, 75) is dated from between 175–225 A.D. and contains portions of John and Luke, Acts, 1–3 John, Jude, and 1 and 2 Peter.[9]

- The **Chester Beatty Papyri**, a very important discovery in 1930, dated at about 200 A.D., contains major fragments of most of the books of the New Testament. There are three papyri in all: one contains the Gospels and book of Acts, another contains a major portion of all of Paul's letters, and a third contains part of the book of Revelation.[10]

---

5   Lee Strobel, *The Case for the Real Jesus,* interview with New Testament scholar Dr. Daniel B. Wallace, Zondervan, Grand Rapids, MI, 2007, 72.

6   Ibid., 83.

7   Lee Strobel, *The Case for Christ,* in an interview with Dr. Bruce Metzger, Zondervan, Grand Rapids, MI, 1998, 79–80. Dr. Metzger was one of the foremost New Testament scholars of the past half-century.

8   Ibid., 80.

9   Randall Price, *Searching for the Original Bible*, 79. (The prefix "P" stands for papyrus.)

10 Ibid.

- The uncial **Codex Sinaiticus**, the oldest complete copy of the New Testament, is dated 350 A.D. Another almost complete uncial, **Codex Vaticanus**, dates from 325 A.D.[11]

The above manuscripts bring the time interval between the earliest manuscripts and the date of the originals down to about twenty-five to fifty years!

By contrast, the time gap between the original of Homer's *Iliad* and its earliest manuscripts is four hundred years. Time gaps for other ancient literature of which we have multiple manuscripts range from four hundred to fourteen hundred years, with most over a thousand years. Yet again scholars do not doubt the authenticity of any of these ancient non-biblical documents.

Sir Frederic Kenyon, who was the director and principal librarian of the British Museum, among the most authoritative scholars to speak on the subject of ancient manuscripts, commented on the fact of the short time gap even before some of the above-mentioned earlier manuscripts were discovered:

"In no other case is the interval of time between the composition of the book and the date of the earliest extant manuscripts so short as in that of the New Testament. The books of the New Testament were written in the latter part of the first century; the earliest extant manuscripts (trifling scraps excepted) are of the fourth century—say from 250 to 300 years later. **This may sound like a considerable interval, but it is nothing to that which parts most of the great classical authors from their earliest manuscripts.** We believe we have in all essentials an accurate text of the seven extant plays of Sophocles; yet the earliest substantial manuscript upon which it is based was written more than fourteen hundred years after the poet's death."[12]

As we have seen, since Kenyon wrote the above, some important manuscript discoveries have been made that further reduce the time interval between copies and originals, especially for certain books of the New Testament.

Here is a more modern quote from New Testament scholar Dr. Daniel B. Wallace: "**The quantity and quality of the New Testament manuscripts are unequalled in the ancient Greco-Roman world.** The average Greek author has fewer than twenty copies of his works still in existence, and they come from no sooner than five hundred to a thousand years later ... **Even the great historians**

---

11 Neil R. Lightfoot, *How We Got the Bible,* 46–48.

12 Frederic G. Kenyon, *Handbook to the Textual Criticism of the New Testament*, London, MacMillan, 1901, 4.

who give us much of our understandings of ancient Roman history are quite incomplete … Livy, for example, wrote 142 volumes on the history of Rome, but only 35 survive."[13]

If modern scholars can trust the ancient Roman historians, how much more the New Testament!

There have been some small fragments discovered that are claimed to be even earlier. The Jesus Papyrus, P 64, also known as the **Magdalen Papyrus**, was redated in 1994 using a scanning laser microscope. It is believed by some to be the oldest New Testament fragment yet found, with verses from the Gospel of Matthew. This new date found for the fragment has been disputed by some scholars. Yet the fragment was scientifically compared with four other ancient manuscripts of other writings, dating from 58–79 A.D. using a scanning laser microscope, by Dr. Carsten Thiede. He concluded that it must have been written very close to the date of the original composition of Matthew's Gospel.[14] Another fragment, 7Q5, found at Qumran, has been dated around 68 A.D. or before and appears to be from the Gospel of Mark.[15]

Whether or not these very early dates for P 64 or 7Q5 turn out to be correct, the time gap, as shown by the other firmly dated early manuscripts above, even at its widest, is still very far below that for other ancient writings.

OTHER EVIDENCE OF NEW TESTAMENT ACCURACY

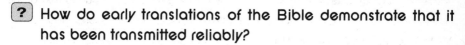 How do early translations of the Bible demonstrate that it has been transmitted reliably?

One indicator of the accuracy of the New Testament comes from the many translations that were made. These are called "versions" by modern scholars. Since Christianity from the beginning was a missionary faith, translation into other languages was necessary to spread the message. Most scholars agree that the books of the New Testament were widely copied and translated from the original Greek language very early on in their history. Translations into Syriac, Latin, and Coptic were made around the second and third centuries A.D. Between fifteen

---

13   Lee Strobel, *The Case for the Real Jesus,* in an interview with Daniel B. Wallace, 83–84.

14   Chuck Missler, *How We Got Our Bible,* tape commentary, Koinonia House, Coeur d'Alene, ID, 2000.

15   "N. T. Ancient Manuscripts," http://biblefacts.org/history/oldtext.html.

thousand and twenty thousand copies of these various versions exist, and they confirm the consistency and accuracy of the text. Here are some of them:

- **Syriac versions:** includes the Peshitta (fifth century, about 350 copies) and Old Syriac, translated from the third to fifth century, but giving evidence of being derived from a second-century text,[16] with the number of manuscripts in the thousands.[17]

- **Latin versions**: more than ten thousand copies, third to sixteenth centuries A.D., the Old Latin translated as early as 150 A.D. This group also includes the Latin Vulgate, fourth century.

- **Coptic versions:** from Egypt, in different dialects, dated from the third to fifth centuries A.D., about one thousand copies.[18]

- Other versions include: **Armenian, Ethiopic, Persian, Gothic, Georgian, Old Slavonic, and Arabic.**[19]

Randall Price comments on the value of the manuscripts plus the different versions: "The provenance (geographical origin) of these manuscripts is from different parts of the ancient world (Israel, Syria, Egypt, Turkey, Greece and Rome), which indicates **they represent *distinct* witnesses to the original text.** Had they been from one provenance only, or had they been collated into a unified text, we would not have the necessary evidence to recover the original text through the science of textual criticism"[20] (emphasis mine).

One of the advantages of having all of these early copies and translations was a check on any alterations that would have been made to the text. If independent translations agreed in a given part of the text, it would indicate that we have the original wording of the text.

Dr. Bruce Metzger comments on the translations: **"Even if we had no Greek manuscripts today, by piecing together the information from these translations from a relatively early date, we could actually reproduce the contents of the New Testament."**[21]

---

16 Lightfoot, *How We Got the Bible,* 25.

17 Price, *Searching for the Original Bible,* 83.

18 Ibid., 82.

19 Ibid.

20 Ibid., 113.

21 Strobel, *The Case for Christ,* interview with Dr. Bruce Metzger, 76.

? **How do the writings of the early church fathers give witness to the reliability of the transmission of the Bible?**

Another powerful attestation to the New Testament text comes from the writings of the early church fathers, who lived from about 70 A.D. to 300 A.D. These writings contain so many quotes of the New Testament that if the entire New Testament were lost we could find it again almost completely from their quotes alone. Dr. Bruce Metzger comments on this: **"Even if we lost all the Greek manuscripts and the early translations, we could still reproduce the contents of the New Testament from the multiplicity of quotations in commentaries, sermons, letters, and so forth of the early church fathers."**[22]

For example, one historian, Sir David Dalrymple, stated that he had found the entire New Testament in the church fathers' quotations, minus eleven verses.[23]

The quotations of the early church fathers were sometimes inexact and imprecise, although many were accurate. The main thing is that they captured the content of the original sufficiently so that comparisons can be made, and once again the reliability of the text is vindicated.[24]

Just from the earliest church fathers alone, up to about the early fourth century, we have more than thirty-two thousand quotes of the New Testament. If you add in Eusebius, this brings the number to almost thirty-six thousand.[25] Some of the earliest of these men were from the generation immediately after the apostles, some even disciples of theirs, and so would have been referencing very early texts.[26] Dean Burgon found more than eighty-six thousand New Testament quotations from early church writings, leaving them in a sixteen-volume unpublished book at the time of his death.[27]

22 Ibid.

23 Charles Leach, *Our Bible. How We Got It*, Moody Press, Chicago, IL, 1898, 35–36, as quoted in McDowell, *Evidence That Demands a Verdict*, 51.

24 Price, *Searching for the Original Bible*, 83.

25 Norman L. Geisler and William E. Nix, *A General Introduction to the Bible*, Moody Press, Chicago, IL, 1968, 353–354, as quoted in McDowell, *Evidence That Demands a Verdict*, 52.

26 Price, *Searching for the Original Bible*, 125.

27 Leo Jaganay, *An Introduction to the Textual Criticism of the New Testament*, transl. by B. V. Miller, London, Sands and Co., 1937, 48, as quoted in McDowell, *Evidence That Demands a Verdict*, 52.

If you include all the church fathers up to the thirteenth century, their quotes from the New Testament number more than one million![28]

When all these are taken together, the trustworthiness of the New Testament text is made about as sure as it could be.

HOW ACCURATE IS THE NEW TESTAMENT?

? Do we have the true original wording of the New Testament today?

There are so many lines of transmission and copies that the original text is very likely to have been preserved. New Testament scholar F. F. Bruce writes: **"The wealth of attestation is such that the true reading is almost invariably bound to be preserved by at least one of the thousands of witnesses."**[29] Frederic Kenyon states: "It cannot be too strongly asserted that in substance the text of the Bible is certain; especially is this the case with the New Testament. The number of manuscripts of the New Testament, of early translations from it and of quotations from it in the oldest writers of the church is so large that **it is practically certain the true reading of every doubtful passage is preserved in some one or other of these ancient authorities. This can be said of no other ancient book in the world."**[30] Kenyon also said, **"No fundamental doctrine of the Christian faith rests upon a disputed reading."**[31] Geisler and Nix stated: "Only about one-eighth of all the variants had any weight, as most of them are merely mechanical matters such as spelling or style. Of the whole, then, only about one-sixtieth rise above 'trivialities' or can in any sense be called 'substantial variations.' **Mathematically this would compute to a text that is 98.33 percent pure."**[32]

? Don't some Bible scholars such as Dr. Bart Ehrman point out that the Bible contains hundreds of thousands of variant readings and that this means we have error-filled copies and nothing close to the originals?

---

28 Strobel, *The Case for Christ,* 83.

29 F. F. Bruce, *The Books and the Parchments,* Pickering and Inglis, London, 1971, rev. ed., 180.

30 Frederic Kenyon, *Our Bible and the Ancient Manuscripts,* Eyre and Spottiswoode, London, 1941, 23.

31 Ibid.

32 Geisler and Nix, *A General Introduction to the Bible,* 365.

Dr. Bart Ehrman in his book *Misquoting Jesus* does indeed say the Bible has up to 400,000 variants and therefore we have more variants than there are words in the New Testament.[33] Ehrman states: *"How does it help us to say that the Bible is the inerrant word of God if in fact we don't have the words that God inerrantly inspired, but only the words copied by the scribes—sometimes correctly but sometimes (many times!) incorrectly? What good is it to say that the autographs (i.e., the originals) were inspired? We don't have the originals! We have only error-ridden copies, and the vast majority of these are centuries removed from the originals and different from them, evidently, in thousands of ways."*[34]

Because Ehrman is an authority on textual criticism, many who have read his writings have had doubt cast on their faith in the Bible. For example, author Lee Strobel shared an e-mail sent to him by a twenty-six-year-old writer who had read Ehrman's book and, as a result, was very bewildered and wondering if he should start questioning the things he had been taught about the Bible since childhood. He wanted an answer no matter what it meant to his faith.[35] This is just an example of how one scholar's pronouncements can have a huge effect on someone's life, and therefore these claims need careful examination.

"No cardinal or essential doctrine is altered by any textual variant that has plausibility of going back to the original."

Dr. Daniel Wallace, textual criticism expert, *The Case for the Real Jesus*, 88–89.

What we need to see here is that not all scholars who have equal credentials agree on the same evidence. For example, highly credentialed scholar Dr. Daniel Wallace comments on Dr. Ehrman's conclusions: **"Ehrman is part of a very small minority of textual critics in what he's saying ... he tries to create strong doubt as to what the original text said, using more innuendo than substance. Readers end up having far**

---

33   Dr. Bart Ehrman, *Misquoting Jesus,* Harper SanFrancisco, San Fransisco, CA, 2005, 89–90.

34   Ibid., 7.

35   E-mail received by author Lee Strobel and reported in his book *The Case for the Real Jesus*, 69.

more doubts about what the Bible says than any textual critic today would ever have. I think Ehrman has simply overstated his case."[36]

So what about these 400,000 variants? How are they counted, and what are they exactly? Taking a look at these two things reveals just how overstated the case against the Bible really is:

- Spelling errors: When one word, the same word, is misspelled in, say, 4,000 manuscripts, that is not counted as 1 variant, even though it is the same mistake, but instead is counted as 4,000 variants! Furthermore, these spelling errors are the most common type of variant, and many of these misspellings in the Greek make no difference in the meaning of the word or sentence, such as saying "a apple" versus "an apple." **According to Wallace, these types of spelling errors that have no impact on meaning, account for up to 70 to 80 percent of the total variants, amounting to about 280,000 to 320,000 of the 400,000 variants!**[37]

- Nonsense errors and other unintentional errors: Nonsense errors are things where words are included that obviously don't fit the context, such as putting in the word "and" when the scribe meant to write "Lord." Synonym errors would be variants such as "When Jesus knew" versus "When the Lord knew." Also, in the Greek there can be several different sentences, each with a different word order, that would be translated exactly the same in English, and each of these is counted as a variant.[38]

- Intentional changes: These came about because the scribes wanted to make the text clearer. An example would be in a lectionary manuscript used in daily readings of Scripture by the early church. Wallace gives such an example: "In the Gospel of Mark, there are eighty-nine verses in a row where the name of Jesus isn't mentioned once. Just pronouns are used, with 'he' referring to Jesus. Well, if you excerpt a passage for a daily lectionary reading, you can't start with: 'When he was going someplace … .' The reader wouldn't know whom you were referring to. So it was logical for the scribe to replace 'he' with 'Jesus' in order to be more specific in the lectionary. But it's counted as a variant every single time."[39]

---

36 Strobel, *The Case for the Real Jesus*, interview with Dr. Daniel Wallace, 72.

37 Ibid., 86.

38 Ibid., 86–87.

39 Ibid., 88.

When you tabulate all these additional variants, you are left with only 1 percent of the variants that really make a difference in meaning, and even most of these are not significant, such as the difference between variants of Romans 5:1 of "We have peace" or "Let us have peace."[40] As for the very few significant variants such as the last twelve verses of Mark 16, or the account of the woman caught in adultery (John 7:53–8:11, missing from two of the oldest manuscripts), these will be discussed later in the book, but for now we can say that even if it turned out that they should be left out (which is not by any means finally resolved), the content of the Christian faith would be unaltered. Dr. Daniel Wallace comments: "No cardinal or essential doctrine is altered by any textual variant that has plausibility of going back to the original."[41]

? **Do any of the remaining variants affect any important doctrine of Christianity?**

Of these 1 percent, not one affects any important doctrine of Christianity. Wallace comments: "Ehrman is making the best case he can in Misquoting Jesus. The remarkable thing is you go through his whole book, and you say, 'Where did he actually prove anything?' Ehrman didn't prove that any doctrine is jeopardized. Let me repeat the basic thesis that has been argued since 1707: No cardinal or essential doctrine is altered by any textual variant that has plausibility of going back to the original. The evidence for that has not changed to this day"[42] (emphasis his).

HOW ACCURATE IS THE OLD TESTAMENT?

The Old Testament text we possess today is also reliable. There are not as many manuscripts available, but this is partly due to the fact that they are much older and the materials used were more easily destroyed. Nevertheless, we have several independent lines of transmission, most of which were done with the utmost care to preserve the text.

? **What are the most significant Hebrew Old Testament manuscripts in existence today?**

---

40 Ibid., 87.

41 Strobel, *The Case for the Real Jesus,* interview with Dr. Daniel Wallace, 88–89.

42 Ibid.

Before the Dead Sea Scrolls, which will be discussed below, the oldest manuscripts of any significant size were dated in the ninth and tenth centuries. Some of the most significant discoveries were as follows:

- **Cairo Codex**—dated 895 A.D., containing only the "former and latter prophets."[43]

- **Leningrad Codex**—dated 1008 A.D., a complete text of the Old Testament. Most of our modern translations are based on this manuscript.

- **Aleppo Codex**—dated 930 A.D., once was complete, but a quarter of it was destroyed by fire.

These and many others from a similar time are manuscripts known collectively as the "Masoretic" text. About three thousand manuscripts in the Masoretic tradition altogether have been discovered to date.[44]

[?] Why are most of the Hebrew manuscripts of the Old Testament dated so much later than the New Testament manuscripts, when the Old Testament was written so much earlier?

One reason why we have so few earlier manuscripts of the Old Testament is that the Jewish scribes had so much respect for the Scriptures that they buried old and worn out copies in a special storage place called a genizah.[45] This is one reason why we don't have any of those earlier copies. Many of these stored away copies were probably destroyed when Jerusalem was attacked, both by the Babylonians in 586 B.C. and again in 70 A.D. by the Romans.[46] And of course, while a few of the Old Testament manuscripts may have been on stone tablets, most of them were written on papyrus, which is perishable.

[?] Are there any older Hebrew manuscripts?

The Nash Papyrus, dating from the Hasmonean Period (169–37 B.C.) was discovered in 1902 and was the oldest manuscript discovered at that point in time. It contained the verses Exodus 20:2–17 and also Deuteronomy 6:4, the text known as the "Shema."[47]

---

43 Price, *Searching for the Original Bible,* 59.

44 Ibid., 56, 59.

45 Ibid., 48.

46 Ibid.

47 Ibid., 61.

The Silver Amulet: The absolutely oldest fragment of the Old Testament was a silver amulet discovered in a tomb in Jerusalem, dating from the seventh century B.C. and containing the text of Numbers 6:24–26, the high-priestly benediction. This discovery alone refutes the critics' theory that all of the first five books of the Bible, the Pentateuch, were composed at the time of the exile in the sixth century.[48]

The Dead Sea Scrolls: By far the most important discovery related to the Old Testament was the finding of the Dead Sea Scrolls, written by a sect of Jewish scribes and first discovered in 1948 in several caves in the Dead Sea region. More discoveries were made in the same area in the 1950s and 60s, with one as late as 2005. Two hundred thirty biblical manuscripts were discovered, with either whole copies or fragments, some very large, of every book in the Old Testament except Esther. They have been dated from 225 B.C. to A.D. 68 and are therefore (except for the silver amulet) the oldest Hebrew manuscripts.[49]

> They…gave the most diligent attention to accurate preservation of the Hebrew Scriptures that has ever been devoted to any ancient literature, secular or religious, in the history of human civilization."
>
> *Gleason Archer, Bible scholar*

? How does the Dead Sea Scrolls discovery confirm the accuracy of transmission of the Old Testament over the centuries? How does it compare to other ancient documents?

Before the Dead Sea Scrolls were discovered, all we had were manuscripts from the ninth and tenth centuries. With such a gap in time between these and the originals, there was a possibility transmission mistakes had been made despite the carefulness of the scribes. When the text of the Dead Sea Scrolls was examined, it demonstrated that in fact the text of the Old Testament had been copied and transmitted with amazing and unparalleled accuracy over a period of one thousand

---

48 Ibid., 92.
49 Ibid., 62.

years! This showed that the accuracy of the Jewish copiers of the Old Testament was unequalled in any other ancient literature.

An example of the accuracy of transmission was found in the Isaiah scroll, dated 125 B.C. When compared to the Masoretic text copy of Isaiah, dated one thousand years later, the differences were next to nothing!

Gleason Archer, a modern Old Testament scholar, states: **"It should be clearly understood that in this respect (to transmission), the Old Testament differs from all other pre-Christian works of literature of which we have any knowledge.** To be sure, we do not possess so many different manuscripts of pagan productions, coming from such widely separated eras, as we do in the case of the Old Testament … But where we do, for example, in the Egyptian Book of the Dead, the variations are of a far more extensive and serious nature. Quite startling differences appear, for example, between chapter 15 contained in the Papyrus of Ani (written in the Eighteenth Dynasty) and the Turin Papyrus (from the Twenty-sixth Dynasty or later). Whole clauses are inserted or left out, and the sense in corresponding columns of text is in some cases altogether different. Apart from divine superintendence of the transmission of the Hebrew text, there is no particular reason why the same phenomena of divergence and change would not appear between Hebrew manuscripts produced centuries apart … .

"Even though the two copies of Isaiah discovered in Qumran Cave 1 near the Dead Sea in 1947 were a thousand years earlier than the oldest dated manuscript previously known (A.D. 980), they proved to be word for word identical with our standard Hebrew Bible in more than 95 percent of the text … The 5 percent of variation consisted chiefly of obvious slips of the pen and variations in spelling … They do not affect the message of revelation in the slightest."[50]

? Who copied the Old Testament, and what methods did they use to transmit the text so accurately?

The Dead Sea Scrolls were an important discovery, since they proved the text had been copied extremely accurately for the thousand years between their age and the age of the oldest standard Hebrew text, called the Masoretic text. The Masoretic text is named after the Masoretes, Jewish scholars who between 500 and 1100 A.D. put the Old Testament text into its final form, including the addition of

---

50 Gleason Archer, *A Survey of Old Testament Introduction,* 28–29.

vowel points. They were the last in a long line of Jewish copyists who meticulously transmitted the Old Testament text. The first copyists of the line were the Sopherim, who copied and transmitted the consonantal Old Testament text from the fifth to the third centuries B.C. After the Sopherim came the Talmudists and finally the Masoretes in about 500 A.D. Each group used highly disciplined methods for producing accurate copies.[51]

The Sopherim counted all the verses, words and letters. If there was any discrepancy between the copy and the original, they knew they had a bad copy. The Talmudists were not allowed to write a single word from memory, without looking at the codex before them. The lines and spaces had to be certain sizes. The columns and rows had to be specific sizes and specific numbers of letters in width and height. The Masoretes counted the number of times each letter of the alphabet occurred in each book. They marked the middle letter and middle word of each book. In fact, they counted just about every conceivable parameter in a text that could be counted, and they used memory devices to record these.[52]

All of these Jewish scholars used so many different safeguards and methods to ensure accurate copying that just to enumerate these methods would take many pages.

Archer comments: **"In conclusion we should accord to the Masoretes the highest praise for their meticulous care ... They together with the Sopherim themselves gave the most diligent attention to accurate preservation of the Hebrew Scriptures that has ever been devoted to any ancient literature, secular or religious, in the history of human civilization."**[53]

[?] **Were there any other independent checks on the transmission of the Old Testament?**

Besides the above-standard Hebrew text, other independent lines of transmission further strengthen the evidence for authenticity of the Old Testament text.

Septuagint version: The Septuagint version of the Old Testament was a translation from Hebrew to Greek starting in about 250 B.C. and continuing over the next few centuries.[54] The main value of the Septuagint is that it is based on a Hebrew

---

51 Ibid., 67–71.

52 Lightfoot, *How We Got the Bible*, 55–56.

53 Archer, *A Survey of Old Testament Introduction*, 72–73.

54 Price, *Searching for the Original Bible*, 69.

text about 1,200 years older than our existing standard Hebrew manuscripts of the Masoretic text. Although there are some variations, the Septuagint text compares closely enough to the Masoretic text to indicate the reliability of the transmission of the Old Testament text through about 1,200 years, especially being an independent line of transmission.[55]

Some significant manuscripts of the Septuagint are:[56]

- The **Chester Beatty Papyri**—dated second to fourth centuries A.D., containing various parts of the Old Testament.

- The **Oxyrhynchus Papyri**—dated first to ninth centuries A.D., contains Pentateuch through Ruth, Psalms, and the Prophets.

- The **Rylands Papyri**—dated second century B.C. to fifth century A.D., containing Genesis, Deuteronomy, Chronicles, Job, and Isaiah.

- **Codex Vaticanus**—dated fourth century A.D.—contains entire Old Testament and Apocrypha.

- **Codex Sinaiticus**—late fourth to early fifth century A.D.—portions of Old Testament and Apocrypha.

Samaritan Pentateuch: Another independent line of transmission is found in the Samaritan Pentateuch, from around 200 B.C., containing only the first five books of the Old Testament. The oldest manuscript is from about 1150 A.D.[57] Although there are many variations from the Masoretic text, the variations are insignificant enough that the Samaritan Pentateuch can serve as another independent witness to the original text.[58]

Aramaic Targums and the Talmud: The Aramaic Targums are Jewish translations into Aramaic written between 100–700 A.D. Targum means "commentary." In some of the texts they paraphrase, and commentary is sometimes included.[59]

Syriac Peshitta: This version was translated into the Old Syriac language in about the second century A.D. It was probably translated from a Hebrew text that was similar to but independent of the Masoretic text.[60]

---

55 F. F. Bruce, *The Books and the Parchments,* 122.

56 Price, *Searching for the Original Bible,* 70.

57 Ibid., 73.

58 Bruce, *The Books and the Parchments,* 122.

59 Price, *Searching for the Original Bible,* 73.

60 Ibid., 74.

Old Latin: translated about A.D. 200, a translation from the Greek Septuagint, valuable in determining what was the earlier Greek text.[61]

All of the above and many other cross checks indicate the incredible reliability of the Old Testament.

MORE EXPERT TESTIMONY OF THE BIBLE'S ACCURACY

One notable expert, Robert Dick Wilson, was one of the greatest experts in the Old Testament, fluent in over forty Semitic languages, who studied the Old Testament text for more than forty-five years. In his book *A Scientific Investigation of the Old Testament* he commented on the incredible accuracy therein: **"I can affirm that there is not a page of the Old Testament concerning which we need have any doubt** … There are twenty-nine ancient kings whose names are mentioned not only in the Bible but also on monuments of their own time … There are 195 consonants in these twenty-nine proper names. Yet we find that in the documents of the Hebrew Old Testament there are only two or three out of the entire 195 about which there can be any question of their being written in exactly the same way as they were inscribed on their own monuments. Some of these go back 4,000 years and are so written that every letter is clear and correct … Compare this accuracy with … the greatest scholar of his age, the librarian at Alexandria in 200 B.C. He compiled a catalogue of the kings of Egypt, thirty-eight in all. Of the entire number only three or four are recognizable. He also made a list of the kings of Assyria; in only one case can we tell who is meant; and that one is not spelt correctly. Or take Ptolemy, who drew up a register of eighteen kings of Babylon. Not one of them is properly spelt; you could not make them out at all if you did not know from other sources to what he is referring. If anyone talks about the Bible, ask him about the kings mentioned in it. **There are twenty-nine kings referred to, and ten different countries among these twenty-nine; all of which are included in the Bible and on monuments. Every one of these is given his right name in the Bible, his right country, and placed in correct chronological order. Think what that means … !"**[62]

---

61 Archer, *A Survey of Old Testament Introduction,* 54.

62 Robert Dick Wilson, *A Scientific Investigation of the Old Testament,* Moody Press, Chicago, IL, 1959, as quoted in Dave Hunt, *In Defense of the Faith,* Harvest House Publishers, Eugene, OR, 1996, 72–73.

We have seen that in both the Old and New Testaments we can have complete confidence that the Bible we have now is for all practical purposes the same as when it was originally written, and any charges of its being tampered with or altered so that the message has been changed cannot be taken seriously.

THE BIBLE VERSUS OTHER "HOLY BOOKS"

? How do other "holy" books such as the Koran or the Book of Mormon compare to the Bible in reliability of transmission?

Not very well. The Book of Mormon, since its publication in 1830, has had more than four thousand changes made to it.[63] These changes were made because of changes in the author Joseph Smith's beliefs, as well as to eliminate hundreds of obvious contradictions and errors, including grammatical errors.[64]

The Koran has had many changes made to it also, with Islamic scholars acknowledging this. Abdollar Sarh, who later defected from Islam, made suggestions to Mohammed about improving the Koran, including additions and deletions. Mohammed actually made these suggested changes.[65] There were no original manuscripts of the Koran, but many versions copied from notes on scraps of leaves, bark, bones, and stones. These versions often contradicted one another.[66]

Caliph Uthman, the third caliph after Mohammed, was responsible for putting together the standardized text of the Koran as it is today. Scholars have shown that Uthman's text contains omissions from older Koran materials.[67] Many rejected his text in favor of their own text. One chapter of the Koran in his text can be shown to be missing 157 verses![68] Uthman ordered the burning of all manuscripts contrary to his, because different groups were fighting over them. These included some versions made by knowledgeable and authoritative Muslims who had Mohammed's

63   Ed Decker and Caryl Matrisciana, *The God Makers II,* Harvest House Publishers, Eugene, OR, 1993, 217–230.

64   Dave Hunt and Ed Decker, *The God Makers,* Harvest House Publishers, Eugene, OR, 1997, revised ed., 124–128.

65   Ergun Mehmet Caner and Emir Fethi Caner, *Unveiling Islam,* Kregel Publications, Grand Rapids, MI, 2002, 45.

66   Ibid., 85–86.

67   Ibid., 86.

68   Abd El Schafi, *Behind the Veil,* Pioneer Book Co., Caney, KS, 2002,, 245–246.

endorsement. Uthman was eventually assassinated.[69] The question is, why did Uthman try to destroy other manuscripts and force people to use his text if there were no conflicting manuscripts? Furthermore, there is evidence that changes continued to be made to the Koran text even after the time of Uthman. For more details, see www.answeringislam.org.

One can see the state of confusion over the Koran's text, and this even though having one official author, Mohammed, and written over a much shorter time period.

SUMMARY

The Bible has been shown to be trustworthy beyond any ancient text in terms of its preservation. While this cannot be used as proof of divine inspiration, nevertheless the remarkable preservation of its text is unique and exactly what you would expect if divine intervention was involved in preserving the Bible. Therefore it is one of the stronger indicators that the Bible is not simply a product of men.

Now that we have shown that what we have today is essentially the Bible as it was originally written, the next step is to examine the events and persons described in the Bible's text to see if there is any external evidence for their validity.

---

69 Ibid., 247–259. Also see Caner and Caner, *Unveiling Islam,* 70–71, 86–87.

CHAPTER SIX

THE SHOVEL DOESN'T LIE

THE VALUE OF ARCHAEOLOGICAL EVIDENCE

Archaeological evidence does not prove the divine inspiration of the Bible, but it does indicate the trustworthiness of the events recorded therein. **If a book such as the Bible can be proven to be reliable in areas where it can be tested, then we have increased confidence in its truth in areas that cannot be tested by archaeological evidence.**

As evidenced by hundreds of discoveries over the last century, the science of archaeology has turned out to be a great friend and ally of the Bible against its most persistent critics. It should also be pointed out that archaeological proof has its limits. We may not find detailed proof of personal, private events in the Bible. Such events may not have left traces that could be reasonably expected to remain thousands of years later. But what we do find confirms the biblical record powerfully.

ARCHAEOLOGICAL EVIDENCE-OLD TESTAMENT

? Was King David a myth?

"The exciting thing here is that you have a historical stele referring to historical events of which the Bible speaks at great lengths."

Professor Avraham Biran, discoverer of inscription bearing the name of King David

For many years King David was considered a legendary character by some scholars. Then an inscription from the ninth century B.C. referring to both the house of David and the king of Israel was found in 1993 at the northern Israelite site of Tel Dan. The inscription contained the words "House of David." Here is a quote from the discoverer of the inscription, Professor Avraham Biran: "In this fragment, a king of Damascus, Ben Hadad, is apparently victorious … But what was really thrilling was to find he defeated a 'king of Israel of the House of David'! **So here you have the mention of the 'House of David' in an Aramean inscription dated … about 150 years after the days of King David.** The following year in another scene of excavation we found two more pieces, and these two pieces link to the first one and give us the names of these kings. The king of Israel that is referred to is 'Jehoram' … who is the son of Ahab. The king of the House of David (Judah) is 'Ahaziahu' (Ahaziah), who is also mentioned in the Bible … **the exciting thing here is that you have a historical stele referring to historical events of which the Bible speaks at great lengths (2 Kings 8:7–15, 9:6–10)."**[1] According to Price, "Professor Biran has more precisely dated the inscription to the time of the Aramean usurper Hazael, whom he believes authored the inscription."[2] The discovery overturned all the skeptic's theories that King David was just a legend.

A recent article in *Biblical Archaeology Review* discusses the Tel Dan Stela and a second reference to David found in a Moabite inscription known as the Mesha Stela.[3]

Author Yosef Garfinkel comments: **"Thus, there is at least one, and possibly two clear references, to the dynasty of David in the ninth century B.C.E.,**

---

1 Randall Price, *The Stones Cry Out,* Harvest House Publishers, Eugene, OR, 1997, 169.

2 Ibid., 169.

3 Yosef Garfinkel, *The Birth and Death of Biblical Minimalism, Biblical Archaeology Review,* vol. 37, no. 3, May/June 2011, 46–53.

only 100–120 years after his reign."[4] The article refers to the theories that King David was a legendary figure as a "modern myth."[5]

This type of discovery has been the rule in biblical archaeology, where a person or an event said to be legendary by some skeptical scholars is subsequently proven to be real. Even when a person has not yet been proven to have existed by archaeology, other indicators are found that show the authenticity of the Bible account of that person.

? What are some examples of archaeological discoveries that verify the Bible accounts?

Many archaeological discoveries verify the Old Testament accounts. To list even most of them would require a book in itself, and many fine books do so. Examples: A Survey of Old Testament Introduction by Gleason Archer, last updated in 1994; The Stones Cry Out by Randall Price, Harvest House, Eugene, OR, 1997; and On the Reliability of the Old Testament, by Kenneth A. Kitchen, Eerdmans Publishing Co., 2003. Below are several more examples of archaeological finds:

1. **Code of Hammurabi**—Babylonian Law code, dated from about 1700 B.C., shows that ancient laws in the Near East were very similar to the Law in the Old Testament, yet different enough to preclude one borrowing from the other.

1. **Merneptah Stela**—Hieroglyphic account of the military exploits of Egyptian King Merneptah, dated at about 1200 B.C. and contains the first mention of the name "Israel" outside the biblical text.

2. **Sennacherib Cylinder**—contains military exploits of Assyrian King Sennacherib, dated about 700 B.C., and confirms the biblical account of the siege of Jerusalem.

3. **Hezekiah's Tunnel**—dated about 700 B.C., a tunnel constructed by King Hezekiah of Judah to provide water during the Assyrian siege of Jerusalem. It is described in the Bible in 2 Kings 20:20.

4. **Mari Tablets**—dated 1700 B.C., confirms customs of the day mentioned in the accounts of the biblical patriarchs.

---

4   Ibid., 47.

5   Ibid.

5. **Tell El-Amarna Tablets**—dated 1400 B.C., confirms the conquest of Canaan by the Hebrews.

6. **Black Obelisk of Shalmanezer III**—dated 840 B.C., confirms the existence of King Jehu of Israel.

7. **Moabite Stone**—dated 840 B.C., confirms history of King Omri and historical accounts in 2 Kings 3 of the Bible.

8. **Cyrus Cylinder**—dated 500 B.C., proclamation of Persian King Cyrus allowing people to return to their home countries. This proclamation is prophesied in the book of Isaiah 44:28; 45:1, and recorded in the book of Ezra (Ezra 1:2–4).

9. **Ebla Tablets**—dated 2300–1600 B.C., thousands of clay tablets confirming early advanced civilization and the existence of written language. Also contains names of cities mentioned in Genesis.

These are but a sampling of many more discoveries that confirm the historicity of the Old Testament.[6]

[?] Has archaeology ever proven the Bible wrong?

Many prominent archaeologists and other scholars have gone on record as stating that there have been no known archaeological discoveries to date that would disprove a biblical reference. An example is Dr. Nelson Glueck: **"As a matter of fact, however, it may be stated categorically that no archaeological discovery has ever controverted a biblical reference."**[7] There are many others. Many articles have appeared in recent issues of popular magazines, and they point out that archaeology not only supports the Bible, but the Bible has been used to help archaeology make discoveries: **"We went about discovering (the gate) with Bible in one hand and spade in the other."**[8]

[?] How about the missing evidence for Abraham or the Exodus? Doesn't this prove they were fiction?

---

6   Price, *The Stones Cry Out,* 66–67; also see Archer, *A Survey of Old Testament Introduction,* 188.

7   Nelson Glueck, *Rivers in the Desert,* Farrar, Strauss and Cudahy, New York, NY, 1959, 31, as quoted in Henry M. Morris, *Many Infallible Proofs,* Master Books, Green Forest, AR, 1996, rev. ed., 312.

8   Yigael Yadin, an Israeli archaeologist, as quoted in Jeffery Scheler, *Is the Bible True? U.S. News and World Report*, October 25, 1999 edition, 59.

Where skepticism remains, it is usually about biblical accounts where it is generally said no direct evidence has been unearthed yet, such as for the Exodus or the existence of Abraham. Some scholars even today are saying the Exodus and Abraham are fictitious accounts. But they have also said that in the past about people like David and others, and one or more new discoveries have forced them to retreat from their former positions.

Abraham

In an article in *Christianity Today,* author Kevin Miller relates how Egyptologist James Hoffmeier had a professor who took the position that Abraham was a fictional character. Hoffmeier described how this professor ignored evidence regarding the historicity of Abraham: "'When he trotted out all the evidence for the first millennium, he made a statement in passing that his reason for that position was that texts from the ancient Near East rarely mention the use of tents.' Made curious by the word *rarely,* Hoffmeier began noticing numerous references to nomads from Syria and Palestine using tents in Egyptian texts he was reading for his hieroglyphics class. To his surprise he also discovered his professor had written extensively on a particular Egyptian text that described nomads and their tents in Syria-Palestine during the second millennium. 'So he knew about this reference to how the Bedouin lived, but he didn't talk about it.' **Hoffmeier says, 'I realized there's a pattern here of minimizing evidence that doesn't fit.'"**[9] (emphasis mine).

[?] **Is there any evidence supporting the existence of Jacob, Joseph, Abraham, or the other patriarchs of the Old Testament?**

Although we might not expect to find personal references to such men in the archaeological records, we can verify that the political, historical, and social conditions fit their life and times in history.

- For example, Joseph was sold for twenty silver shekels, according to Genesis 37:28. Egyptologist Kenneth Kitchen found that this amount matches exactly with Joseph's time period according to the Bible and not any earlier or later periods.[10]

---

9   Kevin D. Miller, "Did the Exodus Never Happen?" *Christianity Today,* cover story, September 9, 1998.

10   Kenneth A. Kitchen, *On the Reliability of the Old Testament,* William B. Eerdmans Publishing Co., Grand Rapids, MI, 2003, 344–345.

- Joseph's appointment by the Pharaoh and his position likewise accord with this time period.[11]

- The treaties made by Abraham, Isaac, and Jacob correspond very closely to the form of treaties in that period and not to other time periods.[12] The description of Jacob's life as a shepherd fits well into the shepherding practices of that region and time.[13]

- Other evidences that fit the times of the patriarchs include: the inheritance rights of an adopted son, confirmed by the Nuzi Tablets (as in Genesis 15:2–4, referring to Isaac's servant);[14] having children by proxy, as in Genesis 16 when Abraham had Ishmael by Hagar;[15] the domestication of camels;[16] the fit of the types of names of the patriarchs to that period; and the great lack of evidence for the use of those names in later periods.[17]

Other specific evidence supporting the accounts of Abraham includes:

- The name Abram has also been discovered in tablets dated around 1550 B.C.[18]

- The names and the political conditions described in the account of the invasion of the Mesopotamian kings in Genesis 14 have been verified by archaeology as fitting the time period described in the biblical account and not later periods.[19]

- The regions where Abraham lived have been shown to have been inhabited in Abraham's time, as well as the existence of the cities of Ur and Haran, contrary to skeptics' theories. The city of Haran, which is portrayed as a thriving city in the Bible at the time of Abraham, has been shown by archaeology to have been abandoned from about 1800 B.C. to 800 B.C. Archaeologist Barry Beitzel comments: **"It's highly improbable (that someone inventing the**

---

11 Ibid., 348–350.

12 Ibid., 323–324.

13 Ibid., 337–338.

14 Ibid., 325.

15 Ibid., 325–326.

16 Ibid., 338–339.

17 Ibid., 341–343.

18 Archer, *A Survey of Old Testament Introduction,* 177.

19 Ibid., 177–178; also Price, *The Stones Cry Out,* 100–102; also Kitchen, *On the Reliability of the Old Testament,* 319–323.

story later) would have chosen Haran as a key location when the
town hadn't existed for hundreds of years."[20]

Kenneth Kitchen refutes the modern claim that the patriarchs were legendary:
**"We are compelled, once and for all, to throw out Wellhausen's bold claim
that the patriarchs were merely a glorified mirage of/from the Hebrew
monarchy period. For such a view there is not a particle of supporting
factual evidence."**[21]

The Exodus

? Should we be able to find evidence for the Exodus?

Egyptologist James Hoffmeier points out that we should not expect to find most
of the records where Egypt might have recorded the Exodus: "'I don't know of any
surviving papyrus documents from Egypt's Delta,'" says Hoffmeier. 'It's too wet.
And papyrus (made from the reed-like plant of the same name) is where most of
the records were kept. The inscriptions that we see on statues and temple facades
tend to be propagandistic, what-we-want-you-to-know messages. And where
papyrus records have survived, they tend to be from the desert areas. **So we
have very few of the day-to-day court records of 3,000 years of Egyptian
history'"**[22] (emphasis mine).

Other archaeologists have pointed out that nomads leave very few traces in the
archaeological record. This would be especially true in a desert setting. They also
point out that if a people such as Israel were inventing their history they would not
be likely to invent a history as descendants of slaves.[23] And the Egyptians did not
tend to record events such as military defeats and catastrophes that would give
them a weak image in the eyes of surrounding nations.

? Is there any positive evidence for the Exodus?

Dr. Randall Price lists some positive evidences for the Exodus in his book *The
Stones Cry Out*: **"We have evidence that foreigners from Canaan entered
Egypt, lived there, were sometimes considered troublemakers, and that**

---

20 Price, *The Stones Cry Out,* 97.

21 Kitchen, *On the Reliability of the Old Testament,* 371–372.

22 Kevin Miller, "Did the Exodus Never Happen?," *Christianity Today,* ibid.

23 Jeffery Scheler, "Is the Bible True?" *U.S. News and World Report*, October 25, 1999, edition,
    54.

Egypt oppressed and enslaved a vast foreign workforce during several dynasties. We also have records that slaves escaped and that Egypt suffered from plague-like conditions."[24]

In *The Exodus Case,* author Dr. Lennart Moeller, a scientist, describes evidence found in and around the Red Sea for the Red Sea crossing event in the Bible.

- Chariot wheels very similar to wheels pictured in Egyptian inscriptions were found on the Red Sea floor.

- Along with them were objects that appeared to be chariots and skeletons of men and horses, all piled together on the Red Sea floor, and the sea bed itself showing where stones and blocks seem to have been cleared aside to form a path.

- Also found were memorial markers on both shores in line with this sea-bed path.[25]

Moeller also describes a unique rock found that may be the rock in the Bible account that produced water in the desert in Rephidim, as well as a new site for Mount Sinai (not the traditional site), with many physical evidences there matching the biblical account of Mount Sinai.[26] There is also scientific evidence shown for the events at Sodom and Gomorrah. For example, in the area that was Gomorrah there is evidence of exposure to a rain of burning sulphur, with sulphur balls still found there, but no sulphur balls in the surrounding areas. Furthermore, this sulphur differs from that found near volcanoes.[27] Overall the book is a very

> By not finding something, archaeologists consider they have proved something. Non-evidence is not the same as evidence."
>
> *Archaeologist David Merling*

---

24 Price, *The Stones Cry Out,* 133.

25 Lennart Moeller, *The Exodus Case,* Scandinavia Publishing House, Copenhagen, Denmark, 2002, 204–229.

26 Ibid., 243–277.

27 Ibid., 37–47.

scientific and cautious treatment of this extraordinary evidence that has been found for the authenticity of many Old Testament events.

? Did the Battle of Jericho really happen?

Kathleen Kenyon, an archaeologist who excavated Jericho in the 1950s, said the city was indeed destroyed, but the time it was destroyed was too early to fit the biblical account. But there are reasons to question this conclusion.

- First, only three of the many Canaanite cities conquered were described as destroyed in the book of Joshua (Jericho, Hazor, and Ai).[28] One of the three cities destroyed according to the biblical account, Hazor, has been shown to have been inhabited and destroyed by fire, as described in the biblical account.[29]

- Some of Kenyon's conclusions using pottery found to establish the date of the destruction have been questioned as well. Bryant Wood analyzed the pottery found at Jericho and concluded the destruction happened about 1400 B.C., rather than 1550 B.C. as Kenyon claimed.[30] Once this time adjustment is made, he makes the case that the archaeological evidence harmonizes very well with the biblical account, including that the walls fell at the time the city was destroyed. Wood found several other evidences for the conquest as well.[31]

- Other archaeologists have found some evidence that indicates a revision of Egyptian chronology may be needed, which would make the Jericho evidence fit closely with the biblical date even assuming Kenyon's conclusions are correct.[32]

- If the Septuagint chronology rather than the Masoretic chronology of Genesis chapters 5 and 11 is followed, this adds about 1300 years to the ancient chronology. The difference in the ages of the fathers given for the times they had their sons in the Genesis genealogies is one of the few variations between

---

28 Kitchen, *On the Reliability of the Old Testament,* 183.

29 Price, *The Stones Cry Out,* 149–151; also Kitchen, On the Reliability of the Old Testament, 185.

30 Ibid., 152.

31 Ibid., 153–155.

32 David Rohl, *Pharaohs and Kings: A Biblical Quest,* Crown Publishing, New York, NY, 1995; also see J. Ashton and D. Down, *Unwrapping the Pharaohs,* Master Books, Green Forest, AR, 2006. Both of these books advocate a shortened Egyptian chronology with overlapping dynasties.

the Masoretic text and the Septuagint, and the Septuagint chronology could conceivably be the correct variation since it is based on earlier Hebrew texts.[33] This would allow the earlier date of Jericho's destruction to fit the biblical chronology, again even if Kenyon was correct.

Therefore, there are several possible solutions to the objections raised about the Battle of Jericho.

[?] If we don't find archaeological evidence, does this disprove the biblical account?

As we have seen, some biblical events are difficult to find in the archaeological record. But this does not prove they did not happen. Archaeologist David Merling, as quoted in The Stones Cry Out, states: **"By not finding something, archaeologists consider that they have proved something. Non-evidence is not the same as evidence. Other conquests, whose histories have never been questioned, have been investigated for evidence of destructions. The lack of evidence among those sites should cause all archaeologists to question the use of non-evidence."**[34]

Biblical archaeology is very much a work in progress, but as problems are solved the biblical record is vindicated again and again.

[?] Are the creation and flood accounts in the Bible borrowed from Babylonian myths?

This is still taught in many seminaries today and is a holdover from the Documentary Hypothesis of the late nineteenth century. Does this Babylonian myth theory fit the evidence? Most who hold this view emphasize the similarities in the accounts. But similarities would indeed be expected if the human race originated from one family and had a common creation or flood account which they took with them as they spread out across the earth.

There are also significant differences. Erwin Lutzer[35] points these out:

---

33 For a defense of the use of the Septuagint chronology in Genesis, see "Ancient Chronology in Scripture," Barry Setterfield, 1999, internet article from web site www.setterfield.org/000docs/scriptchron.htm. Also see by the same author "The Alexandrian Septuagint History," Setterfield, March 2010, www.setterfield.org/Septuagint_history:html.

34 Price, The Stones Cry Out, 156.

35 Erwin Lutzer, Seven Reasons Why You Can Trust the Bible, Moody Press, Chicago, IL, 1998, 70.

- In the Babylonian account there are many gods who quarrel and fight and who sprang from pre-existing matter.

- The Babylonian accounts confuse the Creator with His creation.

- The Babylonian account has the kind of garblings and embellishments to be expected when a historical account has been mythologized. The Genesis account gives a sober history of only one God who created space, time, and matter from nothing.

Some have said the Genesis account is simply the Babylonian account condensed and reworded without the polytheistic elements. But in the ancient Near East the evidence shows that simple accounts are embellished into complex legends, not the other way around. Lutzer quotes A.R. Millard: **"All who suspect or suggest a borrowing by the Hebrews are compelled to admit large-scale revision, alteration, and reinterpretation in a fashion which cannot be substantiated for any other composition from the ancient Near East or in any other Hebrew writing."**[36]

> "Luke's history is unsurpassed in respect of its trustworthiness."
> "This author should be placed along with the very greatest of historians."
>
> *Sir William Ramsey, archaeologist and former skeptic*

A theory that better fits the evidence is that God revealed His creation message to early generations, but as it was passed down through the generations in many different cultures it was corrupted and mythologized as it was handed down, and either God revealed to Moses the original record or Moses had possession of the original account as handed down from tablets written by the patriarchs.

There are several key differences between the flood account in the Bible and the Babylonian account. The ark in the biblical account is very seaworthy and has the dimensions of a modern ocean liner, where the Babylonian ark was a cube that would have been a disastrous design for a ship, being very easy to capsize. Genesis reads like a serious history, where the Babylonian account has many

36 Ibid., 70–71.

mythological elements.[37] Another important difference is that in the biblical account Noah's sin is mentioned, again highly unlikely to be done in a myth concerning the hero of the story.

Furthermore, ancient tablets have been discovered at Ebla, a region that is now part of modern Syria, which predate the Babylonian accounts of creation by about six hundred years.[38]

ARCHAEOLOGICAL EVIDENCE-NEW TESTAMENT

[?] **What reasons do we have to believe the New Testament is authentic history?**

Archaeological discoveries have confirmed people and events in the New Testament as well.[39]

- An inscription was found at Caesarea that confirmed the existence of Pontius Pilate and his title as given in the Bible. Dated around 30 A.D.

- A crucifixion victim was found in Jerusalem that confirms many details of the biblical descriptions, including a nail piercing through an ankle bone and attached to a piece of wood from a cross. Date of origin from about second century B.C. to first century A.D.

- The Pool of Bethesda was found in Jerusalem. Date of origin about third century B.C.

- The tomb of the high priest Caiaphas has been found. Dated in the 40s A.D.

- A Galilean fishing boat, the Kinneret boat, was discovered. Dated 30–70 A.D.

- The Erastus Inscription—monument with name and title of Erastus, treasurer of Corinth described by Paul in Romans 16:23. Dated 50–100 A.D.

---

37 For a complete refutation of the borrowing from Babylon theory, see Andrew Snelling, *Earth's Catastrophic Past—Geology, Creation, and the Flood,* vol. 1, Institute for Creation Research, Dallas Texas, 2009, 81–88.

38 Josh McDowell, *The New Evidence That Demands a Verdict,* Thomas Nelson Publishers, Nashville, TN, 1999, 375–377.

39 See Price, *The Stones Cry Out,* 316–317, for a more complete listing of significant New Testament archaeological discoveries.

- Ancient anchors have been discovered off the coast of Malta which some believe fit the biblical account of Paul's shipwreck described in Acts 27.[40]

The preceding was just a sample; numerous reference books describe these and other finds in great detail. These include: *The Stones Cry Out* by Randall Price; *The New Evidence That Demands a Verdict* by Josh McDowell; *Is the New Testament Reliable? A Look at the Historical Evidence* by Paul Barnett.

[?] Was Luke, the Gospel writer, a reliable historian?

One book that especially lends itself to archaeological verification is the Acts of the Apostles, believed by most scholars to be authored by Luke, the author of the third Gospel. Sir William Ramsay, who was one of the greatest archaeologists to have ever lived, began a study of the book of Acts as a skeptic, believing it was written in the second century and not historical. As he studied he uncovered evidence that indicated otherwise, and he had a complete reversal in his thinking about Luke's accuracy: "Luke's history is unsurpassed in respect of its trustworthiness."[41] Ramsay also stated of Luke: "This author should be placed along with the very greatest of historians."[42]

Josh McDowell lists evidences for Luke's accuracy compiled by Roman historian Colin Hemer, a noted Roman historian: "Specialized details, which would not be known except to a contemporary researcher ... details include exact titles of officials, identification of army units ... correlation of dates of known kings and governors within the chronology of the narrative ... 'undesigned coincidences'

---

40   Robert Cornuke, *The Lost Shipwreck of Paul,* Global Publishing Services, Bend, Oregon, 2003. Four anchors were located by international explorer Cornuke, not at the traditional site, but in St. Thomas Bay, which, unlike the traditional St. Paul's Bay, closely fits the geographical details described in the Acts 27 account. Examination of these anchors shows they were of the correct type and time period to fit the biblical account, found in the correct depth of water; there were four of them as described in the biblical account; and they were in a unique location where ocean currents collide, or "the two seas meet," again as described in Acts. A computer simulation done by the Armed Forces of Malta Search and Rescue Center of the drift course of Paul's ship had the ship arriving not in the traditional site (much to their surprise), but in St. Thomas Bay and on the exact day (day 14) specified in the Acts account (see 187–193).

41   Sir William Ramsay, *St. Paul the Traveler and the Roman Citizen,* Baker Book House, Grand Rapids, MI, 1962, 81.

42   Sir William Ramsay, *The Bearing of Recent Discovery on the Trustworthiness of the New Testament,* Hodder & Stoughton, London, UK, 1915, 222, as quoted in Josh McDowell, *The New Evidence That Demands a Verdict, 63.*

between Acts and the Pauline Epistles ... off-hand geographical references that bespeak familiarity with common knowledge."[43]

McDowell notes that many times historians thought Luke was in error on some points, only to be proven wrong by an archaeological discovery. For example:

- Luke spoke of Philippi as a "part" or "district" of Macedonia. It was believed he erred because the Greek word *meris* did not mean "district." Archaeological evidence unearthed showed, however, that "district" was the exact meaning of the Greek word *meris* that Luke had used.

- Luke referred to Lysanias the Tetrarch of Abilene in his Gospel. Because the only known Lysanias to historians was killed in 36 B.C., Luke was thought to be in error. Then an inscription was found bearing the name of Lysanias the Tetrarch and dated between 14 and 29 A.D., just at the right time period.

- Luke was thought to be wrong about the census taken at the time of Christ, because critics said there was no evidence of a census and that the governor called Quirinius was in power too late, 6 A.D., to be in his position at the time of Christ. They also stated that it was not required for the people to return to their birth homes. But archaeology showed that in fact these censuses were done regularly and that one was indeed taken at the time of Christ and, furthermore, that Quirinius was governor a second time, in 7 B.C. They also found evidence on a papyrus document showing that during the censuses people were required to return to their own homes and countries.[44]

- Luke referred to the Philippian officials as *praetors,* when some scholars thought the titles should be *duumvirs*, but archaeological finds showed that in fact *praetors* was the right title for the Roman magistrates of the colony.[45]

---

43 Josh McDowell, *The New Evidence That Demands a Verdict,* Thomas Nelson Publishers, Nashville, 1999, 65–66, his material being compiled from Colin Hemer, *The Book of Acts in the Setting of Hellenistic History,* Eisenvrauns, Winona Lake, IN, 1990, 104–107.

44 Ibid., 63.

45 Relating to the census, there is evidence a census was taken around 3–2 B.C. for the purpose of the exaltation of Augustus to the "Pater Patriae," which was not a taxation census but a citizen registration for allegiance to the emperor. At this time Quirinius would have possibly been a procurator and put in charge when this census happened. Luke does not actually give Quirinius's title; the Greek word translated "governor" really means a "ruler" or "administrator" at any level; and Luke also does not state that paying taxes was the reason for the census. The Greek word there simply means "registered," not "taxed." For an in-depth article on this position, see http://askelm.com/star/star014.htm, The Census of Quintillus Varus, Associates for Scriptural Knowledge.

- Luke used the title *politarchs* for the Thessalonian officials, but since this title was not found in the classical literature Luke was again assumed to be wrong. Then several inscriptions were found that used the title *politarchs*, and five of them referred to Thessalonica.[46]

There are many more examples of these findings, where Luke was right and the critics were wrong.

? Was John, the Gospel writer, a reliable historian? Weren't his writings more theological and less historical?

John is often portrayed by critics as being very theological with little concern for accurate history. But this view is totally against both the internal evidence of the text and against archaeological discovery. John mentions many historical details that would only be known by a personal witness living at the time and would probably be irrelevant to a later audience. Paul Barnett lists some examples of these:[47]

- John described the Pool of Bethesda as having five porticoes (John 5:2). When the actual pool was unearthed, sure enough, there were exactly five porticoes.

- The Pool of Siloam mentioned by John has also been discovered (John 9:7).

- John describes Jacob's well with familiarity (John 4:4, 11, 19). This well has been discovered also and fits John's description and location.[48]

- John includes a side reference not vital to the narrative, in chapter 10:22–23: "It was at Jerusalem, the feast of the dedication, and it was winter. And Jesus walked in the temple in Solomon's porch." Barnett comments: "The Maccabean feast of dedication occurs in winter, just as Christmas in Australia occurs in mid-summer. Jesus seeks shelter from the weather in a particular place, Solomon's porch, which is part of the temple of Herod. If someone wrote of a person seeking shelter from the sun on Christmas day in the Bennelong restaurant in the Sydney Opera House, it would be reasonable to conclude that he had first-hand knowledge of the Australian climate and of a Sydney landmark in the period after the year 1973 when the opera house was completed. **We conclude that the author of this Gospel had first-hand understanding of the climate of Judaea and of the architecture**

---

46 McDowell, *The New Evidence That Demands a Verdict,* 65.

47 Paul Barnett, *Is the New Testament Reliable? A Look at the Historical Evidence,* Intervarsity Press, Downers Grove, IL, 1986, 59–70.

48 Ibid., 62.

of the temple in the period before A.D. 70 when it was destroyed"[49] (emphasis mine).

- Furthermore, John shows a familiarity with the local geography which indicates he was an eyewitness and not someone writing at a later time period. In fact, John mentions about a dozen places not referred to in the other Gospels. After listing some of these, including the above-mentioned Pool of Siloam and the Kidron Valley (John 18:1), Barnett refers the reader to a quote from Meyers and Strange: "The point we wish to make … is simply that **an unprejudiced reading of the Gospel of John seems to suggest that it is in fact based on a historical and geographical tradition, though not one that simply repeats information from the synoptics"**[50] (emphasis mine).

- Barnett also demonstrates that the historical references in the Gospel of John fit the context of the times[51] and that the details of the lives of the various people he mentions suggest first-hand, authentic history.[52] Barnett sums up the evidence for the historical character and the reliability of the Gospel of John: **"Is the fourth gospel historical in character? The wealth of information relating to places, to the specific content of the pre-A.D. 70 period and the details about named individuals require our acknowledgment that this piece of literature is genuinely historical"**[53] (emphasis mine).

When an author is shown to be trustworthy in areas where he can be tested, this should increase our confidence in all of his writing.

[?] Are there any other historians that confirm the historicity of Jesus?

Several secular historical sources also confirm the historicity of Jesus. Some of these are hostile sources who nevertheless by their writings acknowledge certain facts such as the miracles of Jesus, the time period in which He lived, the manner of His death, reports of His resurrection, His being worshipped as God, and the birth

---

49 Ibid., 63.

50 E. M. Meyers & J. F. Strange, *Archaeology, the Rabbis, and Early Christianity,* London, 1981, 161, as quoted in Paul Barnett, *Is The New Testament Reliable,* 63–65.

51 Paul Barnett, *Is The New Testament Reliable, pp.,* 65–66.

52 Ibid., 66–70.

53 Ibid., 70.

of the Christian church. Some examples of these writers are Flavius Josephus, the writers of the Talmud, Cornelius Tacitus, Suetonius, Pliny the Younger, and others.

What these writers show is the existence of the Christian church in the first century shortly after the time Christ lived and that these early Christians were already dying for rather than denying the facts of the death and resurrection of Jesus Christ.[54]

Was the New Testament invented history?

[?] **Some scholars say the New Testament writers invented many of the details of Jesus' life and sayings and that they put words in His mouth. Is this true?**

Some modern scholars are inclined to dismiss much of the New Testament, especially the Gospels, as inventions of the authors rather than real history. Many people embrace this idea because they don't want to be under the authority of what Jesus said, and so they claim His words were not His words at all, but invented by the Gospel writers to meet some social or political need. But what does the evidence show?

In the writings of the New Testament the authors give no hint they are trying to invent anything, but just the opposite:

- "For we have not followed cunningly devised fables, when we made known unto you the power and the coming of our Lord Jesus Christ, but were eyewitnesses of His majesty" (2 Peter 1:16).

- "That which we have seen and heard declare we unto you, that ye also may have fellowship with us, and truly our fellowship is with the Father and with His Son Jesus Christ" (1 John 1:3).

- "And he that saw it bare record, and his record is true: and he knoweth that he saith true, that ye might believe" (John 19:35).

- "Now in the fifteenth year of the reign of Tiberius Caesar, Pontius Pilate being governor of Judea" (Luke 3:1).

- "I am not mad, most noble Festus, but speak forth the words of truth and soberness. For the king knoweth of these things, before whom also I speak

---

54 A very comprehensive reference covering these secular historians is Josh McDowell, *He Walked Among Us—Evidence for the Historical Jesus,* Here's Life Publishers, San Bernadino, CA, 1988.

CHAPTER SIX: THE SHOVEL DOESN'T LIE

freely, for I am persuaded that none of these things are hidden from him, for this thing was not done in a corner" (Acts 26:25–26).

- "Ye men of Israel, hear these words: Jesus of Nazareth, a man approved by God among you by miracles and wonders and signs, which God did by Him in the midst of you, as ye yourselves also know" (Acts 2:22).

- "For we are not as many, which corrupt the Word of God; but as of sincerity, but as of God, in the sight of God speak we in Christ" (2 Corinthians 2:17).

If the biblical writers invented their accounts, then they were the cleverest liars on earth; yet their writings have inspired many to great honesty and noble conduct. Surely it takes more faith to believe they were liars than that they were telling the truth!

? Could their writings have been made so far after the facts that no one was able to challenge them?

We have already seen some manuscript and archaeological evidence that shows the New Testament was probably written very close to the events it describes. But there is another compelling reason for believing so. Author Dave Hunt discusses how several scholars have pointed out that **if a document claims to be from a certain period, evidence that the events contained therein indeed belong to that period includes public commemorations of the events from that certain time period forward and also some public monuments kept in memory of the events from that time forward. These criterions prevent a fictitious story of an alleged event being foisted on a people long after the event was supposed to have happened.**[55]

For example, it would be like telling Americans there was an attack on Pearl Harbor on December 7, 1941, and that Americans had been holding ceremonies to commemorate this infamous day ever since, when in fact no attack had ever taken place on that day and historical records show this day was never remembered by any ceremony or monument from 1941 until now. The story would be rejected as a forgery, since one would think the American people could check their own history!

The same is true for the New Testament. The writers included accounts of ordinances instituted by Christ, including the Lord's Supper and baptism. As Henry Morris[56] points out, all the people of the second century would have to do would be

---

55 Dave Hunt, *In Defense of the Faith*, 156–157.

56 Henry Morris, *Many Infallible Proofs,* 41–43.

to check their own history to see if the Christian church existed from the first century or if baptism and the Lord's Supper had indeed been celebrated from the first century forward. If the authors were second century or even late first century inventors, why would they risk their credibility by including accounts of these ordinances?

[?] Are there any other reasons to doubt the invention theory?

Many other reasons cast serious doubt on the invention theory.

Eyewitnesses: At the time of writing there were many eyewitnesses, including hostile ones, who could have discredited any inventions. This could be true even forty years later. Many of even the more skeptical scholars will admit this possibility. Josh McDowell quotes Laurence McGinley: **"First of all, eyewitnesses of the events in question were still alive when the tradition had been completely formed; and among those eyewitnesses were bitter enemies of the new religious movement. Yet the tradition claimed to narrate a series of well-known deeds and publicly taught doctrines at a time when false statements could, and would, be challenged."**[57] For example, would any of us more than forty years old believe a story that China was the first nation to put a man on the moon in 1969?

Short time interval: There was also no time for legends and myths to develop as there were in the so-called parallel examples used by these scholars. The Gospels were written down no more than thirty to forty years after the events they describe, while the critics' examples of developing legends span centuries from the events that triggered them.[58]

Oral memorization practices: The Jewish rabbis' method of teaching was to have their pupils memorize their sayings, to the point that it was as reliable as or more so than writing them down to preserve these sayings, and there is plenty of evidence that Jesus used the rabbis' methods in instructing His disciples. He often used the rabbinical device of answering a question with a question and other styles of teaching that have parallels in the rabbinical literature.[59] There was a cultural emphasis on memorization, and Jesus' words were often given in poetic form, a

---

57 Laurence J. McGinley, *Form Criticism of the Synoptic Healing Narratives,* Woodstock College Press, Woodstock, MD, 1944, 25, as quoted in McDowell, *More Evidence That Demands a Verdict,* 211.

58 Ibid., 211–212.

59 McDowell, *He Walked Among Us,* 238-243.

great aid to memorization. So there is evidence for a solid oral tradition in place before the writing of the Gospels.

The Promise of the Holy Spirit: Some scholars also seem to completely discount Jesus' promise that the Holy Spirit would remind the disciples of all that Jesus taught them (John 14:26), and, in general, they discount the supernatural workings of the Holy Spirit to quicken the memory and inspire the New Testament writers. These scholars sometimes don't (and many times don't want to) believe the New Testament is the inspired Word of God.

Other pertinent questions: If they were inventions, why didn't the stories grow in number as time passed and new situations arose?[60] And why weren't any of the many words of Saint Paul put into Jesus' mouth, to give them the ultimate authority? Paul was very careful to distinguish his own words from what were the Lord's spoken words that had been passed on to him. If Jesus didn't say most of the things He was recorded to have said, what reason would they have had to execute Him? And history shows that profound sayings come from individuals, not from inventing communities, so there is no parallel case for their theories.[61]

? Is it more credible to think the people who spent time with Jesus forgot all He really said and then invented sayings of Jesus later or that they simply remembered what He said?

They were martyrs: Even more important, the disciples of Jesus would not have died martyrs' deaths for the product of their imaginations. **People do not die for what they know is a lie.**

Not mass delusion: It couldn't have been mass delusion because the events they wrote about were public events in the open and reported in a great variety of times and places by people of different backgrounds, unlike any known cases of mass hysteria or delusion. Moreover, the New Testament writers were not the types of people who were likely to have hallucinations, and their very sane and practical writings reflect this. And since anyone who became a Christian in that day was immediately in danger of persecution or martyrdom, they had every reason to check out the claims of the disciples before joining them. If they had any reason to believe the apostles were deluded or unstable they would not have received their message.

---

60 McDowell, *More Evidence That Demands a Verdict*, 238.

61 Ibid., 252.

Invention is a greater miracle than the truth: A fabricated New Testament would be a greater miracle than an authentic one.

- More than three hundred prophecies concerning the details of the life of Jesus Christ and other events have been fulfilled. These fulfillments all would have to be included in the fabrication, even the more obscure ones, and have the account still make sense and the details not look contrived.

- Furthermore, this account would have to portray the highest standards of honesty and morals, even though being a total deception, with sworn testimonies to its accuracy included.

- This fabrication would have to be responsible for life transformations and leading people to a relationship with God. How could a book written to deceive people do this?

- This fabrication would also somehow have to stand up to intense archaeological investigation.

- If it were an invention, how could its prophecies have been fulfilled as they have in modern times?

- Would a deceiver have been able to or have the motive for maintaining the incredible consistency found with all other Scripture, including the explaining of all the foreshadowings and symbols of the Old Testament?

- And finally, again, would the authors have been willing to die for such a fabrication?

- And why and how could Jesus fake His birthplace and genealogy? Did He pay off the soldiers on duty to gamble for His robe, give Him vinegar, not break His legs, and yet pierce His side? How did He arrange to be crucified by His enemies on Passover, and why go through all that to die anyway? And how does anyone fake a resurrection?

We can see that the idea the New Testament was an invention of the authors is preposterous. In fact, the only "invention" seems to be the invention of the skeptics' theories.

ARCHAEOLOGICAL EVIDENCE-THE BIBLE VERSUS OTHER "HOLY BOOKS"

? Do other "holy books" have any proven historical errors?

The Koran has some proven historical errors.

For example, the Koran says a Samaritan was the one who made the golden calf for Israel and led them astray (Sura 20:85–88). Yet the Samaritans did not even come into being until after the sixth century B.C., and so there could have been no Samaritans around at the time of the Exodus, for which the latest date given by scholars is about 1200 B.C., more likely in the 1400s B.C.[62]

Mohammed also confused Saul and Gideon in Sura 2:247. He has Saul leading the three-hundred-man army mentioned in the book of Judges, long before the time Saul was born.[63]

The Koran also confuses Mary the mother of Jesus with Miriam, the sister of Moses, and Aaron (Sura 19:28, Sura 3:35).

The Koran reads in many places like a garbled version of the Bible, borrowed from the Bible in parts, but with some confusion of details.[64]

How about the Book of Mormon? The Mormon church has spent decades and much money trying to confirm the Book of Mormon archaeologically; yet they have not found so much as one item of corroboration. This is admitted by Mormon archaeologists. There is also evidence for invention and plagiarism. For example, in portions of the Book of Mormon entire chapters are copied out of the Bible. And in parts of the Book of Mormon allegedly written in 600–500 B.C. there are hundreds of quotes from the New Testament, all in King James English, with not only the chapter and verse divisions (both added long after the time of Christ) intact, but even the italics in the verses. The only reasonable conclusion is that the writer Joseph Smith was using a copy of the King James Bible, and he plagiarized it.[65]

A new discovery causing further problems for the Book of Mormon is that the DNA evidence shows conclusively that the Native Americans could not have descended

---

62 Caner and Caner, *Unveiling Islam,* 90.

63 Ibid.

64 Ibid., 89–90; also see Schafi, *Behind the Veil,* 179–184.

65 Hunt and Decker, *The God Makers,* 125–126.

from the Jews, as the Book of Mormon teaches. Many scholars, some of them even Mormon themselves, admit this proves the Book of Mormon is in error.[66]

In the next section we shall talk about divine inspiration and what it means and the idea of "contradictions" in the Bible.

---

66 *DNA vs. The Book of Mormon,* video by Living Hope Ministries, Brigham City, Utah, 2003.

CHAPTER SEVEN

BIBLE "CONTRADICTIONS"-MUCH ADO ABOUT NOTHING

CLAIMS OF INSPIRATION

? Are there any claims to divine inspiration in the Bible?

The Bible makes the claim to be inspired of God. There are hundreds of claims to divine inspiration throughout the Bible, words such as "Thus saith the Lord," "The word of the Lord came unto me," etc. One of the best known of these claims is in **2 Timothy 3:16: "All scripture is given by inspiration of God."** The words of the Scripture are claimed to be more than just words of men: **"For the prophecy came not in old time by the will of man; but holy men of God spake as they were moved by the Holy Ghost" (2 Peter 1:21)**. These men claimed to know that God was inspiring them: **"The Spirit of the Lord spake by me, and his word was in my tongue" (2 Samuel 23:2).** The Holy Spirit also promised to empower the apostles of Jesus to remember His words: **"But the Comforter, which is the Holy Ghost, whom the Father will send in my name, he shall teach you all things, and bring all things to your remembrance, whatsoever I have said unto you" (John 14:26).** The Holy Spirit is therefore said to be the inspirer of the Bible, and He works through the Bible writers to give us a communication from God.

? What is the definition of divine inspiration?

Inspiration in the biblical sense does not mean the same as a singer or an artist being inspired by their own feelings or experiences or by some human agenda such as political maneuvering or social change. The inspiration claimed in the Bible comes from outside, from a Person apart from humanity. Belief in the Creator God makes this totally reasonable, since if God had the ability to create us He would also have the ability to communicate to us what He wants us to know. **This inspiration would then be defined as God influencing the biblical writers so that, although their particular style, character, and research remained intact, the words they wrote reflected what God Himself wanted to declare to humanity.**

? How would this divine inspiration work itself out in the biblical text?

God would enable the writers to say exactly what He wanted them to say. Jeremiah wrote his prophetic message on a scroll (see Jeremiah 36), which was taken to the king of Judah, who refused to hear it and burned it. The Lord remedied the situation by inspiring Jeremiah to make a complete reproduction of the original scroll. It makes sense that God would not have to be limited to relying on Jeremiah's fallible human memory in reproducing what He wanted to say.

? How much control did God exercise when inspiring the Bible writers?

It makes sense that God would not allow the men to write the Bible unsupervised. The original autographs would have to have been inerrant. What does this mean? It does not mean that every idea had to be said in exactly the same way, without diversity of expression. Sometimes Jesus is quoted with slightly different words in the same context. What is observed in these cases is that although the wording is slightly different the sense of the words is the same in these passages. There is no change in meaning. Sometimes words of Jesus are included in one account that are not included in a parallel account. In these cases one account fills in the gaps in the other, giving a fuller picture of what Jesus said.

Actually, in the oral traditions of the culture of that time, these features are common. Dr. Craig Blomberg, noted author and Bible scholar, was quoted in Lee Strobel's book *The Case for Christ*: "The definition of memorization was more flexible back then. In studies of cultures with oral traditions, there was freedom to vary how much of the story was told on any given occasion—what was included, what was left out, what was paraphrased, what was explained, and so forth … **it's likely that a lot of the similarities and differences among the Synoptics can be explained by assuming that the disciples and other early Christians had committed to memory a lot of what Jesus said and did, but they felt free to recount this information in various forms, always preserving the significance of Jesus' original teachings and deeds"**[1] (emphasis mine).

We no longer have the originals, but as we have seen above we have every reason to believe our copies are trustworthy reproductions. As for textual errors and so-called contradictions, we will be discussing those below.

BIBLE "CONTRADICTIONS"

[?] What about all those Bible contradictions?

There are definitely verses in the Bible that superficially, at least, seem to contradict each other. *We must ask two questions about them: What do these verses show about the Bible, and is there a satisfactory resolution to the "contradiction"?*

One thing the seeming disagreements in Scripture shows is the absence of collusion. They could even have been designed that way as one more evidence of authenticity. **Some of the Bible's verses, when carefully studied in the proper context, exhibit superficial discrepancies and conflicts which resolve themselves on closer examination. This kind of evidence is exactly what is looked for in a court of law to establish credibility and independence of witnesses. If things agree too well they look artificial and contrived.**

There are many books on this subject; one I found that seemed comprehensive is titled *Alleged Discrepancies of the Bible* by John W. Haley, written in 1992 (Whitaker House, New Kensington, PA). I will look at some examples shortly from this work and others.

There are many logical explanations for the perceived conflicts between certain Bible verses.

---

1   Strobel, *The Case for Christ*, 54–55.

- God dealt with people in the Old Testament differently from in the New Testament. Before the cross there was a different spiritual economy. This can be perceived as God progressively revealing Himself to people in a more personal way.

- Another reason is that what is recorded by the Bible, such as the actions of Jacob or Abraham, is not necessarily endorsed by God. All that is necessary is a faithful rendering of what took place.

- When the New Testament writers quote the Old Testament writers, since they were both inspired by the Holy Spirit, He (the Holy Spirit) had a right to modify His own words. Hence the sometimes inexact quotations.

- Some Bible scholars acknowledge that some of the Bible writers record historical events out of chronological order to fit what they are trying to emphasize, but this does not detract from the historicity of the events themselves.

- Some discrepancies, particularly in parallel passages in the Gospels, may be the results of translational differences. F. F. Bruce talks about parallel passages in the Gospels of Matthew and Luke: "Several Greek versions of them were current, which partly explains some of the differences in the sayings of Jesus common to the first and third Gospels; for in many places where the Greek of these Gospels differs, it can be shown that one and the same Aramaic original underlies the variant Greek renderings."[2]

- Another simple explanation would be that Jesus gave the same essential teachings more than once, with slightly varying words each time.

- Also, a large number of perceived discrepancies are the result of taking a Bible verse out of context. Many are also due to the prejudice of the critic. John Haley says in his book *Alleged Discrepancies of the Bible* of the critics Strauss, Colenso, and Theodore Parker: "One can scarcely read the productions of these three, and some others of their school, without the conviction that the *animus* of these writers is often felicitously expressed by the old Latin motto, slightly modified: '*Aut inveniam discrepantiam, aut faciam*—I will either find a discrepancy, or I will make one.'"[3]

---

2   F. F. Bruce, *The New Testament Documents, Are They Reliable?* Intervarsity Press, Leicester, England, 1943, rev. ed. reprinted 1997, 39.

3   Haley, *Alleged Discrepancies of the Bible,* 26.

? Have copying errors corrupted the Bible?

One very large source of discrepancies comes from minor textual errors caused by copyist mistakes. Books of the Bible, before printing presses and copiers, had to be copied by hand. Many letters and numbers in Hebrew and Greek were very similar to each other, and, given the amount of copies made, some small errors were inevitable without a continuous miracle to prevent them. In fact, many theologians think the reason God did not allow perfectly inerrant originals to be preserved was that they might have become idolized and objects of worship. And as we discussed in the section on manuscripts above, scholars who have studied these "slips of the pen" have concluded that no major doctrine of the Bible is affected by them.

Bible scholar Gleason Archer states: "Do we have any objective evidence that errors of transmission have not been permitted by God to corrupt and pervert His revelation? Yes, we have, for **a careful study of the variants (different readings) of the various earliest manuscripts reveals that none of them affects a single doctrine of Scripture.**"[4] It seems God has allowed the Bible to be human enough so the manuscripts do not require a constant miracle and yet still ensure the message will be preserved according to God's purposes.

Actually, many scholars see the discrepancies as beneficial. The discrepancies force one to dig further into the whole Bible to resolve them, and many times a difficult Scripture passage will be explained in another part of the Bible, one passage shedding light on another, which also shows the integrity of the whole book.

EXAMPLES OF SO-CALLED CONTRADICTIONS IN THE NEW TESTAMENT

? How about the contradictions in the account of Peter's denial of Christ?

Let's look at a few of the kinds of items critics are bringing up as they level the charge of "untrustworthy" at the Bible. In Matthew 26, Mark 14, Luke 22, and John 13 there are accounts of Peter's denial of Christ and roosters crowing. In Matthew, Luke, and John, Jesus appears to be telling Peter that before the cock crows once the next morning Peter will deny Him three times. Yet in Mark Jesus tells Peter

---

4   Archer, *A Survey of Old Testament Introduction,* 28.

that he will deny Him before the cock crows twice. Critics point to this and say the accounts disagree and so they can't be trusted.

When some critics find something like this, without considering an alternative explanation, they often immediately jump to the conclusion that each Gospel writer invented his story and then tailored it to whatever political or religious motives he had given the situation. There may or may not have been an actual denial by Peter, they say, but they just can't trust any of the Gospel accounts to be true history because they "contradict" each other. After all, a rooster can't crow once and have it mean the same as crowing twice, can it? So they throw the historical value of the passages out the window and say: "We just don't know, but it makes a nice story."

? So are there any good explanations?

You might say: "Who cares about crowing roosters?" At the risk of ruffling some feathers, I would like to take a second look at this so-called discrepancy.

Author Dave Hunt in his book *In Defense of the Faith* points out that all the roosters tended to start crowing at a time in the early morning called the "cockcrow" or "cockcrowing." This term is used as such in **Mark 13:35: "At even, or at midnight, or at the cockcrowing, or in the morning." In Matthew 26:34, Jesus says: "Before the cock crow, thou shalt deny me thrice."** That is, He may be saying that before that time in the morning when the usual cockcrowing occurs Peter will have denied Him three times. In fact, all four agree on this fact.[5]

Hunt notes also that Mark does not really contradict the other Gospels; rather, he adds more detail. Jesus told Peter: **"Before the cock crow twice, thou shalt deny me thrice" (Mark 14:30).** If we read the account in Mark we find that a rooster crowed right after

"The inspiration of God guiding what each says, though from independent points of view, is seen in that the remarkable blending together of all four testimonies is necessary to provide us with the whole picture."

Dave Hunt, author and lecturer on the Bible

---

5   Dave Hunt, *In Defense of the Faith*, 92.

Peter's first denial. This was not the usual time of the cockcrowing, but the Lord made a rooster crow even earlier, at the time of Peter's first denial. How long was the time between this first cock crowing and the normal time of the "cockcrowing"? Checking the account in Luke, we see the time between the second and third denials was **"about the space of one hour" (Luke 22:59)**, after which was the second, normal cockcrowing.[6]

The above scenario harmonizes all the accounts and is definitely a plausible explanation for the "contradiction." Dave Hunt sums up the so-called "contradiction": **"The honesty of the accounts is revealed in the fact that neither repeats the other but that each provides a piece of information which is necessary to the whole. And the inspiration of God guiding what each says, though from independent points of view, is seen in that the remarkable blending together of all four testimonies is necessary to provide us with the whole picture."**[7] Hunt's description here could easily be applied to the four Gospels in any parts where they differ with one another when describing the same events.

Is it more reasonable to believe an explanation like this or to believe the writers changed what really happened to fit some political motif or that they all carelessly made up their own version just to suit their tastes? Does it not seem more likely that they were each giving earnest accounts aided by the Holy Spirit and He used Mark to provide additional details? Now it is true that each Gospel writer had their own emphasis, such as Luke the humanness of Jesus and John's Gospel the deity of Christ, and the details the Holy Spirit inspires them to record fit these different emphases. But this is totally different from saying the writers were careless or deliberately made up history.

[?] What insight can we gain from these "contradictions"?

These superficial contradictions, which resolve themselves when examined together into a fuller picture, are just the kind of evidence the courts would look for to authenticate the testimony of four eyewitnesses. And in investigating this "contradiction" we uncover additional insight into the account of the denials. In fact, Hunt sees in these additional details God's generosity in providing Peter with the

---

6   Ibid., 93.

7   Ibid.

grace of an early warning to prevent further denials. Like Peter, sometimes we have ignored warnings God has given us and ended up weeping in regret afterward.[8]

? **How about the contradiction in the accounts of the transfiguration of Christ? Matthew 17:1 and Mark 9:2 say the transfiguration happened six days after the previous event presented (Jesus' sermon), but Luke 9:28 says it happened eight days later. How can we trust the Bible when the writers can't even get the number of days right?**

Again more than a superficial examination is needed. In Matthew and Mark it says after (Greek—meta) six days which would mean at least the seventh day or beyond. Luke says "about an eight days." The expression "an eight days" was an expression used for a week, and the word "about" indicates it was not exact.[9]

So we see that the critics have jumped to conclusions a little too quickly. This may tell us more about the critics than it does about the passages. Since they seem to refuse to consider reconciling explanations for their "contradictions," one wonders if they don't want the Bible to be considered trustworthy because then they would be accountable to obey what it says.

? **Do contradictions in the Gospel of John prove it was invented history?**

I was at a conference several years ago and heard a well-known author and scholar speaking on the book of John. This speaker said John's accounts were written from political and spiritual motivations and that John or whoever the author was invented the details to fit his "motif."

He pointed out that, in the Gospel of John, Andrew introduces Peter to Jesus. In the other Gospels the disciples are called from their fishermen's nets by Jesus, and they immediately go off with Him. He also cited the two different accounts of Jesus cleansing the temple. "See," he said, "so many contradictions!" He implied that we can't believe this is real history.

Because this man was a well-known scholar and teacher, I'm sure many accepted his analysis of John's Gospel without question. But in this case a little questioning

---

8   Ibid., 93–94.

9   Ibid., 97.

provides another explanation for the "contradictions." Now, as we said before, most scholars of the Gospels agree that the Gospel writers did not necessarily follow chronological order when they described certain events but grouped certain events together to suit what things about Jesus they were trying to emphasize. But it does not follow that because they sometimes did this they made up stories. Rather they were fitting together in a particular way oral (and possibly earlier written) traditions of real historical events about Jesus.[10]

? So how do we explain the cleansing of the temple "contradictions"?

If John and the others both intended to be chronological here, there would have been two cleansings of the temple. The wording is very different in John's account from the other Gospels (compare John 2:16 with Matthew 21:13). This makes it likely that the writers did not copy from each other. And even if there was only one cleansing it is possible that John, not being necessarily chronological, put it at the beginning of his Gospel for thematic reasons. This does not in any way prove the writers invented the event.

? How about the "contradictions" in the accounts of the calling of the first disciples of Christ?

According to F. F. Bruce, John's Gospel fills in material not covered in the synoptic Gospels, covering the early Judean ministry of Jesus (before the imprisonment of John the Baptist). This material on the Judean ministry of Jesus is not covered in the synoptic Gospels.[11] During that time the disciples such as Peter and Andrew met Jesus but were not called until a later time. Notice that it says in John's account, *"They ... abode with Him that day"* but afterward likely went back to their jobs as fishermen (John 1:35–43). Then they were called into full-time service as apostles (Matthew 4:18–22) and gave up their former occupations at this time. This would better explain their willingness to leave their jobs immediately when Jesus called them to follow Him, because they had met Jesus previously. So, again, plausible explanations can be brought forth, and there is no need to mandate a lack of reliability because of these so-called "contradictions."

---

10 Haley, *Alleged Discrepancies of the Bible,* 9–11.

11 F. F. Bruce, *The New Testament Documents: Are They Reliable?* 55–56.

? Is there evidence that the writer of the Gospel of John was an eyewitness?

John mentions many details that would be characteristic of a first-person observer. He describes specific details on such things as the Pool of Bethesda with five porticoes, the porticoe of Solomon in the temple, the Kidron Valley, Cana in Galilee as opposed to Cana in Sidon, Aenon near Salim, the town of Ephraim, and others.[12] New Testament scholar Paul Barnett describes the above and other details noted in the Gospel of John and then states: **"The evidence relating to buildings and places, historical context and specific people show that this writer was consciously utilizing historical information. There are many more pieces of specific information in the fourth gospel than in the other gospels. This document is a primary, not a derived or secondary, document."**[13]

CONTRADICTIONS IN OTHER HOLY BOOKS

? If all these so-called Bible "contradictions" can be resolved, how about other holy books? Do they have "contradictions" that can be explained in the same manner?

To investigate this, let's look at the Koran.

Many have pointed out contradictions in the Koran, a book said to be divinely inspired by Allah and composed in heaven and revealed to Mohammed who wrote it. It was written down by one man rather than many. Yet there are seemingly real contradictions.

- In the chapter of the Koran called "Al Waqiha," in verses 13–14, it states that the majority of those in paradise will be from the nations who came before Mohammed and the minority will be from peoples who believed in Mohammed. But in the same chapter, verses 39–40, it says that the majority in paradise will be from peoples before Mohammed, and then it adds that there will also be many after Mohammed. Verse 14 says "a few of those of later time," and verse 40 says "a multitude of those of later time." In his book *Behind the Veil*, author Abd El Schafi addresses this problem and notes

12 Barnett, *Is the New Testament Reliable?*, 63–64.
13 Ibid., 73.

that among respected Muslim scholars, whom he exclusively quotes in his book, there is not one explanation they give for what he calls an "obvious" contradiction.[14]

- Other examples of contradictions: Sura 21:76 says Noah's entire family survived the flood. But Sura 11:42–43 says that one of Noah's sons drowned in the flood.[15]

- The Koran denies that it contains any non-Arabic words (Sura 16:103; 41:44); yet there are at least 118 non-Arabic words in the Koran, as admitted by Muslim scholars.[16]

- Sura 7:54 and other texts state that the creation took six days, but in Sura 41:9-12 it takes eight days.[17]

There are several others also.[18] How are these reconciled?

[?] Did Jesus die on the cross, or not, according to the Koran?

One very important contradiction in the Koran refers to the death of Jesus. Sura 4:157-158 says that Jesus was not crucified and did not die but was taken up to heaven. But Sura 19:33 has Jesus speaking of the day He will die and be raised alive. **So there is confusion and contradiction in the Koran about whether Jesus died or not. The fact is, Jesus is the only founder of any religion with an empty tomb, and the Koran is completely confused about one of the most important issues in both Christianity and Islam.** Allah is also quoted in Sura 3:55 as saying, "O Jesus! I will cause thee to die and raise thee to myself." G. J. O. Moshay points out in his book Who Is This Allah? how some have tried to change the meaning of "I will cause thee to die" with "I am gathering thee."[19] But going to the original Arabic of the Koran, Muslim scholars admit this is not the meaning: "As an Arab, I have never known any other meaning than death for this

---

14 Schafi, *Behind the Veil,* 236.

15 Caner and Caner, *Unveiling Islam,* 92.

16 Schafi, *Behind the Veil,* 234–235.

17 Caner and Caner, *Unveiling Islam*, 92.

18 Ibid., 91–93; also see Schafi, *Behind the Veil,* 233–239.

19 G. J. O. Moshay, *Who Is This Allah?* by Dorchester House Publications, Gerrards Cross, UK, 2nd ed., 1995, 121.

expression (Inni muta-waf-feeka), within or without the Quran."[20] Also, Sura 5:110 says that Jesus lived to be an old man.[21]

? What is abrogation in the Koran?

There is another disturbing procedure in Islam called abrogation. This is where one verse in the Koran is said to supersede another, and the former verse is to be forgotten. Right away we see a contrast to the Bible, where Jesus says: **"My words shall not pass away"** (Matthew 24:35). Abrogation as defined in the Koran (Sura 2:106) meant that Mohammed would state some revelation to his followers one day, and then Allah could invalidate and replace it on another day. According to Abd El Schafi, Muslim scholars said this could even happen overnight! There are many such verses.[22]

Muslims will try to defend this concept by saying that circumstances and times change. To this general idea I would agree. In the Bible there came a time, about fifteen centuries after the Mosaic Law was given, that Jesus declared some of the commandments, such as those regarding clean and unclean food, to be no longer binding under the new covenant of grace. Yet Jesus never said to forget the law. Rather, He said He fulfilled its requirements (Matthew 5:17–18). And the law was meant for a certain time in history to teach believers that God was very interested in holy conduct and to show that people could not be justified before God by keeping the law. So there were commands, especially regarding ceremonial law, that were once binding and now are not.

The difference is that in the Koran's abrogation circumstances changed, sometimes overnight, and that Mohammed's followers were told to forget the revelation they received the day before.[23] In the Bible there is no such overnight change of God's revelations or forgetting as unimportant anything God has revealed.

The question that needs to be asked is: are the so-called contradictions in the Bible qualitatively different from the contradictions in the Koran?

---

20 Dr. Anis Shorrosh, *Islam Revealed*, Thomas Nelson, Nashville, 1989, 97, as quoted in Moshay, *Who Is This Allah?* 121.

21 Caner and Caner, *Unveiling Islam*, 93.

22 Schafi, *Behind the Veil*, 219–232.

23 Ibid., 220.

? So the "contradictions" in the Bible can be explained. What do the claims of inspiration prove regarding the trustworthiness of the Bible?

As we have shown, there are satisfactory resolutions to most of the so-called "contradictions" in the Bible. So the claim of divine inspiration is not disproven. But what do the claims of inspiration prove regarding the trustworthiness of the Bible? It is true that anyone can claim anything, and that doesn't mean they are trustworthy. This is how cults operate. They just say, "I am speaking for God! Believe me!" We need some way of testing their claims. We have already seen powerful evidence that the Bible is inspired of God through scientific foreknowledge and prophecy. Another way to test those claims of divine inspiration is to consider who is making them and by what authority. The evidence for Christ's resurrection provides the answer to this. We also need to see how the Bible was put together. These are the subjects of the next chapter.

CHAPTER EIGHT

AMMUNITION FOR THE CANON

THE EVIDENCE FOR THE RESURRECTION OF CHRIST AS PROOF OF THE TRUSTWORTHINESS OF THE BIBLE

? How did Jesus prove the authority of the Bible?

We have already shown we can trust the Bible to be as reliable as any historical document. Jesus taught the authority of the Old Testament Scriptures, and He taught that the New Testament writers would be similarly guided by the Holy Spirit (see John 14:26). The writers of the epistles, such as Paul and Peter, claimed their authority was from Jesus Christ. Also in the biblical accounts Jesus made the claim, when asked by what authority He did and said things, that He would prove His authority by His resurrection.

? What evidence is there for the resurrection of Christ?

The evidence for the resurrection of Jesus Christ turns out to be among the most solid evidence for any fact of history. There are many good reference books on this subject. One very scholarly treatment is The Historical Jesus by Gary Habermas. He outlines certain facts concerning Jesus that are believed by the majority of scholars, even those who are the most critical. Here are some of the facts listed:

- The death of Jesus by crucifixion.
- The disciples' experiences which they believed to be of the risen Christ.
- The transformation of the disciples into bold witnesses.
- The empty tomb.
- The resurrection being the central message of Christianity from the beginning of the Christian church.
- The Jewish leaders published no refutation of the resurrection.
- The very existence and growth of the Christian church.
- Sunday became the primary day of worship rather than Saturday.
- Two skeptics, James and Paul, became believers after reporting experiences of the risen Christ.[1]

All these facts require explanations. And the alternative naturalistic explanations proposed have failed.

Another powerful book on this subject, authored by Habermas and Michael Licona, *The Case for the Resurrection of Jesus,* is called by some scholars and historians the most comprehensive defense of the resurrection available.[2] In this book the authors use just five of the above facts, which they call the minimal facts approach. The facts are as follows:

- Jesus' death by crucifixion.
- The disciples' belief that Jesus appeared.
- The conversion of the church persecutor Paul.
- The conversion of the skeptic James.
- The empty tomb.

Habermas and Licona explain that these facts are so strongly evidenced historically that they are accepted as true history by the vast majority of scholars, even the more skeptical. They point out that one of the strengths of this approach is

---

1   Gary R. Habermas, *The Historical Jesus,* College Press Publishing Company, Joplin, MO, 1996, 158–161.

2   Scholars Maier and Moreland quoted in Strobel, *The Case for the Real Jesus,* 106.

that it does not depend on the inspiration of the Bible or even eliminating so-called contradictions. They comment on this: "Too often the objection raised frequently against the Resurrection is, 'Well, the Bible has errors, so we can't believe Jesus rose.' We can quickly push this point to the side: 'I am not arguing at this time for the inspiration of the Bible or even its general trustworthiness. Believer and skeptic alike accept the facts I'm using because they are so strongly supported. These facts must be addressed.'"[3]

Here is an abbreviated outline of the evidences for the first two of the above facts as discussed in this excellent book:

> "I am not arguing at this time for the inspiration of the Bible or even its general trustworthiness. Believer and skeptic alike accept the facts I'm using because they are so strongly supported. These facts must be addressed."
>
> *Habermas and Licona, The Case for the Resurrection of Jesus*

- Jesus' death by crucifixion: evidenced by five non-Christian sources in addition to the Gospels: Josephus, Tacitus, Lucian, Mara Bar-Serapion, and the Talmud.

- The disciples' belief that Jesus appeared: evidenced by

    o their claims that Jesus appeared to them, documented by nine sources including:

        – The testimony of former church persecutor Paul.

        – Oral traditions which scholars identify from their incorporation into the book of Acts, including creeds and sermon summaries in the book of Acts.

        – Written sources including the four Gospels (treating them solely as additional historical documents without regard to divine inspiration), as well as the testimony of church fathers Polycarp and Clement, who personally knew some of the original twelve apostles. As the

---

3   Gary R. Habermas and Michael R. Licona, *The Case for the Resurrection of Jesus,* Kregel Publications, Grand Rapids, MI, 2004, 44–45.

authors point out: **"The nine sources in the three categories above point to multiple, very early, and eyewitness testimonies to the disciples' claims of witnessing the risen Jesus."**[4]

o   Their belief that these were the actual appearances of Christ was evidenced by their suffering and martyrdom, as testified in at least seven written sources, namely Luke, Clement of Rome, Polycarp, Ignatius, Dionysius of Corinth, Tertullian, and Origen. The authors comment on the value of these sources: **"In all, at least seven early sources testify that the original disciples willingly suffered in defense of their beliefs. If we include the sufferings and martyrdoms of Paul and James the brother of Jesus, we have eleven sources. Even the highly critical New Testament scholar Rudolf Bultmann agreed that historical criticism can establish 'the fact that the first disciples came to believe in the resurrection' and that they thought they had seen the risen Jesus. Atheistic New Testament scholar Gerd Ludemann concludes, 'It may be taken as historically certain that Peter and the disciples had experiences after Jesus' death in which Jesus appeared to them as the risen Christ.'"**[5]

See *The Case for the Resurrection of Jesus* for full elaboration and defenses of the above evidences as well as additional evidences for the conversion of Paul and James and for the empty tomb of Christ.

[?] What (who) is the Jesus Seminar? What do they say?

Some groups such as the Jesus Seminar, who some speak of as if they represented all scholars, say the resurrection didn't happen and no empty tomb existed. They are often quoted on TV or in the paper. People read articles by them in popular magazines, believe these scholars, and reject the resurrection. But are they the most authoritative scholars on the subject of the resurrection of Christ? Not at all.

According to Duke University professor of New Testament Richard Hays, the seventy scholars included in the Jesus Seminar are not representative of a balanced

---

4   Ibid., 55.

5   Ibid., 60.

sample of New Testament scholars. They are sponsored by the Westar Institute, a self-appointed group of scholars considered a maverick group by most New Testament scholars. The Jesus Seminar holds a set of radical and extreme views, and most biblical scholars are very skeptical of their methods and conclusions.[6] Theologian Dr. Gregory Boyd was interviewed by Lee Strobel regarding the Jesus Seminar: **"The Jesus Seminar represents an extremely small number of radical-fringe scholars who are on the far, far left wing of New Testament thinking. It does not represent mainstream scholarship."**[7]

? The "Jesus Seminar" says there was no empty tomb of Christ. But what are the facts?

JohnDominic Crossan of the Jesus Seminar states that the empty tomb did not exist and that all crucifixion victims were put into a pit or common grave, where dogs devoured them.[8] But where is the evidence for this hypothesis? In fact, there are plenty of reasons to believe the opposite. Habermas[9] outlines several of these:

Even if crucifixion victims were normally not buried, we cannot ignore the special circumstances and interest in Jesus' death and burial.

All four Gospels agree on the basic burial account, and no early writings refute these accounts.

The Jews had plenty of reason to keep track of Jesus' body and were said to have propagated a tale about the body being stolen from the tomb, so in effect they were admitting the tomb was empty.

The Roman soldiers would not have forgotten where they buried a body two days before. They would have been interested in keeping track of Jesus in case they were called upon to give evidence of His death, since Jesus had been a controversial figure to the Roman officials.

---

6 Richard B. Hays, "The Corrected Jesus," May 1994 article, http://www.firstthings.com/article/2007/01/the-corrected-jesus-4.

7 Strobel, *The Case for Christ,* 152, 170–171.

8 John Dominic Crossan, *Jesus: A Revolutionary Biography,* Harper/San Francisco, 1994, 152–158, as cited in Habermas, *The Historical Jesus,* 127.

9 Habermas, *The Historical Jesus,* 127–129.

There is evidence for a pre-Gospel of Mark account of the death, burial, and resurrection of Jesus, incorporated into Mark's Gospel. This account has been dated by some scholars as early as 37 A.D.[10]

Since the resurrection was the basis of the start of the Christian church and the message was proclaimed in Jerusalem, enemies had every reason to monitor Jesus' burial closely, in order to produce the dead body. This they could not do. They were not able to give a refutation of the resurrection. All they could do was mock. And Michael Licona points out that even if the authorities were not able to produce Jesus' body for fifty days (the length of time after Jesus' resurrection that the disciples waited before proclaiming His resurrection), a body exhumed even after that amount of time would still be identifiable by its distinctive wounds and stature. Yet there was no mention of any such event or loss of disciples from it in any historical records.[11]

There is an early creed in Paul's letter to the Corinthians, chapter 15: **"For I delivered unto you first of all that which I also received, how that Christ died for our sins according to the scriptures; and that he was buried, and that he rose again the third day according to the scriptures; and that he was seen of Cephas, then of the twelve; after that, he was seen of above five hundred brethren at once; of whom the greater part remain unto this present, but some are fallen asleep. After that, he was seen of James, then of all the apostles. And last of all he was seen of me also, as of one born out of due time" (1 Corinthians 15:3–8)**. Many scholars say this creed meets every criterion for historical reliability and is dated by some scholars as early as 35 A.D.[12] There are similar creed statements in the book of Acts and in Paul's letters.[13]

All of these were written far too close to the actual events for legends to have had time to develop, and the character of their writings, along with the early account in the Gospel of Mark, is simple and contains no embellishments characteristic of legends.[14]

---

10 William Lane Craig, as interviewed in Strobel, *The Case for Christ,* 297.

11 Habermas and Licona, *The Case for the Resurrection of Jesus,* 70–71.

12 Habermas, *The Historical Jesus,* 152–156, 173–175. Also see Strobel, *The Case for Christ,* 314, and Habermas and Licona, *The Case for the Resurrection of Jesus,* 53.

13 Habermas, *The Historical Jesus*, 143–152.

14 Strobel, *The Case for Christ*, 297.

Also, a crucifixion victim who had afterward been buried in a tomb was discovered. This discovery confirmed that some crucifixion victims were indeed buried in tombs.

Women were cited as the primary witnesses to the empty tomb. This would have been covered up or changed in a legend, as women's testimony in the Jewish society of that day was not even accepted as legal in a Jewish court.

Habermas sums up the evidence against the Jesus Seminar's position: **"The agreement of each of the Gospel texts, the lack of any early, contrary documentation, both the Jewish and Roman interest in Jesus's death, the Jewish polemic admitting the empty tomb, the pre-Markan narrative, the witness of the women and the Jerusalem preaching all argue strongly against Crossan's challenge to the traditional burial of Jesus. His allegation that absolutely no one either witnessed the burial by the soldiers or otherwise remembered it is simply unconvincing. *Nothing even approaching strong evidence favors his hypothesis***"[15] (emphasis mine).

? But weren't the accounts of the empty tomb written long after the events themselves?

Some say the accounts could be inventions because the accounts of the empty tomb were supposedly written long after the events themselves. But even some of the most critical New Testament scholars base their material on the conclusions of the Form Critics, the "higher critics" of New Testament scholarship.

- Even though some of the Form Critics try to charge the writers with invention (discussed above), many of them acknowledge an oral tradition that began soon after the date of Christ's resurrection and lasted for no more than thirty years before being written down. Many scholars, including some Form Critics such as Vincent Taylor, point out the fact that eyewitnesses during this time, including hostile ones, would have ensured the accuracy of this oral tradition which led to the writing of the Gospels.[16]

- Furthermore, even 60–70 A.D. isn't a long enough time to ensure all eyewitnesses were dead,[17] and this is the average date given for the writing of the three synoptic Gospels by scholars. Some scholars think there is no

---

15 Ibid., 129.

16 McDowell, *More Evidence That Demands a Verdict*, 209, 273–274.

17 Ibid., 275.

reason why the synoptic Gospels couldn't have been written earlier, maybe in the late 50s, and they give credible reasons for this.

Dr. Craig Blomberg stated in *The Case for Christ*: "Acts ends apparently unfinished—Paul is a central figure of the book, and he's under house arrest in Rome. With that the book abruptly halts. What happens to Paul? We don't find out from Acts, probably because the book was written before Paul was put to death. That means Acts cannot be dated any later than 62 A.D. Having established that, we can then move backward from there. Since Acts is the second part of a two-part work, we know the first part—the Gospel of Luke—must have been written earlier than that. And since Luke incorporates parts of the Gospel of Mark, that means Mark is even earlier. If you allow maybe a year for each of those, you end up with Mark written no later than about 60 A.D., maybe even the late 50s."[18]

The Christian message of the resurrection was indeed proclaimed early, right from the start of the church, and they appealed to the hearer's knowledge of these events. It seems very unlikely that their audience would not know their own history.

FURTHER EVIDENCES FOR THE RESURRECTION

Predictions of the resurrection: The crucifixion of the Messiah and His resurrection were predicted in several places in the Old Testament. For example, Psalm 22 predicts that His hands and feet would be pierced, as well as all the physical symptoms described that match up with what would happen to someone who was crucified. Psalm 16 as well as Isaiah 53 predict His resurrection.

Testimony of experts in history and law: Many experts in history and law have examined the evidence for the resurrection and found it to be as sound as any facts in history. Josh McDowell has assembled many quotes from these experts in his *Evidence That Demands a Verdict* volumes. For example, Simon Greenleaf was the Royal Professor of Law at Harvard University, who wrote a book titled *A Treatise on the Law of Evidence*, which is considered one of the greatest single reference books on legal evidences. After being challenged by his students to examine the resurrection evidence, Greenleaf wrote: **"As one after another was put to a miserable death, the survivors only prosecuted their work with increased vigor and resolution ... They had every possible motive to review carefully the grounds of their faith, and the evidences of the great facts and truths**

---

18 Strobel, *The Case for Christ*, 41–42.

which they asserted ... It was therefore impossible that they could have persisted in affirming the truths they have narrated had not Jesus actually risen from the dead ... If then their testimony was not true, there was no possible motive for its fabrication"[19] (emphasis mine).

New Testament scholar Donald Guthrie states: **"The Christians would not have been prepared to die in order to defend the products of their own imaginations."**[20]

The transformation of the disciples: J. Anderson wrote: **"Think of the number of witnesses, over 500. Think of the character of the witnesses, men and women who gave the world the highest ethical teaching it has ever known, and who even on the testimony of their enemies lived it out in their lives ... Think of the psychological absurdity of picturing a little band of defeated cowards cowering in an upper room one day, and a few days later transformed into a company that no persecution could silence—and then attempting to attribute this dramatic change to nothing more convincing than a miserable fabrication they were trying to foist upon the world. That simply wouldn't make sense."**[21]

Why were these disciples willing to risk death and continue to spread their message even as they were being put to death one by one? Especially when it brought them no gain as far as worldly power and prestige were concerned? What changed them from cowards into bold witnesses? Even the toughest skeptics must admit that "something" extraordinary happened!

The conversion of Paul:

- **Paul was a prominent Jewish leader, a Pharisee, with everything to lose. Why would he throw it all away, risking his very life?** The only explanation that makes sense is that he actually saw the risen Christ as he claimed.

---

19 Simon Greenleaf, *Testimony of the Evangelists, Examined by the Rules of Evidence Administered in Courts of Justice,* Grand Rapids, Baker Book House, 1965, 28–30, as quoted by McDowell, *Evidence That Demands a Verdict,* 192.

20 Donald Guthrie, *New Testament Introduction,* Intervarsity Press, Downers Grove, IL, revised edition, 1990, 233.

21 J. Anderson, "The Resurrection of Christ," *Christianity Today,* March 29, 1968, 5, 6, as quoted by McDowell, *Evidence That Demands a Verdict,* 224.

- Paul's vision was a public event also, with others seeing it although they did not understand what had happened. This is very different from Mohammed's vision, which had no witnesses and had different circumstances also because he gained much power and spoils by spreading his religion.[22]

- **Paul was a church persecutor who was converted,** a fact with multiple testimonies, as Habermas and Licona outline.[23] Not only did he describe his own conversion, but Luke also wrote of Paul's experiences in Acts, and Paul mentions in his letter to the Galatians a story being circulated around Judea within three years after his conversion, telling how the one who formerly persecuted the church was now preaching the faith he once tried to destroy.

- **Paul was so convinced that he was willing to suffer and die, and his suffering and martyrdom are testified to by at least seven independent sources,** including Paul himself, Luke, Clement of Rome, Polycarp, Tertullian, Dionysius of Corinth, and Origen. Habermas and Licona further point out that **Paul converted not because someone else told him, but because he himself was persuaded by an actual appearance of the risen Christ to him.**[24]

- There is no evidence that Paul did or would have been disposed to have had any kind of hallucination based on guilt, wishful thinking, or other mental causes. His conversion by his own testimony was because he saw the risen Christ. Also, even if true, this would not explain the appearances to others.

The conversion of the skeptic James:

- James was the brother of Jesus, who was one of His brothers who initially did not believe in Him. This is definitely reported in the Gospels in several places (Mark 3:21, 31; 6:3-4; John 7:5). **Habermas and Licona emphasize that use of the biblical references is simply evidence of multiple and early attestation, not dependent on biblical inspiration.**[25] According to Moreland,[26] there was no motive for fabricating the skeptical attitude of

---

22 Strobel, *The Case for Christ,* interview with scholar J. P. Moreland, 336.

23 Habermas and Licona, *The Case for the Resurrection of Jesus,* 64–65.

24 Ibid., 65.

25 Ibid., 68.

26 Strobel, *The Case for Christ,* 334–335.

James if it wasn't true, since it was very embarrassing in those days for a rabbi's family not to accept him as Jesus' brothers did not accept Him.

- The creed mentioned before in 1 Corinthians 15 (see above) testifies that the risen Christ appeared to James (1 Corinthians 15:7).

- James becomes a leader in the church at a later time, as testified to in the book of Acts and Paul's letter to the Galatians.

- **James's martyrdom, indicating his belief by his willingness to suffer and die, as was Paul, is testified to by multiple sources**, including Josephus, Hegesippus, and Clement of Alexandria.[27] Habermas and Licona comment: "Although the personal appearance of Jesus to his brother James is reported only once in the New Testament (1 Corinthians 15:7), it has the force of being part of the church's earliest tradition, as reported by Paul. Further, critical scholar Reginald Fuller explains that this is sufficient. **Even without it, 'we should have to invent' such an appearance in order to account for two things: James's conversion from skepticism and his elevation to the pastorate of the church in Jerusalem, the center of ancient Christianity."**[28]

Rebuttals for alternative explanations of the resurrection:

The stolen body theory:

- Their enemies had no reason to steal the body; their friends had no power to do so. Even Joseph of Arimathea, the tomb's owner, would need help to get the body out. If Joseph had been a disciple and stolen the body, he would have come forward when the others were being killed. If he was not a disciple, then surely other members of the Sanhedrin would have known about the deception. And it is not a good idea for the disciples to use the name of a public figure like Joseph anyway if they were planning a deception.

- The tomb was sealed and guarded by either the Romans or the Jewish temple guards.

- The disciples were cowards at that point—they were in hiding.

---

27 Habermas and Licona, *The Case for the Resurrection of Jesus*, 68.

28 Ibid., 68, quote from Reginald Fuller taken by authors from Reginald Fuller, *The Formation of the Resurrection Narratives*, Macmillan, New York, NY, 1971, 37.

- As we have already shown there is no evidence the disciples were deceivers, but that they really believed and were willing to die for that belief.

- This theory does not explain all the resurrection appearances. A story invented by the disciples would not have convinced the church enemy Paul or the skeptic James.[29] They were not convinced by an empty tomb, but by the appearances.

- If the body were moved from one tomb to another by family or friends, as in the "relocation hypothesis,"[30] this would have convinced no one, since it was the appearances that convinced the majority of the disciples. Also, either friends would have come forward and corrected the disciples from preaching His resurrection or enemies would have come forward to produce the body.

Not hallucinations:

- The disciples' experiences happened in public places at many different times and locations to many different people.

- The people who saw Jesus were from all kinds of backgrounds and temperaments. To say they all had the same "hallucinations" at the same time is ludicrous. It would be amazing even if two people had the same hallucination simultaneously.

- The disciples were mostly skeptical at first and were not expecting a resurrection (see Luke 24:11).

- History shows that hallucinations don't transform people as the disciples were transformed.

- Hallucinations don't explain the empty tomb.

- It is not likely that church persecutor Paul or skeptic James was in the frame of mind to have hallucinations or delusions of Jesus from wishful thinking or guilt.[31]

- And why did all the "hallucinations" stop after forty days?

Not legends:

---

29 Habermas and Licona, *The Case for the Resurrection of Jesus,* 93–97.

30 Strobel, *The Case for the Real Jesus,* 145–147.

31 Ibid., 105–108. Also see *Evidence That Demands a Verdict,* 247–255. These two books cover a rebuttal of the hallucination theory in great detail.

- Early eyewitness testimony based on appearances is basis for the origin of the belief in the resurrection, not later legends arising.[32]

- There is no parallel historical case for legends developing so quickly after the events themselves.[33]

- Legends and stories would not have convinced persecutor Paul or skeptic James. Instead they would have suspected some sort of fraud.[34]

- Legends don't explain the empty tomb.

- Resurrection narratives do not contain the embellishments characteristic of later second-century documents. For example, one later Gnostic fabrication has a giant Jesus and a talking cross emerging from His grave.[35]

- There is evidence in the text that the disciples intended to convey real history.[36]

The Jesus Papers: This was a popular book by Michael Baigent that claimed Jesus never died but was somehow resuscitated after being crucified. This idea is a worn-out theory that should have been buried long ago.

- The alleged papyrus documents are gone, and there is no translation or other authentication of them. Most likely they never existed. Dr. Craig Evans comments: **"No papyrus buried in the ground in Jerusalem will survive two thousand years, period … Any archaeologist will tell you that. So there's nothing to this."**[37]

- How would a severely injured, half-dead Jesus convince the disciples He was the risen Lord of glory? Most likely they would have wanted to take Him to a doctor.

- The Romans were expert executioners; they knew a dead man when they saw one.

---

32 Strobel, *The Case for Christ,* 298–299.

33 McDowell, *More Evidence That Demands a Verdict,* 210–213.

34 Habermas and Licona, *The Case for the Resurrection of Jesus,* 84–89.

35 Strobel, *The Case for the Real Jesus,* 44–45.

36 Habermas and Licona, *The Case for the Resurrection of Jesus,* 87–89.

37 Strobel, *The Case for the Real Jesus,* interview with Dr. Craig Evans, 53.

- Baigent's use of the Greek word *soma* to exclusively represent a living body is totally wrong.[38]

- Physicians and historians who have studied crucifixion have concluded that a person could almost never survive it, even in the unlikely event the Romans somehow took someone down from the cross alive.

- Almost all scholars reject the Jesus Papers theory.[39]

The Jesus tomb: There was a tomb, an ossuary or "bone box," found in Jerusalem in 1980 which reportedly had the names of a Joseph, Mary, Mariamne Mara (whom they took for Mary Magdalene), and a "Jesus son of Joseph."A film documentary was made in 2007 by James Cameron and Simcha Jacobovici suggesting it was the family tomb of Jesus. But practically no serious scholars give this idea any credibility because:

- **All the names inscribed in this tomb were very common.** According to Licona,[40] Mary was the most common woman's name in Jerusalem, and Joseph was the second most common man's name. One out of every eleven men was named Jesus. Licona spells out the implications of this: **"As Cameron's documentary said, finding the names of John, Paul, and George is no big deal, but when you add Ringo to the pool, you may have something. The problem, of course, is that when you really examine things, there's no equivalent of 'Ringo' in the Talpiot tomb."[41]**

- According to calculations by physicist Randy Ingermanson, one out of every seventy-nine males in Jerusalem was Jesus, son of Joseph. Hershel Shanks and Ben Witherington III estimate that during the ninety-year period in which ossuaries were used—from 20 B.C. to 70 A.D.—there were about eighty thousand males in Jerusalem. **That means there were approximately a thousand men named Jesus who had a father named Joseph."[42]** He goes on to say that even if all the other names found are taken into account approximately eleven men would still be in Jerusalem that fit this exact profile.

---

38   Ibid., 135, interview with Michael Licona.

39   Ibid.

40   Ibid., 148-149.

41   Ibid.

42   Ibid.

- Furthermore, this does not take into account the fact that there is absolutely no credible evidence Jesus was ever married and much evidence He was single.[43]

- Also, the tomb may have included extended family members as well as immediate family. So the Mary or "Mariamne Mara" who was in the tomb could have been an aunt, cousin, etc.

- DNA tests supposedly showed that "Jesus" and "Mariamne" were not related, and so it was automatically assumed they were married. But this is jumping to quite an unwarranted conclusion! She may have been married to one of several other men in the ossuary, or to none of them, since nothing there indicates who her husband was.[44] Also, the ossuaries often held more than one skeleton, making it difficult to match up the names with the bones.[45]

- Lee Strobel quotes historian Paul Maier: **"This is merely naked hype, baseless sensationalism, and nothing less than a media fraud."**[46]

Again, "natural" explanations for the events of the resurrection require greater faith to believe than the resurrection itself; thus, the resurrection is as sure a fact as any history can be. And this is the fact Jesus used to prove He is who He claims to be, and so it follows that what He says about the authority of Scripture is absolutely true.

> "To my mind, that just shows how careful the early church was ... they weren't 'gung ho,' sweeping in every last document that happened to have anything about Jesus in it. This shows deliberation and careful analysis."
>
> *Dr. Bruce Metzger, renowned Bible scholar*

---

43 Ibid., 149-150.

44 http://www.answersingenesis.org/articles/2007/04/04/so-called-jesus-tomb.

45 Strobel, *The Case for the Real Jesus*, 151.

46 Ibid.

HOW DID WE GET OUR BIBLE?

? How did certain books come to be included in the Bible while others were rejected?

Old Testament

Next, let's explore briefly the subject of how the Bible was put together, starting with the Old Testament. The Torah (the first five books of the Old Testament) was given by God to Moses according to their own testimony and was written down. We see this in the writings themselves: **"And Moses wrote all the words of the Lord" (Exodus 24:4)**. We see the same thing in Joshua 8:32, 1 Samuel 10:25, etc. Each book that was added to the Old Testament, such as Isaiah, Jeremiah, the Psalms, etc., was recognized, soon after it was written, to be of divine authorization and inspiration. The entire collection eventually became known as the Law and the Prophets and the Psalms (see Jesus' words in Luke 24:44).

? Why was there debate about including some books in the Old Testament?

About five of the books in the Old Testament were disputed for a while in regard to their canonicity. Some of the reasons for the disputes seem rather subjective, such as the Song of Solomon sounding like just a human love story and not religious sounding,[47] the book of Ecclesiastes sounding too pessimistic and negative, some proverbs seeming to contradict one another, Esther not containing the name of God (see more on this one later), and Ezekiel being thought of as contradicting the Law of Moses in the Pentateuch. Yet most of the Jewish scholars eventually discerned how these books were to be interpreted and accepted them as Scripture.[48] It was to their credit that they were cautious enough to raise questions.

? Was the Old Testament canon really settled as recently as the Council of Jamnia in 90 A.D.?

The council of Jamnia in 90 A.D. did not determine the canonicity of the Old Testament books but simply confirmed what had already been recognized as the Old

---

47 F. F. Bruce, *The Canon of Scripture*, Intervarsity Press, Downers Grove, IL, 1988, 35. Also see pp. 84 and 276 for more on the debate concerning the Song of Solomon. It was accepted as an allegory of Christ and the church but could equally illustrate the celebration of the love between a man and a woman.

48 Ibid., 27–42.

Testament canon. This council did not add or subtract any books, and there never was one select group that determined canonicity down through the centuries.[49]

New Testament

? **In the case of the New Testament, did the church determine arbitrarily which books were canonical? Did we need an infallible church to gather the New Testament canon?**

The New Testament, in contrast to the Old, was not written over many centuries but was written all in the latter part of the first century A.D. Letters were written to specific churches, as well as to general audiences. The four Gospels we now have were probably consolidated from oral and possibly written material. These writings were read in the churches and were circulated soon after they were written (see 1 Thessalonians 5:27; Colossians 4:16). This was done over a wide geographical area, and since communication was slow and persecutions rampant it took a while for certain books from one area to be known and recognized as authoritative in another area.

"Jesus is the Messiah, he's God's Son, he fulfills the Scriptures, he died on the cross and thereby saved humanity, he rose from the dead–those core issues were not open for discussion. If you didn't buy that, you weren't a Christian."

Dr. Craig Evans, noted Bible scholar

There is evidence within the New Testament itself that some of its books were accepted as Scripture very early on in the church's history. Peter refers to Paul's letters as Scripture (2 Peter 3:15–16), Jude quotes 2 Peter 3:2 (Jude 17), and Paul quotes Luke as Scripture (1 Timothy 5:18). As we have also seen, the early church fathers from the second century on quoted almost the entire New Testament as Scripture.

? **So how was a book accepted as Scripture in the early church?**

---

49 Ibid., 34–36.

Scholars who have studied this have outlined several criteria.

- First, the book had to have been written by an apostle (an eyewitness) or by someone in close association with an apostle.

- Second, the book had to conform doctrinally to what was already generally accepted as sound Christian doctrine, consistent with the known teachings of Jesus and His apostles.

- Third, the book had to have been continually used from the beginnings of the Christian church and accepted as authoritative by the church as a whole.[50]

Dr. Bruce Metzger, one of the greatest experts on the New Testament, comments: **"Basically the church had three criteria. First, the books must have apostolic authority—that is, they must have been written either by apostles themselves, who were eyewitnesses to what they wrote about, or by followers of apostles ... Second, there was the criterion of conformity to what was called the rule of faith. That is, was the document congruent with the basic Christian tradition that the church recognized as normative? And, third, there was the criterion of whether a document had had continuous acceptance and usage by the church at large."[51]**

"This is what history has taught us ... it was not because one group won that it became orthodox; it won because it was orthodox and all others were heterodox."

Archaeologist Randall Price, Searching for the Original Bible

Metzger went on to comment about the fact that even though lists of canonical books from different regions differed slightly, there was still an amazing degree of unanimity among them, especially considering the geographic separation and diversity in the early church.[52] And

---

50 Ibid., see 255–269 for a detailed discussion of the criteria of canonicity by New Testament scholar F. F. Bruce.

51 Strobel, *The Case for Christ,* interview with Dr. Bruce Metzger, 86.

52 Ibid., 86–87.

every New Testament book we now have was quoted by an early church father as authoritative Scripture.[53]

? Why were some books in the New Testament slow to be accepted?

As in the Old Testament, a few books generated some dispute. The book of Hebrews was questioned by some, especially during the time of the Protestant Reformation, because the author was unknown.[54] Revelation was questioned for the same reason, mostly because it differed in style from John's Gospel, and so the traditional authorship of John was disputed.[55] Some doubted the second letter of Peter was authored by Peter. Yet, after careful examination, all of these were eventually accepted as Scripture.[56] Several other books were ultimately rejected, such as the Shepherd of Hermas and the Gospel of Thomas. The fact that the church disputed some books for a while is commendable, showing their caution. In The Case for Christ, renowned New Testament scholar Dr. Bruce Metzger said this concerning the fact that a few books were slow to be accepted into the New Testament canon: **"To my mind, that just shows how careful the early church was ... they weren't 'gung ho,' sweeping in every last document that happened to have anything about Jesus in it. This shows deliberation and careful analysis."**[57]

So why did books such as Hebrews or Revelation get accepted and others such as the Gospel of Thomas get rejected? Arbitrary choice? Hardly. What we have to realize is that a book was not determined to be canonical solely by the church's choice, but rather recognized as canonical by its own intrinsic properties. Dr. Metzger comments again: "The canon is a list of authoritative books more than it is an authoritative list of books. These documents didn't derive their authority from being selected; each one was authoritative before anyone gathered them together. The early church merely listened and sensed that these were authoritative accounts. **For somebody now to say that the canon emerged only after**

---

53 Geisler and Nix, *A General Introduction to the Bible,* 420, 430.

54 Guthrie, *New Testament Introduction,* 671.

55 Ibid., 932.

56 Guthrie's *New Testament Introduction* is the most comprehensive reference the author has found on how each book came to be part of the New Testament. It is a very balanced reference showing the evidence for and against traditional authorship, date, and acceptance of each NT book.

57 Strobel, *The Case for Christ,* 91.

councils and synods made these pronouncements would be like saying, 'Let's get several academies of musicians to make a pronouncement that the music of Bach and Beethoven is wonderful.' I would say, 'Thank you for nothing! We knew that before the pronouncement was made.' We know it because of sensitivity to what is good music and what is not. The same with the canon"[58] (emphasis mine).

> **?** Were there alternative Christianities and rival gospels competing with one another at the beginning of the church, as some scholars say? Did the version of Christianity we have just happen to win out over the others by chance or by force, and were there lost gospels that contain the real truth of Christianity?

This view has been put forth by a number of scholars, including Bart Ehrman and Elaine Pagels, as well as popular books like The DaVinci Code by Dan Brown. They teach that there were many diverse beliefs about Christ in the early church and that the official version of Christianity we have today won out only after a power struggle and elimination of the rival views and gospels. But this view is not accurate, according to New Testament scholar Dr. Craig Evans: "It's not true at all ... the question is, what really did happen in the first century? **What's the evidence? ... the early Christian movement certainly did have disagreements. But these weren't 'Christianities.' There wasn't one Christianity that thought Jesus was the Messiah and another Christianity that didn't; another Christianity that thought He was divine and another Christianity that disagreed ... this is nonsense."**[59]

The evidence shows that most of the so-called "lost gospels" originated long after the canonical Gospels, in the second century, and were heavily influenced by a school of thought called Gnosticism, which was a kind of mystical version of pantheism and Christianity blended together, which depended on secret knowledge (gnosis). Although other heresies were starting to surface in the first century, the early Christians were not dealing with the kind of full-blown developed Gnosticism that some claim.

Evans comments again: **"The New Testament writings reflect the testimony of the first generation church, which very much depended on the testimony**

---

58 Ibid., 90.

59 Strobel, *The Case for the Real Jesus,* interview with Dr. Craig Evans, 34–35.

of Jesus' own handpicked disciples. To take second-century diversity and exaggerate it, and then to try to smuggle those controversies into the first century by hypothesizing that there was some earlier version of second-century documents, is just bogus. Real historians laugh at that kind of procedure."[60]

Strobel asked Evans about what the core message of Christianity was in the first century. Evans replied, **"Jesus is the Messiah, he's God's Son, he fulfills the scriptures, he died on the cross and thereby saved humanity, he rose from the dead—those core issues were not open for discussion. If you didn't buy that, you weren't a Christian."**[61]

In his book *Searching for the Original Bible,* Randall Price outlines how at first the church was not too concerned about a "canon" because they still had living authoritative apostolic witnesses. But in the second century the witnesses were dying off, and more diverse and contrary ideas were being introduced, hence the need for a more structured, established canon of books.[62] As we shall see below, the so-called "lost gospels" were not on the same level as the canonical Gospels at all. Price comments: **"There was not a comfortable diversity in the early church, where 'alternative Christianities' flourished side by side. Rather, there was a pure stream of truth and tradition—coming from Christ and His apostles and preserved through their successors—that experienced conflict with heretical views and groups that arose ... This is what history has taught us ... it was not because one group won that it became orthodox; it won because it was orthodox and all others were heterodox."**[63]

? How about the "Gospel of Thomas"? Why wasn't it included?

The canonical books that were disputed gave internal evidence of being inspired despite questions of authorship or general use, and when we read Hebrews or 2 Peter or Revelation we see they have the same consistency and quality as the other canonical books. In contrast, when we read the books that were rejected we often see many mythological elements and doctrinal contradictions. For example, the

---

60 Ibid., 35.

61 Ibid., 35.

62 Price, *Searching for the Original Bible,* 159–176.

63 Ibid., 193.

Gospel of Thomas is generally thought by most scholars to have been written in the second century, about 170–180 A.D.[64]

Although it may contain some accurate information about some of the sayings of Jesus, additions and Gnostic elements are present which conflict with the canonical Gospels. For example, in the Gospel of Thomas "Jesus" says: "Split wood; I am there. Lift up a stone, and you will find me there."[65] These are definitely Gnostic elements, namely pantheism, the idea that all material is God. And look what "Jesus" says about women at the end of the Gospel of Thomas: "Let Mary go away from us, because women are not worthy of life … Lo, I shall lead her in order to make her a male, so that she too may become a living spirit, resembling you males. For every woman who makes herself male will enter into the kingdom of heaven."[66] We see the blatant doctrinal contradictions.

Randall Price comments on the preceding verse: "This is because in Gnostic thought only the male mind is capable of 'knowing' and therefore of attaining salvation, which is based on knowledge. Apparently, women also are not 'living spirits'!"[67]

As we can see, the "Jesus" in the Gospel of Thomas is a totally different Jesus from the Jesus of the canonical Gospels. Grant and Freedman, in their modern translation and commentary on the Gospel of Thomas, deny its connection with the real Jesus: **"The Gospel of Thomas … is probably our most significant witness to the early perversion of Christianity by those who wanted to create Jesus in their own image … Ultimately it testifies not to what Jesus said but to what men wished he had said."**[68]

? How about the "Gospel of Judas"?

The "Gospel of Judas" is written in Coptic, and the earliest copy dates from about the third century. The news media and popular books have portrayed it as a new discovery, but this false gospel was known all the way back in the days of Irenaeus in the second century. Irenaeus mentioned it in his work Against Heresies

---

64 See detailed discussion about the dating of the Gospel of Thomas, including its affinities with the second-century document *The Diatessaron*, with Dr. Craig Evans in Strobel, *The Case for the Real Jesus,* 35–39.

65 *Gospel of Thomas,* 94.22–28, as seen in Robert Grant and David Noel Freedman, *The Secret Sayings of Jesus,* Barnes & Noble Books, New York, 1993, 177.

66 Ibid., 197.

67 Price, *Searching for the Original Bible,* 182.

68 Grant and Freedman, *The Secret Sayings of Jesus,* 20.

and called it invented history, written by a Gnostic group.[69] The Gnostics believed matter was evil, including the human body, and so part of their "salvation" was to be liberated from the body. So in the Gospel of Judas they make Judas into a hero who comes from another planet, and he is made a hero because he arranges for Jesus to be killed and thus "liberates" Him from that evil earthly body![70] Needless to say, this is a total reversal of the account of the canonical Gospels and is right along the lines of Gnostic thought. It is just another example of the remaking of "Jesus" by the Gnostics into their own imaginary character.

[?] How about the "Gospel of Mary" or the Apocryphon of John?

The same lack of reliable history is true of the other "gospels," which have been found in Egypt and other sites, such as the "Gospel of Mary," where "Jesus" was deduced by some to have been married to Mary Magdalene, or the Apocryphon of John, where the Gnostic Jesus was supposedly explaining the hidden meanings of some of the Old Testament accounts to his disciple John. Grant and Freedman comment on these and other Gnostic fragments discovered: *"We therefore have, in Till's edition, fifth century Coptic versions of three Gnostic gospels or semi-gospels which go back to the second and third centuries of our era. There is no reason to suppose that any of them contains the faintest reminiscence of authentic words of Jesus."*[71] Significantly, these authors seem to be trying to give an unbiased, even sometimes favorable treatment of these documents; yet they honestly admit their shortcomings.

I think we can see that the Gnostic "gospels" are in fact the legendary works the critics are looking for.

[?] Did we need an infallible church to write and collect the books of the Bible?

The church didn't need to be infallible, but it makes sense that the same Holy Spirit that inspired the Scriptures would also enable the early church to recognize by that Spirit which books were inspired, rather than leaving it to arbitrary human determination alone. *So fallible people were nevertheless inspired by an infallible Spirit to write Scripture.* God used their different styles and their own perspectives but ensured that the essentials of His message would remain. And we

---

69 Price, *Searching for the Original Bible,* 187–188.

70 Ibid., 185–186.

71 Grant and Freedman, *The Secret Sayings of Jesus,* 60.

have seen that God has preserved the message despite having imperfect copies (which would have required a continual miracle) and different translations from the original languages.

Some may say the Scriptures were determined at the council of Carthage in 397 A.D. But this council only confirmed and ratified the twenty-seven books that had already been recognized as authoritative for the preceding two centuries.[72] And, as Lutzer comments, it must be noted that any of the councils had no special power that was not also vested in any ordinary Spirit-filled Christians. The discerning power of the Spirit was indeed shared by all (see John 14:26; 16:13; 1 John 2:27).

SUMMARY-CLAIMS OF INSPIRATION AND TRUSTWORTHINESS

The claims to divine inspiration allow us to say that either these men were inspired of God or they were the worst deceivers in all of history. Is it possible the Bible that has inspired the highest standards of morality and honesty and that portrays the greatest figure in history, Jesus Christ, faultless even before His enemies, could have been written by wicked deceivers? That would seem to be a greater miracle than if the claims to divine inspiration were true. And there is no evidence they were deluded fanatics. On the contrary, they have given the world the sanest precepts for living found anywhere. That insane men could write such a sane book would again be a great miracle. So there is no getting away from the miraculous in any case.

Here is a quote from Charles Wesley, one of Methodism's founding fathers: **"The Bible must be the invention either of good men or angels, bad men or devils, or of God. Therefore: 1. It could not be the invention of good men or angels, for they neither would or could make a book and tell lies all the time they were writing it, saying, 'Thus saith the Lord,' when it was their own invention. 2. It could not be the invention of bad men or devils, for they would not make a book which commands all duty, forbids all sin, and condemns their souls to hell for all eternity. 3. Therefore, I draw this conclusion, that the Bible must be given by divine inspiration."[73]**

In the next chapter we will look at some very unusual but nonetheless powerful additional evidences that show the Bible to be more than just a human product.

---

72 Ibid., 175–176.

73 Robert W. Burtner and Robert E. Chiles, *A Compendium of Wesley's Theology*, Abingdon Press, New York, 1954, 20.

CHAPTER NINE

THE NUMBERS ADD UP

INTRODUCTION

One of the more amazing things about the Bible is the numerical design evident in the original language of the text. This should not be surprising since we find the same design in God's creation, which can also be described by mathematics. The Designer of the universe and the Author of Scripture could incorporate mathematical design into each. In this section of the book and the next we shall see powerful evidence of supernatural design in the text of the Bible.

[?] Are the numbers in the Bible thematic?

There are many significant numbers in the Bible that are used repeatedly, and each time they appear they seem to consistently denote a particular theme. For example, the number twelve seems to be associated with divine government, such as the twelve apostles, the twelve tribes of Israel, etc. One number in particular, the number seven, is by far the most frequently appearing and important number in the Bible. The number seven, when it appears, seems to speak of completeness and perfection, associated with God. When the number six appears, it seems to be associated with man, falling as it does one short of seven, as man falls short of perfection. Other numbers also appear to have consistent themes associated with them.

We will concentrate in this section on what is evidently the most important number in Scripture, the number seven. Patterns of sevens, or heptadic structures, appear in a great variety of ways in the Bible. As we get started, let's acknowledge up front that some of the numerical structure could be satisfactorily, though not necessarily, explained by the human author designing it into the text.

Even some of these possible human designs seem rather difficult, however. For example, in Psalm 119, the largest chapter in the Bible, we have twenty-two stanzas of eight verses each. Each of the eight verses in a given stanza begins with the same letter of the Hebrew alphabet. So the first stanza in Psalm 119 has each verse begin with *aleph*, the second stanza with *beth*, and so on through all twenty-two letters. This would be difficult, but not impossible, for a human author to do, and it shows a mathematical and alphabetical structure in the text.

THE DESIGN OF SEVENS IN THE PLAIN TEXT OF THE BIBLE

As far as sevens go, we first will look at some of the simpler ways the number seven shows up. Now, the number seven appears in the structure of the biblical text in so many ways that to do each of them justice would require many books. Here are some easy ones.

- For example, there are seven days of creation.

- There are seven cattle and seven ears of corn in Pharaoh's dreams in Exodus.

- Seven lamps in the Menorah, as in Exodus 25:37.

- Seven feasts of Israel, as in Leviticus 23.

- Seven years between sabbatical years, as in Leviticus 25:4.

- Naaman washed seven times in the river to have his leprosy healed, as in 2 Kings 5:10, 14.

These are very obvious sevens, and for someone who already is convinced of the divine inspiration of the Bible they would be viewed as having been inspired by God; but someone who is not yet so convinced could explain them as solely the style and creation of the human writer of the passages. But let's keep this in mind as we look at some further examples.

- In the Gospel of John there are seven "I am" statements of Jesus. These are distributed throughout the Gospel of John, not in a single chapter or list.

- There are also seven discourses of Jesus in John's Gospel, as well as seven miracles.[1]

- In the book of Revelation there are seven letters to seven churches.

- Here is one the author discovered in the book of Hebrews: Seven times Jesus is said to be offered **once** as a sacrifice for our sins in the book of Hebrews, spread out over chapters 7 (one time), chapter 9 (three times), and chapter 10 (three times), with slightly different wording each time, but the same message, namely that Jesus offered one sacrifice of Himself for sins, and this was sufficient for our redemption. This fits with the theme that His offering for us was complete (as the number seven seems to symbolize), with no repetition necessary.

These latest examples mentioned are much less obvious than the first group but could still be explained as the creations of a very careful and clever author, who was really going out of his way to put everything significant in groups of seven and yet not have it seem obvious at all without paying close attention. But the divine design of the Holy Spirit of God starts to show itself as a strong possibility here, even though not proven to the satisfaction of some. One example Missler mentions is how many times Jesus is referred to as "just," seven times, scattering over more than one author: Acts, Matthew, Luke, 1 Peter.[2] Did these authors collude just to have this come out to seven?

Seven letters, seven churches, seven kingdom parables correlate: Furthermore, the seven letters in Revelation are to seven churches, and interestingly enough Paul just happens to have written to exactly seven churches in his epistles. Some authors such as Chuck Missler have shown that the themes of the seven letters in Revelation can be correlated to the types of things Paul addressed to each of the seven churches he wrote to, as well as both of these thematically correlating with the seven kingdom parables in Matthew 13. To explain these to show the correlations I will refer you to Chuck Missler's tape commentary *The*

1   Missler, *Cosmic Codes,* 418.

2   Ibid., 419.

Letters to Seven Churches.[3] Some of these correlations are not obvious at first but are definitely there. Would John, Paul, and Matthew, writing at different times and places, have bothered to make sure these letters and parables matched up this way, both in number and theme? As you can see, we are starting to see things that are very hard to explain unless one mind is behind them, the mind of the Holy Spirit. And we are only just getting started!

COMPLEX NUMERICAL DESIGN—
THE WORK OF IVAN PANIN

The sevens we have seen so far are on the surface of the text. It turns out mathematical designs underlie the text as well. Some of the most extensive and fascinating discoveries about sevens in the Bible come from a Russian named Ivan Panin, who was exiled from Russia and studied in Germany before coming to the United States to Harvard University in the late 1800s.[4] In his early years he was a committed atheist but then became a Christian and soon began an amazing quest to which he devoted more than fifty years of research, uncovering numerical patterns in the Scriptures. He wrote more than forty-three thousand handwritten pages on this subject! Ironically, he came from an atheistic country and saw when he came to the USA that many religious leaders were abandoning faith in the divine inspiration of the Bible.

? **How did Panin handle variants between New Testament manuscripts in his numerical studies?**

Ivan Panin was a brilliant scholar and a master of literary criticism.[5] One of the things that led him to Christ was his discovery that numeric patterns were in the original Greek text of the Bible.[6] There were, of course, different existing manuscripts of the Greek text, with variants between them, although the variations were relatively few and minor, amounting to a very small percentage of the text, as discussed in the section on manuscripts above.

---

3   Chuck Missler, *The Letters to Seven Churches,* tape/CD set, Koinonia House, 1993.

4   Missler, *Cosmic Codes,* 93.

5   Keith Brooks, *The Works of Ivan Panin,* introduction, retrieved 15 Jul 2004, http://www.bereanpublishers.co.nz/Apologetics/Book_Info_On_Ivan_Panin.htm.

6   Ivan Panin, *A Holy Challenge for Today,* edited by J. S. Bentley, 1987, 8–9.

He examined the variants between these Greek texts using his numeric tests. Where he found intricate, interlaced patterns of sevens in many places in the text that seemed beyond chance or human contrivance (as we shall see), for him that settled which was the correct variant of the text.[7]

Many times in using his numeric tests he was compelled to choose the variants contained in the older Sinatic and Vaticanus manuscripts also used by Westcott and Hort, but he also made some corrections to the text they came up with.[8]

In just about every place where they wanted to take out whole sections and major passages such as Mark 16:9–20 or John 7:53–8:11, Panin, using his tests for patterns of sevens, ended up correcting their editing and leaving these disputed passages in, as they are in the Textus Receptus (the Received Text) on which the King James Version is based.

One example of a passage Westcott and Hort wanted to leave out was Mark 16:9–20 (the last twelve verses of Mark, on which we will go into greater detail below), but Panin includes it, having found many patterns of sevens therein. So he concluded, using his numeric pattern testing methods, that the Sinai and Vaticanus Codexes were correct in most places but that the Received Text (Textus Receptus) also correctly contained verses that many modern scholars, following Westcott and Hort, tried to say did not belong there. In one of his books Panin comments on these deletions by Westcott and Hort: **"The guillotining of the Last Twelve Verses of Mark, and of the Incident of the Woman Taken in the Act of John VII. 53, VIII.11 ... is passing grievous."**[9]

The key thing was that Panin looked at all the variations between texts and applied his meticulous numeric tests to them. It is important to note that Panin almost always used existing variant readings catalogued by other textual scholars and did not just add his own words to make the numeric phenomenon work.[10] He explained any "corrections" he made to the text in places where textual scholars are uncertain, such as splitting one particular Greek word into two words as a legitimate variant form.[11] As we shall see, Panin most likely had discovered a powerful way, if

---

7   Ibid., 8.

8   Ibid., 19–25.

9   Ibid., 26–27.

10   Ibid., 51–56, 65–66.

11   Ivan Panin, *The Last Twelve Verses of Mark,* The Association of the Covenant People, n.d., 20.

not the only way, to determine the true original text of a given passage in the Bible, in the small percentage of places where manuscripts disagreed.

? What were Panin's methods?

Panin worked for long hours each day, counting letters and words. He even compiled several of his own concordances in which he put in all the various forms of the Greek words.[12] This whole process of making these concordances alone took several years. He also noted the numerical value of each word and letter. He gives an example in his book on the last twelve verses of Mark's Gospel, where he starts with the Greek text as rendered by Westcott and Hort and then shows how he applies his tests to it.[13] Panin apparently used meticulous methods for textual criticism on a par with the best scholars.[14]

Again it could very well be that Ivan Panin found the way to determine with his numeric tests the correct original form of the Greek text and could therefore settle the disputes between critical scholars, some who champion using the older Vaticanus and Sinaiticus texts and some who favor the Received Text. Actually Panin's findings seem to prove both sides correct on different points. Unfortunately his work has fallen into obscurity with modern scholars' academics. It's as if they pretend it doesn't exist. But let's examine what he found to see what it proves.

Example of numerical design-Matthew's genealogy

One of the many patterns of sevens Panin found was in the genealogy in the first chapter of Matthew's Gospel. To get an idea of what was found, here is a challenge presented by author Chuck Missler in his book *Cosmic Codes*.[15] Design a genealogy, even a fictitious one, with the following properties:

- The number of words must be divisible by seven exactly, with no remainder.

- Next, the number of letters must also be divisible by seven exactly. This might seem fairly easy so far. But more restrictions are coming here.

- The number of vowels must be divisible by seven exactly. So must the number of consonants.

---

12 Ibid., 37–50 for an example of one of his concordances.

13 Ibid., 5–36.

14 Bible Numerics Examined, Part 2, Dr. Ivan Panin, Russia's Gift to Christianity, The Cutting Edge, 7 May 2003, http://www.cuttingedge.org/news/n1363.cfm.

15 Missler, *Cosmic Codes*, 92–94.

- The number of words beginning with a vowel must be divisible by seven exactly. So must the number of words beginning with a consonant. Does this seem harder now? We aren't finished.

- The number of words that occur more than once must be divisible by seven exactly.

- So must the number of words that occur in more than one form. And the number of words that occur in only one form.

- The number of nouns, the number of words that aren't nouns, the number of names, with only seven other kinds of nouns allowed, the number of male names and the number of generations. All divisible by seven exactly. Do you think you could do this? Need a computer?

The genealogy in Matthew 1, the section from verses 1–11, meets all of the above criteria in the Greek. Could this be simply by chance? Or could any of us, even with a computer, easily design such a genealogy? Remember that the Bible writers didn't have PCs back then.

One section of this genealogy runs from verses 1–11 as described above, the other from verses 12–17, the whole genealogy being from 1–17.[16] The section divisions seem to be the important thing, not the verses themselves, which were partitioned up in the sixteenth century.

Greek, like Hebrew, has numerical values that are assigned to each letter, and so each word has a numerical value, given by adding up all the values of each letter. In verses 1–17, the 72 vocabulary words add up to a numerical value of 42,364, which is exactly 7 x 6,052. These words exist in 90 forms (unique spellings), which have a total numerical value of 54,075, which is 7 x 7,725 exactly.[17] There are similar properties of sevens found in Matthew 1:18–25, the section on the birth of Christ.[18]

To contrive such a passage as the genealogy above, even with unlimited letters and arbitrary combinations of numbers possible, is extremely difficult. Each new word or phrase has to fit the interlocking wheels-within-wheels type pattern. Remember that the men who penned the Bible were ordinary men without computers! They were also separated from each other by centuries in some cases. And why would they bother to do this, rather than just write a plain text?

---

16 Ibid., 94.

17 Ibid., 95.

18 Jeffrey, *The Signature of God,* 236–237.

ANSWERING THE SKEPTICS

Some skeptics have posted attempted rebuttals on the internet. They put forth examples they claim prove that what Panin found was not significant and could happen in any large text. The author has gone to several of their web sites.[19] For example, using numerical values assigned to English letters in a similar pattern to the Greek, A=1, B=2, J=10, K=20, etc., they construct small sentences. Or they pick a sentence out of a book and look for features that give numbers divisible by seven. Sometimes they may have adjusted the sentence until they have exactly seven words and twenty-eight letters (if they did, they don't admit it), which is not horribly difficult. They may also have added, or even found without adding, several other heptadic features. They mention features such as:

- The sum of each word's last letter's numerical values divisible by seven.

- The sum of all the first letter's values also divisible by seven.

- All the nouns with seven letters.

- Several other words with seven letters.

- The numerical value of every seventh letter added together also divisible by seven.

- The number of consonants or vowels divisible by seven.

- Place values (the number position where the letter appears in the alphabet) of letters divisible by seven, and other similar things.

All of these are not featured in one sentence or paragraph but instead are in several small, usually unconnected sentences. The importance of this will be seen shortly.

? What do the critics' examples show?

What they show is that anyone clever enough might be able to, especially if they have computers to help, design several features of seven into a simple sentence, arbitrarily choosing the parameters. It also shows that if you just by trial and error select various features, after trying at least seven features, odds are you will get one that is divisible by seven, even without adjusting the sentence. With numerical

---

19 Brendan McKay, "Miracles in Edgar Allen Poe," 26 Jul 2011, http://cs.anu.edu.au/bdm/dilugim/poe.html. Notes from visitor 6006, 26 Jul 2011, http://cs.anu.edu.au/bdm/dilugim/vis6006.html. Also Mark Perakh, www.talkreason.org/articles/ignoramus.cfm., 2000.

values the chance is one in seven for each feature that they will be divisible by seven. With an unaltered sentence, the more features of seven in that sentence, the more difficult it becomes for chance to produce such patterns. This is especially true if the features divisible by seven show consistent patterns over several sentences or paragraphs, rather than a single short sentence.

My unremarkable sentence

After reading their material, I tried an experiment myself, using one critic's numerical values for English letters. I decided I would use a sentence of similar length to what the critics used in their examples. I constructed a sentence: "I DON'T BELIEVE THE SKEPTIC IS FAIR." I had to adjust it slightly from my original wording to make sure I had exactly seven words and twenty-eight letters. I found that the numerical value of the sentence, using the critic's numerical values assigned to the letters, was equal to 1554, or 7 x 222! (The sentence's numerical value had by itself a one in seven chance of being divisible by seven.) And I also noticed, without any adjusting, that the verb and the noun in the sentence both have seven letters! So I have five features of seven, three without any design efforts on my part. Have I proven these five features could appear by chance despite apparent odds of 1/7 to the 5th power, or 1/16,807?

- The first two features of my sentence, the number of words and letters, were designed, just as the critics probably did above. But the chances of both number of words and letters coming out as multiples of seven are not all that improbable by themselves. I think that if you take the average length of a given short English sentence a length of seven words must be a very common number anyway, definitely more common than two words, or thirty-two words.

- The number of letters by chance would have odds of one in seven of being a multiple of seven. But remember: I tweaked the sentence to get that number. By itself the total numerical value of all the letters has a one-in-seven chance of being a multiple of seven, so those are not bad odds for my hitting it by chance.

- The key words are "by itself." I'm sure I could adjust, as the critics likely did, other words and letters to get other numerical values to come out divisible by seven. But without adjusting, the chance of many of them all coming out to sevens would still remain quite low, which the critics must admit. (I noticed in some of their examples the features of sevens are fairly unrelated, looking as if they used the above method of trial and error until they had several features divisible by seven and discarding the rest.)

- And how about the noun and the verb having seven letters too? I think that in the English language, again, seven-letter words are extremely common, maybe a significant fraction of the total, whereas words with two letters or sixteen letters are much less common. My point is in a given sentence there are bound to be several words with seven letters. (In fact, there are two in the sentence previous to this one!) So my remarkable sentence isn't all that remarkable after all, and neither are the critics' contrived sentences.

I tried several more sentences and some short paragraphs. My testing showed that for the numerical values and place values of letters and words the number of successful trials (features divisible by seven) came out about what I would expect mathematically, namely about one in seven hits. This really makes me wonder about some of the critics' examples such as "visitor number 6006"[20] where the writer appears to have found many patterns of seven just in the place values of the first and last letters of his sentences, simply by chance. Even apart from a question of godly inspiration for the text, since the claim is that this all happens by chance, I would have to question that claim because he lists about eight patterns of seemingly very related patterns of seven for these values which have a probability of one in seven each. He either got extremely lucky to the tune of 1/5,764,801 (seven to the eighth power), or perhaps he did some doctoring of the sentence, probably with a computer. But I don't think even these critics trust luck that much to claim that chance produces all these patterns.

I realize some of these critics were trying to answer the claim some have made that men could not deliberately duplicate some of these features of seven. But the author is not attempting to say men couldn't do some of this, especially with the data processing tools we have today. What I am trying to show is that the patterns Panin found could not be due to chance alone. I don't think the Bible writers were sitting around with computers trying to put sevens in the texts they wrote.

? How are my example and the critics' examples different from Panin's work?

- **Limited variations available:** First of all, Panin, as we already mentioned, had very limited variations he could use of the Bible texts. **With the Matthew**

---

20 See note 19.

genealogy he had extremely few variants. As we saw, it would be very difficult to deliberately design a genealogy similar to the one in Matthew's Gospel, even with unlimited variations and a fictitious genealogy. **How could it happen just by chance?**

- **Consistent patterns over large areas of text rather than isolated sentences:** As you look at the examples the critics and I have used, you see small sentences with mostly unrelated features that are divisible by seven, which is what you would expect when you test a large number of parameters and pick the ones that by chance come out to a multiple of seven. But what we have in Panin's examples such as Matthew's genealogy are many **related parameters of seven** completely covering at least **several paragraphs**, not just occurring in isolated short sentences. Remember that heptadic features such as numerical value of words or number of letters must have their individual probabilities of one in seven multiplied together, and as you add up the number of these parameters in a given text the odds get smaller for chance occurrence.

- **Type of features of seven:** I also noticed that the critics' examples don't deal with number of vocabulary words and word forms, in which Panin found extensive and consistent patterns across many paragraphs. **Adding or subtracting the number of words, word forms, and vocabulary words, as well as their numerical values, so that they all simultaneously divide evenly by seven is much more difficult to coordinate by deliberate design than just adding or subtracting individual letters.** This is very different from making many short sentences, each with different arbitrary parameters, even if those parameters happen to match some of the types Panin found.

- **Extent of features:** Furthermore, notice that **many of these same parameters,** such as numbers of vowels and consonants, vocabulary words, words with one form and more than one form, and their numerical values **occur over many sentences, paragraphs, even whole books** as we shall examine below. And as we shall see, Panin often found **other number schemes** such as elevens or thirteens **simultaneously imbedded in the same text**. This would be difficult to obtain by chance or human design. If you doubt this, try using the same procedure the critics and I used to construct a small sentence to build a large paragraph and obtain the same extensive parameters of sevens and other numbers Panin found.

- **Breakdown of patterns:** Furthermore, **these patterns break down according to logical divisions in the Bible.** For example, as we shall see below, there are interlocking patterns of different numbers all across the names of the Bible writers, the numbers of books in the Bible, and the entire book of Genesis. And the patterns are broken down according to logical divisions of the Bible such as the Law, the Prophets, and the "Writings." This will be easier to see by looking at the examples below.

Remember that this would all be without deliberate adjusting, according to the random chance thesis of the critics. In Matthew's first chapter the genealogy is a large section, followed by another section on the birth of Christ, and these sections both contain the same types of features, rather than small sentences with more diverse types of heptadic features, as the critics put forth.[21] I didn't see any large paragraphs in any of their examples, much less whole chapters and books, as Panin found.

As we shall see below, the sheer number and complexity of the features Panin found, when taken together, cannot be by chance and are even shown to be impossible to explain in most instances by deliberate design (if anyone is still seriously thinking the Bible writers would be trying to do this!).

OTHER NUMERICAL PATTERNS

Panin found patterns of other numbers along with sevens also. He found these in the Old and New Testaments, with some features extending across the entire Bible. Here are some abbreviated examples taken from his books.

Design of thirteens in the number of books and their classification in the Old Testament:

Here is a sample of what Panin found in the number and classification of Old Testament books. Two things to note: one is that Panin used the order and grouping of books in the Old Testament as they appeared in the Hebrew original language, namely the Law, the Prophets, and the Writings, ending with 2 Chronicles rather than with Malachi as in our modern versions. (In Panin's example above,

---

21 Panin, *A Holy Challenge for Today,* 57–64.

anonymous books meant books that do not indicate within their author by name, such as Genesis, Joshua, Judges, etc.—thirteen in all.)[22] The other is that these books were written by many authors, most of whom did not even know each other, and they were written over a period of thousands of years.

- There are 39 books, or 3 x 13 total.

- The anonymous books are 13; the non-anonymous are 26, or 2 x 13.

- The Law and the Prophets are 26 books; the Writings are 13.

- The Law is books 1–5, the Prophets are books 6–26, and the Writings books 27–39. If you add up the numbers 1, 5, 6, 26, 27 and 39 you get 104, or 8 x 13.

- The sum of the order number of the books 1–39 is 780, or 60 x 13.

These order numbers are divided so that the two books named after women, Ruth and Esther, which have order numbers 31 and 34, have as the sum of their order numbers 65, or 5 x 13, and the remaining book's order numbers sum to 715, or 55 x 13.

The sum of the figures of the remaining book's order numbers of 715 is 13.

Panin gives very high mathematical odds for just these few features of thirteen being by chance. And he found many more of these running just through the number of books in the Old Testament.[23] Panin therefore found patterns of thirteens in just the number of books of the Hebrew Bible, tying it together as one book.

Panin found similar patterns in the New Testament books, both in their numbers and other features as well. He mentioned that these patterns found would act as an automatic check against anyone tampering with the number of books in the Bible and also the designed order of those books. Removal or addition to these experimentally indeed bears out his conclusion.[24]

Designs of sevens in the names of the writers of the Old Testament

Panin also found a design of sevens in the names of the writers of the Hebrew Bible.

22 Ibid., 2–3.

23 Ivan Panin, *Inspiration of the Hebrew Scriptures Scientifically Demonstrated,* 1928, reprinted in 1980 and 1990, 10–12.

24 Panin, *Verbal Inspiration of the Bible Scientifically Demonstrated,* 55.

- The 26 non-anonymous Old Testament books mentioned above were written by 21 different writers (7 x 3). Panin figured the numerical value of each name. Using these numeric values, Panin found patterns of sevens in the 21 names.

"No one man, nor any set of men with about a thousand years between them, could have devised such schemes."

Ivan Panin

- Twenty-one writers are 3 x 7; 14 of them have odd numeric values, seven even values.

- Their total numeric value is 3,808 (544 x 7), which if you factor it out is 7 x 17 x 2 x 2 x 2 x 2 x 2 (seven factors).

- The numeric value of the Law and the Prophets writers' names is 2,933 (7 x 419) which has 21 for a sum of the factor figures (7 + 4 + 1 + 9). The numeric value for the Writings writers' names is 875 (125 x 7). Of the Writings the numerical value of the name of David is 14, and the remainder Solomon to Nehemiah 861 (123 x 7).[25] Panin goes on to describe a total of 12 features of seven running across the names of the writers of the Hebrew Bible. Notice the breakup of these features according to logical divisions of the Bible.[26]

Designs of sevens in the first verse of Genesis

Panin found many features of seven in the first verse of Genesis. Some critics have claimed that they can reproduce similar features easily in random sentences. Grant Jeffrey has pointed out some of the patterns of seven in this first verse of Genesis. They attacked his claim that a group of Harvard scientists tried and could not produce these patterns[27] (eleven patterns of seven in this verse were mentioned in his book such as the verse having 7 words, 28 letters, first three words with 7 letters, three key words with 7 letters, numeric value of first and last letters of all seven words divisible by seven, etc.), since the critics themselves have constructed

---

25 Panin, *Inspiration of the Hebrew Scriptures*, 12–13.

26 Ibid., 13.

27 Jeffrey, *The Signature of God*, 232–234.

sentences with similar simple features.[28]   But the critics' attacks fail for other important reasons.

First of all, Panin found more than just those eleven simpler features in the verse. **He kept finding more and more features of sevens, the last count he mentioned being fifty features of seven and counting. And some of these were much more complex than the critics mentioned.**

- For example, Panin found many patterns of sevens in the numerical values of both the vocabulary words and in the total numerical value of all the words. (Vocabulary words are the number of unique words. Different forms of the same word count as one vocabulary word.)

- He also found patterns of sevens involving words with one form and more than one form. These sound very similar to what was found in the Matthew genealogy above.

Panin comments: **"Three distinct schemes of sevens, with thirty features thereof, are thus presented as forming only the smaller part of an elaborate design of sevens running through this verse; the three separate schemes thus presenting rings within rings and wheels within wheels; ... But in addition to this threefold scheme of sevens there are other designs running through this verse."**[29]

What the critics don't mention in their attacks is very important. They don't read on in Panin's book to see the many interlocking number schemes found in just the first verse of Genesis.[30] Just the sheer number and consistency in types of patterns here is much different from the critics' examples, which they claim show up by chance! I noticed they did not claim they could even deliberately produce similar patterns. Instead of their insulting claims that Panin wasted fifty-plus years of his life finding and writing about mathematical patterns they claim could be produced by chance, they should study the text objectively and explain how **all** the features could appear by chance. But in this the critics fail completely.

---

28 See note 19 above.

29 Ibid., 17–21.

30 Ibid., 15–21.

Designs of first and last words across Genesis and the whole Old Testament and individual names

Panin found schemes of thirteens, elevens, and thirty-sevens in this verse, Genesis 1:1, all interlocking in such a way as to be beyond contrivance. Furthermore, **he found a large number of these same types of patterns in the whole first chapter of Genesis, in fact through the entire book of Genesis!** This is very important because he not only found these patterns, but they were very consistent in structure across the entire book of Genesis.[31] And it doesn't end there. **Panin found these patterns, with the same types of numerical features, running throughout the entire Hebrew Bible, showing it was in fact one book.**[32]

We will give just one example Panin found of patterns which tie the whole Old Testament together.

He saw that the first and last words of Genesis had numeric patterns in them. He noticed also that these patterns ran through the first and last words of such divisions of the Old Testament as the Law by itself, the Law and Prophets together, and even the Old Testament as a whole:

- The numeric value of the first word of Genesis is 913, and that of the last word of 2 Chronicles is 116. When you add those together, they equal 1,029, or 3 x 7 x 7 x 7.

- The numeric value of the first and last words in Genesis is 1,295, or 7 x 37 x 5.

- The numeric value of the first and last words of the Law and the Prophets is 532, or 7 x 16.

- Panin goes on to tabulate six different features of the first and last words in the Old Testament as a whole and also its various divisions, involving both place values and numeric values in intricate patterns.[33]

Another scheme of design found through the whole Hebrew Bible involved single names, such as Jeremiah, Moses, Isaiah, David, and Abraham. By now we see how complex and mind-boggling are the patterns found. And what is important to notice here also is that these were different authors in different centuries. How could they have collaborated to come up with these patterns for specific persons' names? In his closing chapter on the Hebrew Old Testament Panin concludes: **"No**

---

31 Ibid., 24–31.

32 Ibid., 35.

33 Ibid., 35–36.

one man, nor any set of men with about a thousand years between them, could have devised such schemes, least of all carried it out so successfully to the minutest detail of the hundreds that present themselves."[34]

? Did Panin contrive it all?

It would be almost impossible for Panin to be able to contrive the properties or adjust the text to make it fit the patterns of sevens. Referring to the New Testament, as we noted above, Panin had an established text to work with, with only a limited amount of variants for some words. Even without a restricted text, it would have been an almost impossible task. In many cases Panin found the patterns of sevens in text where no variant readings existed, and so no leeway was possible in the reading of the text. The methods he used for textual editing using variants were as good as or better than those used by textual critics. And remember that Panin devoted his whole life to this task, without wealth or fame for it.

Panin and others also examined texts outside the Bible in Greek and Hebrew and found no similar patterns of sevens. Dr. Daniel Turney is quoted in one of Panin's books: **"A sincere effort to find numerics in Homer proved unsuccessful, but as soon as I tried 3 John my labours were abundantly rewarded. I took up this because it was short, and in Panin's writings I had not seen it discussed. My investigation thus began with as little to guide me as in the case of the Iliad, but the result was so perfect a scheme of numerics as to leave no room for doubt."[35]**

Panin also presented his work to the qualified skeptics of his day. Somehow I think he would have checked his math! And again it is an insult to this brilliant man's intelligence to think he would have just chosen arbitrary parameters of seven until he found those that worked, to contrive it all, when he received no reward for his work and spent many long tedious hours over it.

I found one website that is very informative about Ivan Panin: www.cuttingedge. org/news/n1363.cfm., titled *Bible Numerics Examined—Part 2*. They give some additional historical background on Panin and his methods and the implications of his findings.[36]

---

34 Ibid., 60–61.

35 Panin, *Verbal Inspiration of the Bible Scientifically Demonstrated*, 25.

36 *Bible Numerics Examined, Part 2, Dr. Ivan Panin, Russia's Gift to Christianity,* The Cutting Edge, May 7, 2003, http//www.cuttingedge.org/news/n1363.cfm.

？ The last twelve verses of Mark: evidence for their authenticity?

Panin found thousands of patterns of sevens throughout the entire Bible, thousands of them. As an example, let's look at the last twelve verses of Mark—a passage that many textual critics, including Westcott and Hort, tried to say does not belong in the Bible. There has been much controversy about these verses in Mark. Many scholars exclude them because they are not found in some of the earliest manuscripts [Codex B (Vaticanus) and Codex Aleph (Sinaiticus)] from the fourth century. There is evidence, however, that they indeed are part of the Gospel. A very competent defense of these verses was written by the great scholar Dean John W. Burgon.[37] One reason he gives for their authenticity is that several early church fathers, who wrote before the date of those early manuscripts, quote from them.[38] Another is that there is a suspicious-looking blank space in the early manuscript Codex B where these verses would have been written.[39] But there is an even more compelling reason. Ivan Panin not only determined that these verses belonged in the text, but he came to this conclusion because they contained an incredible amount of patterns of seven just as he had found in other biblical texts.

？ Did Panin find a method for discerning the original text of the New Testament?

Before we look at some of these numerical features, let's consider that one pretty sure way of settling what the original text of a passage was would be that it exhibited these intricate properties of sevens. If we found such patterns in a version of the text, the most reasonable conclusion would be that we have the original wording and spelling as inspired, or very close to it.[40] What would be some alternative conclusions if we found such properties? Did we just happen to stumble on a version that is not the original, yet by pure chance, through errors in transmission, has all these remarkable properties? This would seem preposterous. We have great difficulty constructing such complex features of a passage on purpose, even

---

37   John W. Burgon and editor David Otis Fuller, D.D. *Counterfeit or Genuine: Mark 16? John 8?* Grand Rapids International Publications, Grand Rapids, MI, 1978.

38   Ibid., 48–49.

39   Ibid., 67.

40   Ivan Panin, *The Last Twelve Verses of Mark,* The Association of the Covenant People, n.d., 17–23.

without the restrictions imposed on us by the biblical text. So it seems that finding these properties could be a stamp of God's inspiration.

Patterns of seven in Mark 16:9-20

Ivan Panin devoted a whole book just to the last twelve verses of Mark.[41] I have included a detailed description of his findings on this passage which will serve as an example to illustrate the extent and consistency of numerical patterns Panin had also found in many other parts of the whole Bible.

Let's look at the last twelve verses of Mark, Mark 16:9–20. This passage has natural divisions—the appearance of Christ to Mary Magdalene (verses 9–11), Christ's appearances (verses 12–14), the speech of Christ (verses 15–18) and the conclusion (verses 19–20).

- There are 175 (7 x 25) words in this section.

- The total vocabulary words are 98 (7 x 14).

- The number of letters in the vocabulary words is 553 (7 x 79).

- The number of vowels in the vocabulary words is 294 (7 x 42); the number of consonants is 259 (7 x 37).

- Of the 98 vocabulary words, 84 (7 x 12) are found before in Mark; 14 are only found in this passage.

- In the Lord's speech, verses 15–18, 42 (6 x 7) vocabulary words are found, whereas the remaining words not found in this division are 56 (7 x 8).

- And there is more. The total number of word forms in the whole passage is 133 (7 x 19).

- Forms occurring only once are 112 (7 x 16); there are 21 forms that occur 63 times.

- The 21 forms that occur more than once have 231 letters (7 x 33).

- Out of the 175 total words, 56 (7 x 8) of these are in the Lord's speech; 119 (7 x 17) are in the rest of the passage.

- As noted above, the natural divisions of the whole passage are: the appearance to Mary Magdalene (v. 9–11), Christ's appearances (v. 12–14), the speech of Christ (v. 15–18) and the conclusion (v. 19–20). These sections

---

41   Ibid.

have: 35 (7 x 5) words in verses 9–11, 105 (7 x 15) in verses 12-18, and 35 words in verses 19–20, for a total of 175. In verse 12 there are 14 words, 35 words in verses 13–15, and 56 (7 x 8) in verses 16-18. So even the subdivisions of the divisions are broken up into multiples of seven.[42]

- Let's look at the numerical value of words. The total numerical value of the letters in the whole passage is 103,663 (7 x 14,809).

- Verses 9, 10 and 11 form natural subdivisions; the numeric value of this division, 17,213 (7 x 2,459), is thus: The value of verse 9 plus 11, the two outside subdivisions, is 11,795 (7 x 1,685), the middle subdivision verse 10 is 5,418 (7 x 774). Also, verses 12–20 have a value of 86,450 (7 x 12,350).

- In verse 10, the numerical value of the first word is 98 (7 x 14), the middle words are 4,529 (7 x 647), and the last word is 791 (7 x 113).

- The numerical value of the total word forms is 89,663 (7 x 12,809).

And so on. There are similar elaborate schemes of seven in the numerical values of the vocabulary words and also in the word forms. We have looked at multiple features of seven in this passage. Ivan Panin found seventy-five in all![43] **Panin is also emphatic to state that the same types of patterns seen in the complex example above are in fact found throughout the entire Gospel of Mark.[44] So the fact that some scholars dispute this passage does not affect the phenomenon as a whole, but a powerful argument is made here for its inclusion.**

Would an ambitious scribe writing this passage be able to do all this? The detail I have shown here is also shown by Panin in his other examples throughout the Bible. **In other words, what he found here is the same type of patterns he found not only in Mark's Gospel, but throughout the entire Bible.** Even with a computer it would be difficult to impossible to design any such text and have any paragraph make any sense at all, much less by a human scribe in the third to eighth century as some critics allege. This obviously indicates much more than chance or human effort alone.

---

42 Ibid., 10–11.

43 Ibid., 16.

44 Ibid., 28–29.

Other reasons why Mark 16:9-20 should be considered authoritative

As far as why Panin thought this passage in Mark should definitely be included, he notes the following: "Three words are used in Mark 16:9–20 for the divine persons: God, Jesus, and Lord. These three words occur in the Gospel of Mark *including this passage*, 48, 81 and 18 times respectively, 147 in all, or 7 x 7 x 3, a multiple not only of 7 but of 7 x 7; and the numeric value of these 147 occurrences is 103,635, or 7 x 7 x 2,115, again a multiple of 7 x 7. **This clearly designed result is possible only with the four occurrences of these words *in this passage*. In other words: with the removal of this passage a design of sevens now running through these three words in the whole Gospel is destroyed. This passage is thus at once proved to be a necessary integral part of the Gospel as a whole."**[45] As we shall see, there is also a design that runs through the first and last words of all the New Testament books, of which the first and last words of Mark are of course an integral part.

[?] Were all the books of the New Testament written "last"?

Author Chuck Missler describes another phenomenon Panin found.[46] This involves the number of unique vocabulary words used by a given New Testament author. There are words in the Gospel of Matthew, for example, that occur nowhere else in the New Testament. They occur 42 times (7 x 6) and have 126 (7 x 18) letters. Now, if Matthew deliberately designed in this feature, the only way he could have known these specific words would not be used by the other New Testament writers would either have been: 1) a prior agreement with the other writers, so they would not use certain words he wanted to use and to make sure the number of his unique words totalled a multiple of seven (which seems totally ridiculous since there would be no reason for them to do this, and many of them wrote at different times and places, and so such collaboration would have been impossible), or 2) his book was written last, and he had all the other New Testament books before him.

There is much evidence against Matthew's Gospel being written last and no reason evident that he would attempt to produce this phenomenon even if he could. But there is an even bigger problem. The Gospel of Mark also exhibits these same phenomena. So this suggests that the Gospel of Mark had to have been

---

45 Ibid., 30, emphasis his.

46 Missler, *Cosmic Codes,* 95–96.

written last. The same thing happens in the writings of John, James, Peter, Jude and Paul. **Each New Testament writer has a set of unique words the number of which is divisible by seven exactly. So the absurd conclusion we would come to would be that each one had to have been written last!**

The only other possibility would be for each author when he was ready to finish the last of his writings (as if he would bother with doing this) would find out about and get copies of the writings of all the other writers who wrote before him (whose writings somehow he would have to know in advance would someday be part of a collection called the New Testament), figure out what words all the other writers collectively did not use that he used and then restrict what he wrote to have the number of his unique set of words divisible by seven exactly. The ridiculous unlikelihood of such a theory is its own refutation.

The only conclusion remaining is that one mind oversaw this phenomenon in the New Testament writings, and it was to be revealed to our skeptical generation in modern times as proof of divine inspiration. Notice that this feature of unique words for a given writer also ties the entire New Testament together as one book.

Tying together the New Testament—the first and last words of each book

In his tape commentary *How We Got Our Bible* Chuck Missler[47] discusses some other heptadic features that also tie the New Testament together.

- The beginning and ending words of each New Testament book are 54 in number (since there are 27 books, 27 x 2 is 54), which consist of 28 (7 x 4) vocabulary words, and the total numerical value of all these words together is divisible by 7, as is the numerical value of the largest and smallest words.

- There are several other features of sevens involving sums of place values of words, numerical values of words, etc.

- There is another scheme of sevens running through the forms of the 28 vocabulary words.

- There are also similarly complex schemes of nines, thirteens, and seventeens running through these 54 first and last words of the New Testament books.

- There are also sophisticated patterns associated with single words that run throughout the New Testament.

---

47   Missler, *How We Got Our Bible,* tape commentary, Koinonia House, 2000.

By the way, try taking the first and last words of each chapter of any other large book and see what you get!

There are also sevens that are more extensive in that they tie the entire Bible together. These involve at least thirty-six authors, who, not knowing one another in most cases or even living at the same time period or location, nevertheless produced the following features in the biblical text.

Tying together the whole Bible

Designs of sevens in words, phrases, and names throughout the Bible

Missler[48] lists some examples of sevens found in words, phrases, and names through the Bible that tie it together as one book:

- The term "Hallelujiah" occurs 24 times in the Psalms and 4 times in Revelation, for a total of 28 times in the Bible.

- "Hosanna" occurs once in the Old Testament (OT) and 6 times in the New Testament (NT) for a total of 7.

- "Shepherd" occurs 12 times in the OT and 9 times in the NT for a total of 21.

- "Jehovah Sabaoth" (Lord of Hosts) occurs 285 times in the OT and 2 in the NT for a total of 287 (7 x 41).

- The name "Isaac" occurs 112 times in the OT and 14 in the NT totalling 126 times (7 x 18).

- The phrase "The stone that the builders rejected has become the headstone of the corner" occurs 1 time in the OT and 6 times in the NT for a total of 7.

- "Love thy neighbor as thyself" occurs once in the OT and 6 times in the NT for a total of 7.

- The name "Aaron" occurs 443 times in the OT and 5 in the NT for a total of 448 (7 x 64).

These are too consistent to have gotten there by chance. They all happen to be very significant names and phrases in the themes of the Bible. They therefore appear deliberate; yet how could the authors have contrived them? Why would they if they could? These numerical features tie the whole Bible together as a book that evidences design by one mind, the mind of God.

---

48 Missler, *Cosmic Codes*, 292.

CHAPTER NINE: THE NUMBERS ADD UP

**The design of sevens and elevens with the name of Moses and others—
were these deliberately planned by the Bible writers?**

The name of Moses occurs 847 times (7 x 121) in the whole Bible. It turns out
that a design of sevens and elevens runs through these occurrences of the name
Moses. Designs run throughout the whole Bible involving the names of other
Bible writers as well. Regarding the name of Moses, Panin made the following
deductions in his book *Verbal Inspiration of the Bible Scientifically Demonstrated*:
**"If the Bible writers themselves planned this distribution of this name with
its double scheme of sevens and elevens, they accomplished this only
by an understanding among themselves:** ... Moses then began this scheme
deliberately in his four books, expecting that subsequent writers (those of the New
Testament fifteen hundred years after him) would insert his name just enough times
to keep the design in suspense—always in full view of each writer—until it gets to
John, who by inserting it just once at last completes the centuries-ago planned and
waited-for design.

**"Moses thus foreknew the number of books in the Bible, their order
numbers, the number of times his name was to occur in each book,
and more of the like ... such an understanding among a score of men in
different lands, centuries apart, could originate and be kept up only by
a miracle, and one continued for centuries: the very miracle required for
verbal inspiration"**[49] (emphasis mine).

[?] Did someone revise the Bible to make this design come out?

I will quote Panin again: "One other possibility: Someone may have revised the
Bible so as to distribute the name of Moses among the different books to produce
these numerics. It was then either one who lived after Revelation was written, in which
book Moses was found; or its writer, John himself, since without its one occurrence
here the design is not completed. But the Hebrew text of the Old Testament was
already settled centuries before John; was most zealously watched over by the
Jews to jot and tittle. And, as these numerics run through both Testaments, the
needed alterations must have been made by a hated Christian, which the Jews
would have promptly disowned. This much as to deliberate alterations of the Old
Testament. Any tampering with the text of the New for introducing these numerics,
even by the apostle John himself, would be exposed at least by the Diotrepheses

---

49 Panin, *Verbal Inspiration of the Bible Scientifically Demonstrated*, 57.

of the day, who shrank not from disfellowshipping him. Moreover, alterations in the New Testament without any in the Old would here be of no avail.

"But even apart from all this only miraculous skill could carry out this design even with Moses' name alone. David's case with his 1,134 occurrences presents the same need. The same is the case with the rest of the seven names which form the special group with Moses and David discussed ... And again, several of the numeric features run already in the Old Testament alone independent of the New.

"On mere human grounds then these phenomena, even those for Moses alone, are inexplicable. And this is one case in thousands. The explanation that these numerics got into the Bible by the design of man is thus equally untenable with the one of mere chance."[50]

Panin describes in detail a scheme of elevens running through the number of books in the whole Bible, similar to the one described above for the Old Testament books alone. He sums this up: "Thus a mere glance at barely the table of contents of the Bible reveals eleven distinct features of elevens. The chance for any number being a multiple of eleven is only one in eleven. The chance for any two numbers being multiples of eleven is only one in 11 x 11, or 121 ... the division in three out of the eleven features not only by elevens but by two elevens diminishes the chance here 2 x 2 x 2, or eightfold. The chance for these eight features of elevens to be here accidental, undesigned rather than designed, is thus only one in ... 1,714 millions (sic).

"Now were this fact in connection with the Bible books to stand alone, it might be dismissed as a mere curiosity. But it does not stand alone: it is a mere sapling in a forest extending over kingdoms, a flakelet in a snowstorm over half a continent, a grain of sand on Long Beach, yea, a mere drop in the very ocean that washes it."[51]

Panin challenged the skeptics

After skeptics refused to believe his research, Panin boldly issued them a challenge in one of the major newspapers of his time, the *New York Sun*, in 1899. He issued this challenge to some of the greatest atheist scholars of his day: "I herewith respectfully invite any or all of the following to prove that my facts are not facts: namely Messrs. Lyman Abbott, Washington Gladden ... and Dr. Briggs, and

---

50 Ibid., 57–58.
51 Ibid., 40–41.

any other prominent higher critic so called. They may associate with themselves, if they choose, all the contributors to the ninth edition of the Encyclopaedia Britannica, who wrote its articles on biblical subjects, together with a dozen mathematicians of the caliber of Professor Simon Newcomb. **The heavier the caliber of either scholar or mathematician, the more satisfactory to me. They will find that my facts are facts.** And since they are facts, I am ready to take them to any three prominent lawyers, or better still, to any judge of the superior or Supreme Court, and abide by his decision as to whether the conclusion is not necessary that Inspiration alone can account for the facts, if they are facts."[52]

Not one of the above men attempted to refute his facts, but they simply ignored them. These facts stand today unrefuted, as a testimony to the divine inspiration of the Bible. One can't mention the sevens in the Bible without taking into account the fifty-plus years of work which Ivan Panin put into his research. And as you read his writings you see that his motive was simply to lift up Jesus Christ. Grant Jeffrey quotes Ivan Panin in *The Signature of God*: **"My friend of the world, whoso you are: Either Jesus Christ is mistaken or you are. The answer that neither might be is only evading the issue, not settling it. But the ages have decided that Jesus Christ was not mistaken. It is for you to decide whether you will continue to be."**[53]

CAUTIONS, DESIGNS IN NATURE, AND CONCLUSION

Cautions: There are many other significant numbers mentioned in the Bible besides the number seven, as we mentioned above. **Caution must be used when dealing with the meanings of numbers. For example, many "mystics" over the centuries have tried to find hidden meanings beyond and in disregard of the plain text, and these ideas have led to what is called "numerology." This has led to unsound doctrine and overemphasis on subjects not related to the message of the Bible.** The Gnostics were one group that made many heresies from mystical numerology. But, avoiding these kinds of extremes, there does seem to be some meaning behind the numbers, and in the numerical design we can see irrefutable evidence for divine inspiration.

---

52 Jeffrey, *The Signature of God*, 237–238.

53 Panin, as quoted in Jeffrey, *The Signature of God*, 239.

Designs in nature similar to biblical designs: We see numerical design, including sevens, in nature and in human experience. There are 7 colors in the light spectrum. There are 7 musically whole tones. Many animals have gestation periods that are multiples of 7, such as 98 days for lions, 147 days for sheep, etc. There are mathematical spirals in nature such as in shells, the human ear, the ram's horn, the DNA molecule, galaxies, etc. These spirals have precise mathematical properties.[54] There are even precise mathematical patterns in the seed arrangement in sunflowers, patterns in leaves, and in the way the leaves are arranged around the plant stems. In fact, they seem to adhere to a number scheme discovered by an Italian mathematician, Filius Bonacci, or Fibonacci as he was called. This Fibonacci number scheme is a sequence where each number in the sequence is the sum of the two preceding numbers, such as the sequence 1, 1, 2, 3, 5, 8, 13, 21, 34, etc. Many more examples could be given.[55]

? Pi and e in the Bible?

It makes sense that the one who created the universe and the mathematical constants of nature would also inspire a message that is mathematically designed. The author can't resist giving one more example to ponder, pointed out by author Chuck Missler.[56] In Genesis 1:1, a verse we have already looked at for other reasons, we examine the numerical values of each of the Hebrew letters and the numerical value of the Hebrew words. This is for you mathematicians and engineers out there. If you take the formula:

$$\frac{\text{The number of letters x the product of the letters}}{\text{The number of words x the product of the words}}$$

and apply that to this verse, you get 3.1416 x 10 to the seventeenth power; 3.1416 is the value of pi to four decimal places.

There is a number which is called e, the base of the natural logarithm. It is used often in advanced engineering and mathematics. Now if you take the verse John 1:1, which is also about the beginning, "In the beginning was the Word, and the Word was with God, and the Word was God," and apply the same formula above, you get 2.7183 x 10 to the 65 power; 2.7183 is the value of e to four decimal places! What a coincidence! Or is it?

54 Jeffrey, *The Signature of God*, 240.

55 Missler, *Cosmic Codes*, 449–454.

56 Ibid., 464–465.

Conclusion: Numerical designs in the Bible are evidence for divine inspiration

The numerical study of Scripture shows proof there is one mind behind the text, since other explanations fail to account for these phenomena. This becomes especially true when you consider that all these features interlock within the same text of the Bible, a text that has been also verified historically and archaeologically. This is all very mind-boggling, but we are not finished by a long shot. In the next section we will look at another phenomenon hidden even deeper in the text of the Bible, the sometimes controversial "Bible codes."

CHAPTER TEN

CODES OR COINCIDENCE?

WHAT ARE THE "BIBLE CODES"?

With the invention of high-speed computers a phenomenon has been discovered in the Bible involving what is called Equidistant Letter Sequences, or ELS. This phenomenon has also been called the "Bible codes," and a best-selling book by Michael Drosnin in 1997[1] helped to popularize it among the general public. But this is not the first time the "codes" had been discovered; for that we need to go back about six hundred years. Rabbi Bachya, from Europe, discovered one of the simpler ELS "codes," which was more recently rediscovered by Rabbi Michael Dov Weissmandl.[2]

"Torah" encoded in the first five books of the Bible: This code was found in the Torah. If we take the Hebrew text of Genesis, start at the beginning and count in forty-nine letters, we get a Tau or "T." If we count forty-nine more letters we get an "O"; forty-nine more we get "R"; then forty-nine more, an "H", which spells TORH, or Torah. Then if we take the second book, Exodus, start from the beginning and count in forty-nine letter intervals, we get "Torah" again! If we try this in the next book,

---

1   Michael Drosnin, *The Bible Code,* Simon and Schuster, New York, NY, 1997.

2   Grant Jeffrey, *The Mysterious Bible Codes,* Word Publishing, Nashville, TN, 1998, 43–44.

Leviticus, it doesn't work. But if we do this in the next book, Numbers, and in the following book, Deuteronomy, in each case we get HROT, or Torah spelled backward.

If we go back to Leviticus, start from the beginning and count in seven-letter intervals, we get the name of God, the Tetragammaton, YHWH. So in the first two books "Torah" points forward to the name of God in Leviticus, and in the last two books "Torah" points backward toward the name of God. As Chuck Missler has noted in his discussion of this finding in *Cosmic Codes*, the Torah always points to God![3] Although the letters TORH might be expected to show up at equidistant letter intervals several times based on the number of letters in Genesis and the relative frequency of the above four letters in Hebrew, it is the fact that they begin with the first "T" of each book, in both Genesis and Exodus, that makes the probability exceedingly remote.[4]

Could the scribe have inserted this "code"? Perhaps in this case, although it would be difficult, and the question also arises as to whether this would be expected of the writer.

Some of the ancient Jewish sages such as Rabbi Nachmanides wrote about the phenomenon of codes. Many of them taught that all of history is somehow encoded in the Torah alone. For example, Rabbi Eliyahu ben Shlomo in the 1700s, also called the Vilna Gaon, wrote in the introduction to *Sifra Ditzniut*: "The rule is that all that was, is, and will be unto the end of time is included in Torah from the first word to the last word. And not merely in a general sense, but including the details of every species and of each person individually."[5] While this sounds extreme, modern computers have been finding many details of history apparently encoded in the biblical text, some of which we shall examine later on.

PIONEERING COMPUTER RESEARCH ON BIBLE CODES

The name "Israel"

In 1982 a study was done using computers to find these ELS codes in the book of Genesis, which was performed by three Jewish mathematics and computer specialists, Drs. Eli Rips, Moshe Katz, and Doron Witztum. One example of what

---

3   Missler, *Cosmic Codes*, 128.

4   Ibid., 126–129.

5   Jeffrey, *The Mysterious Bible Codes*, 39–40.

they found was uncovered when they ran a search for the name "Israel" in the first 10,000 letters of Genesis. They did the search looking for ELS sequences from 100 to -100 (-100 meaning the word spelled backward at an interval of every 100 letters). The word "Israel," although expected to appear statistically about 5 times by chance in this section of text, appeared only twice, at ELS intervals of 7 and -50, and these were clustered in Genesis 1:31–2:3. This verse is called the Kiddush, which is recited before each Sabbath. The numbers seven and fifty are also associated with the Sabbath, which relate to the seventh weekday and the fiftieth Sabbath year, the year of Jubilee.[6]

As Missler discusses in *Cosmic Codes*, the probability of "Israel" appearing only twice at a given interval in the above verses is 1 in 1,200, and the probability of its appearing at the exact intervals of 7 and 50, positive or negative, is 1 in 400,000. And further significance is given by the relationship of this code to the Sabbath.[7]

[?] What are some important factors in searching for "codes"?

In searching for these codes, some critical questions are whether the encoded word/words are found at low ELS intervals (less than a thousand), whether or not the words relate to the text they are found in, and/or if several related words are found close together.

Again, could these have been made by clever scribes? Maybe some of the simpler ones. But we shall see that some would be very complicated and difficult to do even with computers, much like the structures of seven seen in the last section. In addition, some of these codes are prophetic, which precludes their being a product of human intellect alone, as we shall see in ensuing examples.

[?] Are there any prophetic codes?

Missler[8] describes one example of a prophetic code that is found in Genesis 38. This is the story of Judah and Tamar, where they eventually gave birth to twin sons named Pharez and Zerach. In the book of Ruth we find out that Boaz was descended from Pharez. Boaz's son was Obed, who was the father of Jesse, who was the father of King David. The amazing part is that these five names, Pharez, Boaz, Obed, Jesse, and David, are all encoded in Genesis 38, at forty-nine-letter

---

6   Missler, *Cosmic Codes,* 136.

7   Ibid.

8   Ibid., 457–460.

intervals, in chronological order. **What are the odds of this occurring by chance, especially in the correct chronological order? And it is not likely that the writer of Genesis, even if some say he could have written it after David was born, would have bothered to encode these names in that particular story.** As we shall see, there is some prophetic encoding which reaches even into modern times, which should not be surprising, given the prophecy we have already seen in the plain text. How do we explain all this?

[?] What was the "famous rabbi" experiment?

The most famous experiment with the Bible codes to date was conducted by Rips, Rosenberg, and Witztum in 1994, popularly called the "famous rabbi" experiment. In this experiment a computer search was done for pairs of encoded words that reveal the names and dates of the births or deaths of thirty-four of the most famous rabbis during the years 90–1900 A.D. They did this by selecting the thirty-four with the longest biographies in a well-known Hebrew reference book called The Encyclopedia of Great Men in Israel.[9] The dates of death are significant as well as birthdates because the Jewish people considered the date of death of a famous rabbi as important as the day of his birth.

When this experiment was run, the researchers found the names of every one of the thirty-four rabbis encoded and paired in close association with their birth or death dates. These all were encoded in the 78,064 letters of Genesis. It has been calculated that the odds that these specific rabbis' names could occur in such close proximity to their birth or death dates by chance would be 1 in 775 million.[10] The researchers published an article in the refereed journal *Statistical Science*.[11]

The skeptics ask for more proof

Before publishing, the referees for *Statistical Science* were of course skeptical. After all, this document was written thousands of years before all of these men had lived. They suggested that maybe it was by chance or that the researchers played with the program until they got the results they wanted or didn't report failures. So these referees demanded that these same researchers run the experiment on a second set of famous Jewish rabbis selected by the referees themselves. The

9 M. Margalioth, *The Encyclopedia of Great Men in Israel,* Joshua Chachik, Tel Aviv, Israel, 1961

10 Jeffrey, *The Mysterious Bible Codes,* 49.

11 Doron Witztum, Yoav Rosenberg and Eliyahu Rips, "Equidistant Letter Sequences in the Book of Genesis," *Statistical Science,* vol. 9, no. 3, August 1994, 429–438.

Statistical Science referees selected an additional thirty-two prominent Jewish rabbis and sages from the same encyclopedia. They also did an analysis on the computer programs being used to make sure they were not biased and were properly constructed.

The results

To their surprise, the results on the second set of rabbis gave similar results to the first set. The editors of *Statistical Science*, after a long review period of about six years, could not find anything wrong with the results of the experiment and so published the above article. Robert Kass, the editor of *Statistical Science*, commented on the study: "Our referees were baffled: their prior beliefs made them think the book of Genesis could not possibly contain meaningful references to modern-day individuals; yet when the authors carried out additional analyses and checks the effect persisted. The paper is thus offered to *Statistical Science* readers as a challenging puzzle."[12] The same article concluded with the following statement: "We conclude that the proximity of the ELSs (Equidistant Letter Sequences) with related meanings in the book of Genesis is **not due to chance**" (emphasis mine).[13]

These scientists performed an extremely thorough scientific investigation, and subsequent to publishing the article all of the referees now consider the codes a credible phenomenon.[14]

? Have there been any attempted refutations of the famous rabbi experiment?

Attempts have been made to find similar codes in other Hebrew texts, including the Samaritan Pentateuch, which has slight variations in hundreds of places from the Masoretic text. No significant codes have been found there. But recent claims have been made that the results of the famous rabbi experiment were duplicated in a Hebrew text of Tolstoy's War and Peace, taking a portion of its text about the same length as the book of Genesis. An alleged refutation of the Witztum, Rosenberg, and Rips study was published in 1999 in Statistical Science.[15] They

---

12 Robert Kass, *Statistical Science,* August 1994.

13 Ibid., 434.

14 Missler, *Cosmic Codes,* 139.

15 Brendan McKay, Dror Bar Natan, Maya Bar Hillel and Gil Kalai, "Solving the Bible Code Puzzle," *Statistical Science,* vol. 14, no. 2, 1999, 149–173.

also published an article on the internet on September 20, 1997, titled "Equidistant Letter Sequences in Tolstoy's War and Peace" in which authors Bar Natan and McKay claim the same results in Genesis were found in Tolstoy's famous novel.[16]

These articles also attempted to discredit Witztum, Rips, and Rosenberg's research by claiming they "cooked" the input data in order to get their results. They claim there are no codes and that any results are from manipulating the data. In the abstract of their 1999 *Statistical Science* article mentioned above, McKay, Bar Natan, Bar Hillel and Kalai stated their case: "In reply, we argue that Witztum, Rips and Rosenberg's case is fatally defective, indeed that their result merely reflects on the choices made in designing their experiment and collecting the data for it. We present extensive evidence in support of that conclusion. We also report on many new experiments of our own, all of which failed to detect the alleged phenomenon."[17]

Even the editor of *Statistical Science,* Robert Kass, seemed to backpedal on his previous remarks mentioned above: "When the article … by Witztum, Rips and Rosenberg was examined by reviewers … none was convinced that the authors had found something genuinely amazing. Instead, what remained intriguing was the difficulty of pinpointing the cause, **presumed** to be some flaw in their procedure that produced such apparently remarkable findings. Thus, in introducing that paper, I wrote that it was offered to readers 'as a challenging puzzle.' Unfortunately, though perhaps not so surprisingly, many people outside our own profession interpreted publication of the paper as a stamp of scientific approval on the work."[18]

One can see in Kass's statement that there is an *a priori* skepticism about any possible supernatural effects and that any seemingly remarkable results are assumed to be from a flaw in the experiment, rather than genuine, even before any comprehensive attempt at rebuttal was published. One also wonders if the *Statistical Science* editor regarded all his former referees as incompetent!

Recent follow-up experiments and defenses of the famous rabbi experiment

A more recent article reports on a follow-up experiment to answer some challenges to the original WRR famous rabbi study. This experiment, performed

---

16 McKay, Bar Natan, et al., *Astounding Discoveries in War and Peace,* May 1997 (website not available).

17 Ibid., 150.

18 Ibid., 149, emphasis mine.

by Harold Gans, Zvi Inbal and Nachum Bombach, was even more statistically rigorous and not only confirmed WRR's results, but extended the original findings to include the names of the rabbis' communities.[19] The website titled *The Light of Torah Codes*,[20] which is the current reference site for Torah codes constructed by some of the original code researchers, has many similar articles and presents the latest research on the codes.

One of the current defenders of the codes found in the Torah, the first five books of the Bible, is computer science professor Robert Haralick, whose web site, **www. torah-code.org**, contains many recent articles on the subject. He has helped the code researchers develop even more stringent and rigorous statistical protocols for verifying the code phenomenon. A detailed paper by Haralick describing these criteria used can be found at http://www.torah-code.org/papers.shtml.[21] In this paper he lists fourteen different methods to test whether or not a given set of codes is real. In a follow-up paper he then applies these tests to both the WRR famous rabbi data set and the data set used by McKay in *War and Peace*. He concluded after applying these tests that the results demonstrated the codes found by Witztum, et al. (WRR), were not explainable by chance, but that the supposed codes McKay and his associates found in *War and Peace* could possibly occur by a chance process.[22]

All of these articles on both sides are very technical, and I do not claim the competence to completely follow all of their arguments. Nevertheless, I think what can be concluded is that, even though the debate goes on, the assertion that the "famous rabbi's experiment" has been disproven is by no means certain, and it may be even more likely that it has been the critics that have been refuted. **The fact is, there are highly credentialed scientists and mathematicians who believe the code phenomenon is genuine. And it seems as if the critics have not come up with anything to refute the latest stringent tests imposed by the researchers to prove the code phenomenon.**

19 Harold Gans, Zvi Inbal and Nachum Bombach, *Patterns of Equidistant Letter Sequence Pairs in Genesis,* presented August 23, 2006, at the 18th International Conference on Pattern Recognition, Hong Kong, retrieved August 19, 2011, from web site http://www.torahcodes.net/gans.pdf.

20 http://www.torahcodes.net.html.

21 Robert M. Haralick, *Basic Concepts for Testing the Torah Code Hypothesis,* 18th International Conference on Pattern Recognition, August 20-24, 2006, Hong Kong, retrieved August 19, 2011, from http://www.torah-code.org/papers.shtml.

22 Ibid.

Remember that more is going on here than a pure statistics debate; worldviews are at stake. All the theist has to do is prove one supernatural line of evidence, even if all others are disproven. On the other hand, the naturalist atheist has to disprove all lines of supernatural evidence or face the scary possibility of accountability to a Creator God for his life. I think the latter is the more daunting task. And, as we see, the more powerful and varied the evidence that piles up for the supernatural, the more hopeless it looks for the naturalistic worldview.

Prophetic codes–the Mishneh Torah

Another example involves a twelfth-century rabbi, the famous Jewish sage Moses Ben Maimonides, also known as "RAMBAM," derived from his Hebrew name. His most famous book was called *Mishneh Torah*. His Hebrew name RMBM is encoded at 4-letter intervals in **Exodus 11:9: "That my wonders may be multiplied in the land of Egypt."** RAMBAM was also a famous doctor in Egypt. The first word of the title of his book *Mishneh Torah*, "Mishneh," is also encoded in the same verse, Exodus 11:9, at 50-letter intervals. The second word in the title, "Torah," is encoded in Exodus 12:11, also at 50-letter intervals. The beginnings of the two encoded words are exactly 613 letters apart in the Hebrew. The numbers 613 and 50 are key here.

What makes this very interesting is that the book *Mishneh Torah* refers to the 613 commandments and laws of God given in the Torah. Between the giving of the first commandment in Egypt and the 613th commandment given at Sinai, there were exactly fifty days, a time span marked by the Feast of Weeks. The passage that part of this book title is encoded in, Exodus 12:11, speaks of the first command given to all Israel, on Passover eve, to mark the beginning of months. The odds of all this occurring by chance in the text were calculated at 186 million to one by Dr. Daniel Michelson of the UCLA mathematics department.[23] Note that this also couldn't be a deliberate human construction because it deals with a twelfth-century A.D. book.

Names of trees encoded in Genesis

Another example shows that the names of all twenty-five kinds of trees mentioned throughout the Old Testament are encoded at small ELS intervals from -2 to -18, in the passage beginning at Genesis 1:29 and going through Genesis 2:9. It starts with: **"And God said, Behold, I have given you every herb bearing seed,**

---

23   Jeffey, *The Mysterious Bible Codes*, 84–85.

which is upon the face of all the earth, and every tree, in the which is the fruit of a tree yielding seed; to you it shall be for meat" (Genesis 1:29), and ends with: "And out of the ground made the Lord God to grow every tree that is pleasant to the sight, and good for food; the tree of life also in the midst of the garden, and the tree of knowledge of good and evil" (Genesis 2:9).

No other passage in the Old Testament contains the encoded names of these twenty-five trees at intervals of less than twenty.[24] And this passage is about trees, so you can see the relatedness of the codes to the plain text. In addition, the passage mentioned above contains seventeen animals that are mentioned in the Old Testament, the name Torah five times and the name Yeshua ten times, all interwoven in a complex pattern.[25] Yet the text does not seem artificial or contrived.

[?] Are there codes of the name of Jesus (Yeshua)?

One thing we might expect to be emphasized in any "codes" in the Bible is the name Jesus, or *Yeshua* in the Hebrew. Rabbi Yakov Rambsel has been researching Yeshua codes in the Hebrew Scriptures.[26] He has indeed found the name of Yeshua encoded in every major messianic prophecy in the Old Testament.[27] Rambsel does not use a computer to find these codes, so his work has been a tedious process.

One of the problems with the Yeshua codes is that the Hebrew name of Yeshua has only four letters, two of these letters being the most common letters in Hebrew, and the other two occurring fairly frequently also. What this means is that the name Yeshua would be expected to occur many times by chance alone.[28] The task then is to separate what is statistically significant. The key again is the occurrence in clusters, inside texts which are well-known references to the Messiah. For example, Rambsel found that in Isaiah 53, a well-known messianic prophecy, is the only occurrence of the phrase "Yeshua is My Name."[29] Also, within Isaiah 53 are encoded the names of forty other important individuals at short ELS intervals. Another is found in Leviticus 21:10, where every third letter it spells: "Behold, the blood of

---

24 Ibid., 85.

25 Ibid., 87.

26 Yacov Rambsel, *YESHUA: The Name of Jesus Revealed in the Old Testament,* Frontier Research Publications, Toronto, Ont., 1996.

27 Jeffrey, *The Mysterious Bible Codes,* 89–102.

28 Missler, *Cosmic Codes,* 149.

29 Jeffrey, *The Mysterious Bible Codes,* 91.

Yeshua!" Statistically this code in Leviticus should occur about 1 time in 69,000 at three-letter intervals.[30]

Names of the disciples encoded in Isaiah 52-53, the "Suffering Servant" passage

There are many others, but let's look at what Rambsel found in the passage known as the "Suffering Servant" passage, from Isaiah 52:13–53:12. Rambsel discovered in this passage the names of Jesus Christ and more than forty other individuals who were associated with Him at His crucifixion.[31] Remember: Isaiah 53 was written more than seven hundred years before the time of Christ and was translated into Greek three centuries before, and the Hebrew writers had no known incentive to encode these names even if they could have. What we will see is although you might expect to find these names in a large Hebrew text by chance, it is their appearance in combination in a relevant text that indicates more than just chance occurrence.

In *Cosmic Codes* Missler[32] discusses the probability of chance occurrences of the names of some of these individuals:

- The name of Peter appears at an interval of every 19 letters. This name is encoded in more than 300 places in Isaiah so by itself would not be convincing. But let's keep going.

- The name of John occurs at the ELS interval of every 28 letters starting from Isaiah 53:10. This is more unlikely because John only appears 9 times in the whole book of Isaiah.

- The name of Andrew occurs at the ELS interval of 48. Since Andrew only occurs 5 times in the entire book of Isaiah, the evidence is starting to accumulate against chance alone.

- The name of Philip occurs at the ELS of 133 with only 15 other occurrences in Isaiah. (Remember: Isaiah has sixty-six chapters.)

- The name Thomas appears also (at the ELS of 35), and even though there are 200 other occurrences in Isaiah, the combination of all these relevant names is becoming more significant.

---

30 Ibid., 95.

31 Ibid., 104–133.

32 Missler, *Cosmic Codes,* 155–158.

- Similarly, the names of Simon (ELS of 47) and Thaddeus (ELS of 50) also appear.

Two Jameses

There is more. The name James appears twice at intervals of -20 and -34. What makes this significant is there were two disciples of the original twelve called James: James the son of Zebedee, and James the son of Alphaeus. There was a third James, the brother of Jesus, but he was not a disciple before the cross, becoming a disciple after the resurrection. How interesting then that the name James is encoded precisely two times.[33]

Three Marys

There were also three Marys at the cross: Jesus' mother, Mary the wife of Cleopas, and Mary Magdalene. Certainly Mary is a common name, with more than six hundred occurrences in Isaiah and twelve in this passage alone. But three of the encoded Marys are closely linked together, using the same letter *yod* in the word *yaarik* in Isaiah 53:10, which also is the same *yod* that forms the first letter of the encoded names Yeshua and John. Remember John 19:25–27, where Jesus entrusts Mary to John's care. So this close linking of three Marys with John and Jesus is very significant.[34]

No Judas!

Another striking fact: a particular person's name does not show up. The name Judas, although appearing more than fifty times in Isaiah, does not appear in Isaiah 53. Remember: Judas was the traitor who left the group and was eventually replaced by Matthias as the twelfth disciple. And, sure enough, Matthias, at the ELS of 11, does appear.

So what you have here is more than forty names in fifteen sentences, close together, at short ELS intervals and in a relevant text that was written centuries before the days of Jesus and His disciples! These are very unlikely "coincidences." Chuck Missler used the following paragraph in his book *Cosmic Codes* to illustrate the unlikelihood of a chance explanation for this type of phenomena:

---

33   Ibid., 156–157.

34   Ibid., 158.

"Upon this basis I am going to show you how a bunch of bright young folks did find a champion: a man with boys and girls of his own; a man of so dominating and happy individuality that Youth is drawn to him as is a fly to a sugar bowl. It is a story about a small town. It is not a gossipy yarn; nor is it a dry monotonous account, full of such customary "fill-ins" as "romantic moonlight casting murky shadows down a long winding country road." Nor will it say anything about twinklings lulling distant folds; robins caroling at twilight, nor any "warm glow of lamplight" from a cabin window. No. It is an account of up-and-going activity; a vivid portrayal of Youth as it is today; and a practical discarding of that worn-out notion that 'a child don't know anything.'"[35]

What you may not notice at first is that not one letter e is used in this entire paragraph! Now, if you found a paragraph of this length or longer in a book, would you conclude that it got there by chance? We don't realize how hard it would be not to use the letter e. It was in fact quite a challenge for the author to write, the author apparently having to disable the e key on his typewriter to keep from using it![36] How much harder to encode words in a paragraph and have the text still make sense and have proper grammatical structure.

Chuck Missler comments on the ELS codes debate: **"The skeptics point out, with substantial validity, that the ELS codes are facilitated by the nature of the Hebrew language and its density due to the shorter alphabet and its absence of vowels ... The rebuttal to their being simply a chance phenomenon are their occurrence behind relevant plaintext, the clustering of related codes, and the absences of any significant alternative candidate names within the cluster."**[37] He also thinks it is possible the Hebrew language may even have been **designed** to facilitate these ELS codes!

PROPHETIC CODES?

Some current events seem to be encoded in the Bible. We have already mentioned some of the words found concerning Hitler and the Holocaust. These were found within a few short passages, Deuteronomy 10:17–22 and also Deuteronomy

---

35 Earnest V. Wright, *Gadsby, A Story of Over Fifty Thousand Words Without Using the Letter E*, 1939, Wetzel Publishing Company, Los Angeles, as quoted by Missler, *Cosmic Codes*, 161–162.

36 Ibid., 162.

37 Ibid., 163.

31:16–33:21. There are words relating to the Gulf War in the early 90s encoded in a few passages in Genesis.[38] There are also, in Genesis 32, 34, 35, 36 and 44, words encoded relating to the Oklahoma City bombing, words such as "Oklahoma," "Timothy," "McVeigh," "day 19" and others.[39] Several internet articles claim there are a cluster of codes in Ezekiel 37 relating to September 11, 2001. All these are clustered in a few passages, not spread out over the entire Bible or even one book of the Bible. Most of them are also at significantly short ELS intervals, which argue against their being by chance.

? Rabin assassination predicted?

One significant code seems to have to do with the assassination of Prime Minister Yitzchak Rabin. A group of words such as "Rabin," "will be murdered," "Yigal," "Amir," "Israel," "5682" (the year of Rabin's birth in the Hebrew calendar), "5756" (the year of Rabin's death in the Hebrew calendar) and others are all found at ELS intervals ranging from 1 to -285 in the passage Genesis 48:13–49:3.[40] This is a very dense cluster at low ELS intervals, so it is statistically significant. Chuck Missler gives another example concerning Rabin in Genesis 15:17, a passage that deals with the covenant God makes with Abraham concerning the promised land for Abraham's descendants. In the original Hebrew language there are no spaces between the words, but the spacing is inferred. Missler shows that if the inferred spacing is slightly changed without changing the letters, the Hebrew reads: "decreed God into Rabin evil fire fire" ("An evil fire (twice) into Rabin God decreed").[41]

It is a Jewish custom that a reading from the Torah is done in synagogues throughout the world, beginning at Rosh Hashanah and continuing throughout the Jewish year. The scheduled reading for November 4, 1995, was Genesis 15. This was the very day Rabin was assassinated by two gunshots. Missler comments that at the time Rabin was viewed by most of Israel as having betrayed their right to the land God gave them by agreeing to turn over portions of the land. He said he would never negotiate with the PLO; yet he began secret talks with them after being

---

38   Grant Jeffrey, *The Handwriting of God,* Frontier Research Publications, Toronto, ON, 1997, 134–136.

39   Ibid., 136–138.

40   Ibid., 132–133.

41   Missler, *Cosmic Codes,* 117–118.

elected. Rabin even said: "The Bible is not Israel's title deed."[42] Thirty days after he said that, Rabin was killed.

Is this all coincidence? Or have significant events in our time been prophetically encoded in the Bible? As Missler points out, the perpetrator of the crime is in no way relieved of his responsibility if this is in fact an actual prophecy.[43] But it has to be explained somehow.

THE BIBLE CODES-MICHAEL DROSNIN'S BOOKS

As was mentioned above, an author by the name of Michael Drosnin wrote a book in 1997, *The Bible Code*.[44] To his credit he helped to make the idea of the Bible codes known to the general public, instead of just being the realm of private research by professional mathematicians. He wrote a follow-up book in 2002, called *Bible Code II, The Countdown*,[45] and a third in 2010, *Bible Code III, Saving the World*.[46] Although he has written three entertaining books that publicized the code phenomena, his methods and conclusions have drawn much criticism, both from detractors of the Bible codes and from the leading code researchers themselves. In fact, most of the criticism of the idea of Bible codes has been leveled at Drosnin's first book, the critics acting as though they have disproven the phenomena by their attacks. Most of the leading code researchers have stated that the methodology Drosnin uses is not statistically sound.

[?] Did Drosnin warn Rabin before his assassination?

Drosnin claims to have found a code concerning the assassination of Rabin and claims he even went to warn Rabin when he had discovered this code. But his approach is roundly denounced by the leading code researchers. His claim to have found the prediction of Rabin's assassination is based on an entirely different finding than has been presented above. For example, he claims to have found the words "assassin will assassinate" associated with Rabin. But Hebrew experts, including the code researchers, have shown that his translation of Hebrew into "assassin

---

42 Ibid., 119.

43 Ibid.

44 Michael Drosnin, *The Bible Code*, Simon and Schuster, New York, NY, 1997.

45 Michael Drosnin, *Bible Code II: The Countdown*, Penguin Books, New York, NY, 2002.

46 Michael Drosnin, *Bible Code III: Saving the World*, Worldmedia, Inc., 2010.

will assassinate" is erroneous.[47] Furthermore, he finds this code at a very high ELS interval of 4772, which greatly reduces its statistical significance.

? Do the leading code researchers endorse Drosnin's work?

Doron Witztum, the leading code researcher, denounces Drosnin's methods. "Mr. Drosnin's work employs no scientific methodology. No distinction is made between statistically valid codes and accidental appearances, which can be found in any book ... It is impossible to use Torah codes to predict the future ... Additionally, just like there is a code that Rabin would be assassinated, I also found a code saying that Churchill would be assassinated ... It is therefore unwise, and one could say irresponsible, to make 'predictions' based on ELSs of words appearing near each other."[48]

It has not been verified whether Drosnin ever actually warned Rabin. But using Drosnin's methodology, the words "Churchill" and "will be murdered" are found encoded together. If someone had found the "code" and had then warned Churchill, he would have been wrong.

Drosnin's first book does report some of the statistically sound discoveries made by code researchers such as Dr. Rips. But Rips, in public statements on the internet, says the following: "While I did meet and talk with Mr. Drosnin, I did not do joint work with him." "I do not support Mr. Drosnin's work on the codes, nor the conclusions he derives." "There was an impression that I was involved in finding the code relating to Prime Minister Rabin's assassination. This is not true."[49]

Although Drosnin admits the Bible codes must have a supernatural origin, he rejects the conclusion that the author was God and tries to come up with a "space alien" idea instead. In view of this idea and the fact that the real code experts question his methods we can say that Drosnin's books may be good entertaining reads but are not to be used as the sole criterion to judge whether or not the phenomenon of the Bible codes is real. Therefore any refutations of his books do not disprove the Bible code phenomenon.

---

47 John Weldon, *Decoding the Bible Code. Can We Trust the Message?* Harvest House, Eugene, OR, 1998, 67 .

48 Ibid., 42–43.

49 *Public Statement by Eliyahu Rips,* internet document, retrieved May 3, 2003, from http://www. thei.aust.com/torah/coderips.html.

OTHER OBJECTIONS TO THE BIBLE CODES

[?] Were assassination "codes" found in Moby Dick?

There has been an often repeated claim that several assassinations are predicted in the text of *Moby Dick*.[50] There is a refutation of this claim published on the internet also.[51] They point out that, first of all, many words are claimed to be encoded that are actually in the surface text, which eliminates a large portion of the "codes" found. Another thing they bring out, which is not conspicuously shown on the critics' website, is that for each "code" found the ELS interval is huge, sometimes in the hundreds of thousands, and that the author (McKay) uses a huge matrix of letters. This makes the letters look close together when in reality they are found across most of the book.

They also specifically examined some of the claimed encoded assassinations. For Prime Minister Indira Gandhi: "IGANDHI" was found at an ELS of 102,857. (Any ELS of more than 35,000 is rejected immediately by researchers, and no valid code has been found anywhere with an ELS of more than 7,000 that we know of.) An ELS that high is outrageous. The word stretches across the whole book![52]

The alleged encoding of the assassination of Reverend Martin Luther King: Quoting again from the paper: " 'MLKING' was found at an ELS of -26,026 (which is getting better but still much too high); 'to be killed by them' and 'prepare for death' are found in the surface text, not encoded ... 'TENN' ... is encoded at around 26,000, and 'gun" is encoded twice. (All of these three-letter words he has can be found encoded anywhere in any book.)"[53]

The others cited by the paper are similar. The main points are that McKay found the names encoded over huge ELS intervals, which easily can occur by chance, and instead of intersecting other encoded words at short intervals they intersected phrases which are actually in the surface text. Since the preceding articles about codes in *Moby Dick* were written, some very rigorous methods have been applied

---

50 Brendan McKay, *Assassinations Foretold in Moby Dick!,* 1997, http://cs.anu.edu.au/~bdm/ dilugim/moby.html.

51 The Biblecodes.com. *Claim: Assassinations Are Foretold in* Moby Dick, Answers to Claims, retrieved from website on May 5, 2003, from address http://www.thebiblecodes.com/claims/ assassinations.html. (website no longer active).

52 Ibid., 2.

53 Ibid., 2.

to the Bible text in Genesis and other long texts which will be described briefly below.

❓ So are the Bible codes just a chance phenomenon that can be found in any large text like *Moby Dick* or *War in Peace?* How does one prove otherwise?

Fortunately, statistical methods can distinguish a statistically significant "code" from a random occurrence.

- One of the tests is to select the input data "a priori," that is, rather than looking for related words by trial and error, instead to specify in advance the words you are looking for in the text.[54] Here are some analogies. If you have a newspaper headline with several names in it, and you find those same names encoded in a very large book, spread out over the book, it could easily be explained by chance. Or, if the names were very common and there were not too many of them, there could even be a chance occurrence of all of them on just one page of the book. What would be very unlikely to happen by chance is to find several rare names that had been pre-specified in a newspaper headline, on one single page of a very large book, the large book being totally unconnected with the newspaper headline. This final scenario of the rare names on one page is analogous to what is found in the Bible code phenomena.[55]

- The area of the letter matrix in which you find these pre-specified words is called the measure of compactness of the data. This essentially is a measure of how close together the words are encoded and how small the ELS skip intervals are. This area needs to be very stringently specified. Haralick notes that one of the reasons McKay's experiment was able to look like it refuted the WRR famous rabbi experiment was that the compactness protocols were not quite tight enough in the WRR experiment.[56]

---

54 See articles in Counterpoint-Torah Codes Revisited, retrieved August 24, 2011, from http://www.torahcodes.net/new/pages/critical1.html. This includes interviews with code researchers Art Levitt and Harold Gans.

55 The Light of Torah Codes, Disciplined Codes, retrieved August 19, 2011, from http://www.torahcodes.net/new/pages/precision.html.

56 Robert M. Haralick, *Testing the Torah Code Hypothesis: The Experimental Protocol, <http://www.torah-code.org/papers.shtml>.*

- Another measure is the length of the ELS skip interval, the smaller the better. A value between one and ten is ideal.[57]

- Yet another important test is to analyze control texts along with the Bible text. These texts are called "monkey" texts, because they simulate scores of monkeys mindlessly hammering away at typewriters and producing all kinds of random letter sequences. The monkey texts for the book of Genesis or Torah examples are made by taking the biblical text and randomly shuffling the words, the letters, the verses, the chapters or other parameters. In this way you have a large random text that uses the same letters as the original Bible text. A monkey text can also be any large book such as *Moby Dick* or *War and Peace.* For a code in the Bible to be statistically significant, it needs to appear in a smaller area of the text or have a smaller compactness measure than the majority of the monkey texts.[58] When these tests are performed on books such as *Moby Dick* or *War and Peace,* the so-called "codes" found in them are demonstrated to be explainable by chance, whereas in Genesis or the Torah, their probability value is too low for chance to explain.[59]

[?] Do different versions of the Old Testament invalidate the code phenomenon?

Israeli researchers of the Bible codes have used the standard Masoretic text also known as the Koren text. The Koren text differs from the Dead Sea Scroll text by only 169 letters out of the 304,805 letters in the first five books of Moses (the Pentateuch), a tribute, as we mentioned above, to the meticulous copying done over the centuries.

The Biblical Hebraica Stuttgartensis (BHS) text is the most commonly used Hebrew text by scholars. According to Jeffrey, it varies from the Masoretic Koren text in some of the spellings of the words, 130 letters in all, out of 304,805 in the Pentateuch.[60] Yet most if not all of the ELS codes can be found in both texts.

---

57 Haralick, *Similar Patterns,* retrieved August 24, 2011, from http://www.torah-code.org/controversy/similar_patterns.shtml.

58 Robert M. Haralick, *Monkey Text Populations,* retrieved August 24, 2011, from http://www.torah-code.org/monkey_texts.shtml.

59 Haralick, *Skeptical About the Reasoning of the Bible Code Skeptic,* retrieved August 24, 2011, from http://www.torah-code.org/papers/skeptical_inquirer_02_15_07.pdf. This article addresses in particular the claims of codes in *Moby Dick* and *War and Peace.*

60 Jeffrey, *The Mysterious Bible Codes*, 22.

The more the spelling varies, of course, the more the code would be affected. As Jeffrey discusses,[61] the type of error is also important. If it were a deletion it would throw off a code; but if it is just a substitution and the ELS code skipped over that substituted letter, the letter count does not change and the code is intact. So there is a tolerance built into the text. The researchers also note that the existence of the codes in fact confirms they are using the correct text.[62]

? Vowel points weren't added to the original Old Testament text until many centuries after Christ. Wouldn't the adding of the vowel points mess up any code that had originally been there?

As far as vowel points go, this objection shows the critics don't understand the structure of Hebrew text. Ancient Hebrew consisted entirely of consonants, with the vowel points added by the Masoretic scribes between the sixth and ninth centuries A.D., to help pronounce the words correctly.[63] The key point is that vowel points are added above and below the consonants, similar to the dotting of an i or j, and so they do not change the letter count or affect any ELS codes present. But let's assume, for the sake of argument, that adding the vowel points did affect the codes. Wouldn't it be an equally unexplainable miracle if they added vowel points and out popped the codes?

WOULD GOD PUT CODES IN THE BIBLE?

Some feel that analysis of Bible codes smacks of elitism, with the knowledge going to a select few experts. Admittedly, sophisticated analysis is sometimes needed to determine whether a genuine ELS code is present. Many will object by saying God has put nothing in His Word that the average person can't understand. What we need to know for salvation and growth, for example, is spelled out in plain language. But is it necessarily true that God has never put anything into the Bible that is not easy to find? **Proverbs 25:2 says: "It is the glory of God to conceal a thing: but the honor of kings is to search out a matter."**

---

61 Ibid., 24.

62 The Light of Torah Codes, *Accuracy of the Torah Text,* retrieved August 19, 2011, from www.torahcodes.net/new/pages/accuracy.html

63 Jeffrey, *The Mysterious Bible Codes,* 24–25.

Acrostics in the Bible

There are acrostics, for example, in some of the psalms, as already mentioned concerning Psalm 119. And something very interesting is found in the book of Esther. The book of Esther was one of the books of which it was disputed whether or not it should be included in the Old Testament canon, simply because it did not contain the name of God. Indeed, the name of God does not appear in the plain text; the root meaning of the name "Esther" is "hidden." What we find in Esther is that the name of God does appear, but it is in hidden form. Chuck Missler describes how, in key verses, the name of God is hidden eight times in the text: four times in acrostic form as the Tetragammaton "YHWH," once as an acrostic "EHYH" ("I AM"), and three times as equidistant letter sequences at ELS intervals of seven and eight.[64]

Now the acrostics shown above are within the capabilities of a clever scribe to produce, unlike some of the more complex codes already seen. The point here is that hidden designs in the text are not out of character for God and His Word.

The value of the Bible code phenomenon

Many Christians find the whole idea of the Bible codes to be quite uncomfortable, especially because of the potential for misuse, such as in trying to predict future events as in fortune telling. Of course, people also greatly misuse the plain text of the Bible, so there will be misuse, no matter what.

I believe God may have put the codes there just for a testimony to this skeptical, computer-age generation and not to provide doctrines or prophecy. It is one more valid indicator of the incredible design of the Word of God. The Bible can be both easy to understand for a child and yet at the same time contain depth and complexity befitting its Author, beyond all human knowledge and understanding.

---

64 Missler, *Cosmic Codes,* 81–86, for a complete discussion of acrostics in the book of Esther.

CHAPTER ELEVEN

EVIDENCE FOR THE DIVINE FINGERPRINT

INTRODUCTION

As the Scripture is studied in greater depth, more and more evidence surfaces that this book was designed as a whole, by one mind, right down to the places, people, and numbers contained in it, and that the whole Bible points to the Savior Jesus Christ. Christ Himself made the claim: **"The volume of the book it is written of me" (Hebrews 10:7)**, and that the Law and the Prophets point to Him: **"And he said unto them, These are the words which I spake unto you, while I was yet with you, that all things must be fulfilled, which were written in the law of Moses, and in the prophets, and in the psalms, concerning me" (Luke 24:44)**.

There are, of course, all the messianic prophecies discussed earlier. But there are also those things Bible scholars call types, shadows, and allusions, which can also be prophetic but are much more subtle than obvious prophecies. This would necessarily mean they are very unlikely to have been perceived as types or shadows until after they were fulfilled, which would in turn make fabrication of details to "fit" to these types very unlikely, as will be demonstrated. In fact, we will see that it would require a greater miracle to believe that some people deliberately fabricated a story and a person to match all of the types, shadows, and allusions than if the foreshadowed events and people were real. The consistency of idioms used by many different human writers across many centuries also points to inspiration by one mind. So let's look at some of these.

THE GENESIS GENEALOGY: A HIDING PLACE FOR THE CHRISTIAN GOSPEL?

In Genesis 5 a genealogy of ten names begins with Adam and goes to Noah. Each name in the Bible of course has a specific meaning, as names do today. As Chuck Missler points out, to get to the proper meaning, a study of the original roots making up the name is needed, and sometimes this is not provided by a standard lexicon or concordance.[1]

When these ten names in Genesis 5 are studied in this way, something remarkable emerges. The ten names are, in order, Adam, Seth, Enos, Cainan, Mahalaleel, Jared, Enoch, Methuselah, Lamech, and Noah. Adam, of course, means "man." In his book Missler lists the root meanings of the other names in the genealogy: Seth means "appointed," Enosh means "mortal," Cainan (or Kenan) means "sorrow," Mahalaleel means "the Blessed God," Jared means "shall come down," Enoch means "teaching" or "commencement," Methuselah means "His death shall bring," Lamech means "despairing," and finally Noah means "rest" or "comfort." Now put these meanings in a sentence(s) in the order the names appear in the genealogy: "Man is appointed mortal sorrow. The Blessed God shall come down teaching that His death shall bring the despairing comfort."[2]

Does that sound like the Christian gospel? Would the Jewish writers have been conscious of this as they were recording this genealogy thousands of years before? No, what you have here is prophetic evidence for the author being God Himself, who "can see the end from the beginning." If the names had any different meanings or were in another order, the message would not be there or would be garbled.

---

1   Missler, *Cosmic Codes*, 71.

2   Ibid., 71–75.

A type is a figure used to foreshadow something in the future. An antitype is the future fulfillment of the type. There is an interesting verse in the prophetic book of Hosea that seems to describe this type of prophecy: **"I have also spoken by the prophets, and I have multiplied visions, and used similitudes, by the ministry of the prophets" (Hosea 12:10)**. So the Bible itself alludes to this phenomenon.

ABRAHAM AND ISAAC-PROPHETIC TYPES

One of the most powerful examples of types and antitypes is found in Genesis 22, the famous account of Abraham and Isaac, where Abraham is asked to offer his son Isaac as a sacrifice. The antitype is, of course, Jesus Christ and His sacrifice of Himself. Let's take a close look at this passage, with the Gospel accounts of Jesus in mind.

In **Genesis 22:2** it says: **"And he said, Take now thy son, thine only son Isaac, whom thou lovest, and get thee into the land of Moriah; and offer him there for a burnt offering upon one of the mountains which I will tell thee of."**

Of course we know from reading the rest of Scripture that God doesn't want human sacrifice. But looking at this whole thing prophetically, it begins to make more sense.

? How does the account of Abraham and Isaac in Genesis 22 foreshadow the sacrificial death of Christ?

Abraham's "only son": First of all, God calls Isaac Abraham's "only son." Yet we know Abraham had another son Ishmael at the time. Of course, Isaac is the son through whom it is promised future blessings will come, and so God seems to say here it is as if Isaac was Abraham's only biological son. God for His purpose views Isaac as Abraham's only son to fit the antipype, Jesus, who is God's only Son.

Same location: Furthermore, as Missler discusses, Mount Moriah where Abraham is directed to go is really a ridge, with the peak being at a location in the same region that would later be known as Golgotha. This is the location where Jesus would be crucified and made an offering for sin two thousand years later.[3]

---

3   Missler, *Cosmic Codes,* 192–193.

Parallels to the crucifixion event: Let's continue in Genesis 22:3–5: "And Abraham rose up early in the morning, and saddled his ass, and took two of his young men with him, and Isaac his son, and clave the wood for the burnt offering, and rose up, and went unto the place of which God had told him. Then on the third day Abraham lifted up his eyes, and saw the place afar off. And Abraham said unto his young men, Abide ye here with the ass, and I and the lad will go yonder and worship, and come again to you."

Notice that two men were with him, but they were not a part of the offering. Two men were crucified with Christ, but they were also not part of His offering.

Notice the expression the "third day." The journey was for three days, and during that time, because of God's command, Isaac had been as good as "dead" to Abraham for three days.[4] Yet Abraham said they would "come again unto you" to the others, meaning he believed that since God had said Isaac would have many descendants, somehow God would resurrect Isaac. This is not speculation, since Abraham's belief in resurrection is spelled out in **Hebrews 11:17–19: "By faith Abraham, when he was tried, offered up Isaac; and he that had received the promises offered up his only begotten son, of whom it was said, that in Isaac shall thy seed be called: accounting that God was able to raise him up, even from the dead; from whence also he received him in a figure."** In other words, Abraham did not actually sacrifice Isaac but was ready to, believing God would simply raise Isaac from the dead. This passage also says that **figuratively Isaac was raised from the dead, by being spared from the original command to be killed.**

Continuing in Genesis 22:6–8: "And Abraham took the wood of the burnt offering, and laid it upon Isaac his son; and he took the fire in his hand, and a knife; and they went both of them together. And Isaac spake unto Abraham his father, and said, My father: and he said, Here am I, my son. And he said, Behold the fire and the wood: but where is the lamb for a burnt offering? And Abraham said, My son, God will provide himself a lamb for a burnt offering: so they went both of them together."

Notice that the wood was laid upon Isaac's back. Remember how the wooden cross was laid upon Jesus' back as He was on His way to

---

4   Ibid., 194.

execution. And Abraham's explanation for the missing lamb is very important. Notice the wording. "God will provide **himself** a lamb." **Two thousand years later God the Father would actually carry out the offering of His Son, the Lamb of God, for sin. And in the same location.**[5]

The substitutionary sacrifice: We know that in the following verses Abraham binds Isaac and is ready to slay him when the angel intervenes and stops Abraham. Incidentally, many scholars think Isaac was not a little boy at this time, but somewhere around thirty. This would imply that he willingly cooperated and did not resist. But regardless, look at **verses 9–13: "And they came to the place which God had told him of; and Abraham built an altar there, and laid the wood in order, and bound Isaac his son, and laid him on the altar upon the wood. And Abraham stretched forth his hand, and took the knife to slay his son. And the angel of the Lord called unto him out of heaven, and said, Abraham, Abraham: and he said, Here am I. And he said, Lay not thine hand upon the lad, neither do thou anything unto him: for now I know that thou fearest God, seeing thou hast not withheld thy son, thine only son from me. And Abraham lifted up his eyes, and looked, and behold behind him was a ram caught in a thicket by his horns: and Abraham went and took the ram, and offered him up for a burnt offering in the stead of his son."**

So we see the ram offered as a substitute in place of Isaac, illustrating the idea of a substitutionary death.[6] All the sacrifices of the Old Testament, such as the Passover lamb, were meant to illustrate the idea of a substitutionary death, that is, the idea that innocent blood had to be shed to cover our sins. This is fulfilled in Jesus Christ, the innocent Lamb of God who died in our place and took upon Him our sins.

A prophecy given: Finally, let's look at **verse 14: "And Abraham called the name of that place Jehovah-jireh: as it is said to this day, In the mount of the Lord it shall be seen."**

Abraham gave this place the name "In the mount of the Lord it shall be seen." Did he know that what would be seen two thousand years later in this location was the

---

5   Ibid., 191.

6   Ibid., 194.

Father offering His Son for the sins of the world? Did Abraham know his experience was so profoundly prophetic of the sacrifice of Christ?[7]

For more on this section on Genesis 22, refer to Chuck Missler's book[8] and his account of the types and shadows in this passage. Abraham is a type of the Father, and Isaac of Jesus. Once you look closely at the text, the correspondence of the details of the types with their antitypical events in the crucifixion of Jesus Christ is indeed striking, as we have just seen.

[?] Could the fulfillment of this prophetic type have been fabricated?

Having looked at this, we need to ask some questions. **Would a Jewish writer have made so many allusions accidentally that ended up fitting the history of Jesus so well?** Or would a faker inventing Jesus pick out things for his story such as a three-day period or wood laid on the son's back (which just happened to match what they do during a Roman crucifixion)? Would he pick this particular geographic location for the crucifixion and then be able to have it stand up to archaeological scrutiny? How would he know Jesus would be crucified in this location? Would such details even be bothered with?

We can see that such an invention hypothesis is absurd.

OTHER OLD TESTAMENT PEOPLE AND EVENTS AS TYPES AND FORESHADOWINGS

Joseph as a prophetic type of Christ: There are many other types and shadows in the Scripture. Joseph, the one with the "coat of many colors," is the son of Jacob who was sold by his brothers as a slave and ended up becoming a prince in Egypt.

In Genesis 37:4–5, 8, he is hated by his brethren because of his words. The antitype is fulfilled in John 5:18, 7:7, 8:40, and many other places where Jesus is hated because of His words. In Genesis 37:18 Joseph was conspired against; in 37:23 he was insulted and stripped; in 37:28 sold (see Matthew 26:14–16, where Jesus was sold out by Judas for thirty pieces of silver); in 37:31–32 Joseph's blood

---

7   Ibid., 194.

8   Ibid., 189–195.

was presented to the father (antitype fulfilled in Hebrews 9:12); in 39:16–19 he was falsely accused, with no defense given, as Jesus was at the cross. In chapter 40:1–3, he was numbered with two transgressors (the baker and the wine steward), as Jesus was numbered with two thieves. Concerning the two transgressors, in Genesis 40:13, 19, Joseph's message to them meant blessings to one and judgment to the other, just as Jesus' message was with the two thieves. In chapter 40:20–22 Joseph had predicted the future, and it came true. In chapter 41:39–40 Joseph was exalted over the others and set over the kingdom (of Egypt). In chapter 41:46 Joseph was thirty years old when he began his work (as was Jesus in Luke 3:23).[9]

There are too many more to list here. Take them together, all one hundred-plus, then imagine these all just being coincidental or picked out by a faker. A similarly long list of types can also be made for Moses, who was an intercessor for his people, again with just too many details to be coincidence or contrived.

The book of Ruth foreshadows the history of Israel and the church: In the book of Ruth the typology is a little more subtle; yet it is discernible. Chuck Missler in points out the ways this little book is a prophetic type. The hero of the story is Boaz, in the role of "Goel," or "kinsman redeemer." His commitment to redeem the land as a near kinsman returned the land to its rightful owner, Naomi, and he took a Gentile bride, namely Ruth. Many types can be seen, too many for a complete list here, even though Ruth is such a small book. Naomi is a type of Israel, driven from her land. Ruth is the Gentile bride, as is the Gentile church the bride of Christ. Naomi gets back her land, as does Israel. The redeemer takes a Gentile bride, as does Jesus as he takes Gentiles into the church. Boaz has to be a near kinsman to perform the redemption (Jesus became human), and Boaz also had to be willing to do it (as Jesus was).[10]

Other Old Testament persons as types of Christ: Other Old Testament people seem to be types of Jesus in different aspects of His life and ministry, even though not so comprehensively as Joseph or Moses. For example, Elijah performs many similar miracles, such as the raising of the dead and the widow of Zarepath fed with the barrel of meal and the oil that miraculously did not run out (1 Kings 17), similar to what Jesus did as He multiplied the loaves and fishes. Jonah was a type of Christ in his being in the belly of the fish for three days (referred to by Jesus in

---

9   See Missler, *Cosmic Codes,* 399–404.

10   Ibid., 271–272.

Matthew 12:40). Ezekiel was a type of Christ in that he spoke in parables (Ezekiel 17:2, 20:49; compare with Matthew 13:3). David was a type, as king (2 Samuel 7:1–17, Psalm 22:16). Jeremiah was a type of Christ in his grief and trials (Jeremiah 3:20, 5:1–5, 8:20–22). Melchizedek was a type as a king and priest (Genesis 14:18–20).[11] Again, are these all just coincidence? Or would a faker bother putting together details from all these people with so many different forms of typology to make up just one person?

? How is Noah's ark a type of the resurrection of Jesus Christ and salvation through Him?

Here's a provocative example. The ark of Noah is referenced in the New Testament as a type of the resurrection of Jesus Christ and salvation through Him (1 Peter 3:18–22). In the Genesis account we see that God specified the exact day the ark came to rest: the seventeenth day of the seventh month, which represented a new beginning on the earth (Genesis 8:4). The Jewish New Year is celebrated in the fall, on the first day of the month of Tishri. When God had established the Passover in Exodus, He told Israel to consider the month of Nisan in the spring to be the first month of the year to them (Exodus 12:2).

The Jews therefore have two calendars: one civil calendar starting in the month of Tishri, and one religious calendar starting in the month of Nisan. In the book of Genesis the traditional calendar (civil) is still being referenced, with the month of Tishri being the first month, Nisan being the seventh month. The "seventh month" of Genesis, Nisan, is therefore the month in which the Passover would later be instituted. We have already seen that Christ was crucified on Passover, the fourteenth of Nisan. When did Jesus rise? Three days later on the seventeenth of Nisan! The day of Jesus' resurrection was therefore the seventeenth day of the seventh month on the traditional calendar. As noted by Missler in his discussion of this typology, **the new beginning on the earth in the time of Noah occurred on the anniversary in anticipation of our new beginning, the resurrection of Christ!**[12] Coincidence, or design?

? Do the feasts of Israel have prophetic significance?

---

11 Ibid., 397.

12 Ibid., 251–252.

Passover: Let's take a close look at the feasts of Israel, starting with the Passover, celebrated on the fourteenth of Nisan—as already noted, the day Christ was crucified. With Passover there are many other types and shadows of the death of Christ on the cross and also types anticipating salvation by His shed blood.

- The Passover feast commemorated the night when the blood of the lamb sacrificed was put on the doorposts of the houses of Israelites so that the angel of death would pass over the houses so marked. It didn't matter whether the occupants of the house were Jewish or not, the blood was what delivered them from the judgment. Notice the parallel with the blood of Christ redeeming Jews and Gentile alike.

- The Passover lambs were to be without blemish or spot (see 1 Peter 1:19 and Hebrews 9:14 for references to Jesus being as an unblemished lamb and without spot).

- On the fourteenth day of Nisan all the Passover lambs were to be killed, but the text says: **"and the whole assembly of the congregation of Israel shall kill it in the evening" (Exodus 12:6)**.

- No bones of the Passover lambs were to be broken (Exodus 12:46), and we know that when Jesus was crucified no bones were broken, which was a very unusual break in protocol for crucifixion in that day (see John 19:31–36).

- The Passover lambs were inspected on the tenth day of Nisan. Jesus presented Himself as king in Jerusalem on the tenth of Nisan.[13]

- In the Passover ceremony they mix wine with water, and if you ask a rabbi they do not know why they do this other than that it is tradition.[14] Now look at John 19:33–34, where it says that blood and water came out of Jesus' side when he was pierced.

- The Matzah, the unleavened bread used in Passover, is baked so that it is both striped and pierced. (Jesus' body was striped during the scourging and then pierced after His death.)[15]

---

13 Ibid., 247.

14 Ibid., 248.

15 Chuck Missler, *The Feasts of Israel,* tape commentary, Koinonia House Publishers, 1994.

- In fact there are three Matzahs—the middle one is broken, wrapped in a cloth, and then hidden, and they don't know why they do this other than, again, tradition![16]

When you add all these features together there seem to be way too many to be just coincidental. And yet too subtle for a faker to use.

A "code" about Jewish holy days: Here is another interesting observation. **Genesis 1:14 says this: "Let them be for signs, and for seasons, and for days, and years."** The word "seasons" here is Hamoyadim, which means "the appointed times." As Missler points out, the larger the word, the smaller are its chances of being found in a text at a given ELS interval. Hamoyadim appears only once in the book of Genesis, at the ELS interval of every seventy letters, centered around where the word "seasons" appears in the text of the above verse.[17]

According to Missler,[18] it just so happens that there are exactly seventy "appointed times" for holy days in the Jewish year: fifty-two Sabbaths, seven days of Pesach which includes Passover, the Feast of Unleavened Bread, the Feast of First Fruits, one day for the Feast of Pentecost or Hag Ha Shavuot, one day for Yom Teruah (the Feast of Trumpets, coinciding with Rosh Hashanah), one day for Yom Kippur, seven days for the Feast of Booths, or Sukkot, and finally one day of Shmini Atzeret (the Eighth Day of Assembly). These all add up to seventy holy days. Statistically this word for appointed times would be expected to occur about five times in Genesis. The odds against its occurring by chance in one location only and centered on the verse that contains that very same word in the plain text has been calculated at seventy million to one![19] Another strange "coincidence."

The other feasts of Israel also have typological allusions to Jesus Christ. We don't have the space here to go into all of them, but **let's ask an important question to those who would say the person of Jesus was invented to fit all of these types. Would a Jewish writer make up a Messiah fitting all of these very subtle features of the Jewish Feasts, only to say then that the Jews rejected Him?**

---

16 Ibid.

17 Missler, *Cosmic Codes,* 246.

18 Ibid., 245.

19 Ibid., 245–246.

FORESHADOWINGS OF CHRIST'S SACRIFICIAL DEATH

Numbers: the bronze serpent as a type of Christ's sacrifice: Here's another rather obscure one. In the book of Numbers, chapter 21, Israel was complaining against God, and a plague of venomous snakes was sent as a judgment against Israel, and people were being bitten in the camp by them. But God provided a remedy by having Moses put a brass serpent on a pole. Whoever looked upon this brass serpent on the pole would then be healed. How strange this sounds, until you dig into the typology behind it. John in his Gospel points it out for us, where a reference to this brass serpent ties it to the crucifixion of Christ: **"And as Moses lifted up the serpent in the wilderness, even so must the Son of Man be lifted up: that whosoever believeth in him should not perish, but have eternal life" (John 3:14–15)**. The snake-bitten, dying Israelites, by faith, would simply look on the brass serpent to be healed.

Missler points out that in the Bible brass is used consistently as representing the judgment of God, and serpents represent sin. So the brass serpent would represent sin judged, raised up on a pole.[20] New Testament references show Jesus was in fact made to be sin for us: **"For he hath made him to be sin for us, who knew no sin; that we might be made the righteousness of God in him" (2 Corinthians 5:21). "For what the law could not do, in that it was weak through the flesh, God sending his own Son in the likeness of sinful flesh, and for sin, condemned sin in the flesh" (Romans 8:3). "Who his own self bare our sins in his own body on the tree" (1 Peter 2:24a).**

So we see that Jesus was made sin and sin was judged, our sin, through His death on our behalf and that He "bore our sins … on the tree." So now we see what that strange episode in Numbers 21 is foreshadowing. Would anyone see that typology until after Jesus had lived it out and they realized spiritually what was going on? Yet it was prophetic of what Jesus would accomplish for us. He who was sinless, being only in the "likeness" of sinful flesh, became "sin judged," "lifted up" on the tree, so we could become His righteousness.

[?] Is there prophetic significance in the details of the Jewish tabernacle and sacrifices in the Law of Moses? Do these also point to Christ?

---

20 Ibid., 249.

There also have been many types found pointing to Christ in the design of the tabernacle and in the Old Testament sacrifices. Some of these are quite subtle, requiring careful study, but they are found to be consistent.

The Most Holy Place: For example, as mentioned above, in the whole Bible brass as a material seems to be consistently used in connection with God's judgment and purification from sin, starting with the brass or brazen altar where the sin offering is made in the tabernacle. You could not enter into the Most Holy Place in the tabernacle except by this altar of sacrifice. The high priest who entered the Most Holy Place to sprinkle the blood of the sacrifice on the mercy seat was a type of our great High Priest Jesus Christ, who offered His own blood for our sins in the heavenly Most Holy Place: **"Neither by the blood of goats and calves, but by his own blood he entered in once into the holy place, having obtained eternal redemption for us" (Hebrews 9:12).**

The scapegoat: The scapegoat offering in Leviticus 16 on the Day of Atonement foreshadows the sacrifice of Christ. On this day two goats were taken; one was killed as an offering for sin, and his blood sprinkled on the mercy seat in the Most Holy Place by the high priest. The other goat was not killed, but the high priest confessed all the sins of the people over this goat, and he was then sent out into the wilderness: **"And the goat shall bear upon him all their iniquities unto a land not inhabited" (Leviticus 16:22). So the two goats represented both a blood sacrifice and one who bears away the sin of all the people.**

The offerings and materials of the tabernacle: Many other types and foreshadowings would require a book in themselves to explain and develop here. We will get into a few of these when we discuss consistency in use of idioms below. Some of these involve the materials used in the tabernacle, the overall layout of the tabernacle, the implements used such as the menorah with its seven lamps (Christ is the "light of the world"), the table of shewbread (pointing to Christ, the "Bread of Life"), the ark with the mercy seat pointing to the atonement of Christ, the sprinkling and pouring out of the blood of the sin offering, innocent, unblemished animals used for sacrifice pointing to Christ as the innocent, unblemished Lamb of God, etc. The main thing to see is how numerous they are, how subtle and yet real they are, and how consistent. **After doing an in-depth study of these details of the Jewish tabernacle, it becomes harder and harder to imagine a New Testament inventor incorporating all of these details into his invention or**

even for the inventor noticing them to even bother with. Rather, all of these details point strongly to an overall design in the entire Bible by one mind.

THE CAMP OF ISRAEL AS A FORESHADOWING

In the book of Numbers, chapter 1, a census is taken of the men of Israel more than twenty years old and directions for how they should arrange their camp. The numbers are given for each tribe and totalled at the end of the chapter. Then in chapter 2 the details of how this multitude is to lay out their camp are given. When they set up the camp, the tabernacle was at the center, with the Levites encamped around it. The twelve tribes, excluding Levi, were grouped into four camps around the center where the Levites were, three tribes per camp as specified in Numbers 2. Each of the four camps was given a direction, that is, one camp was to be set up east of the tabernacle, the next one south, and so on. Now how could these passages contain any kind of foreshadowing or types?

Chuck Missler notes in *Cosmic Codes*[21] that the rabbis always precisely obeyed what instructions they were given, including how they camped. When they were told to camp east, this meant due east, not southeast or northeast. If their camp was wider than that of the Levites, they would then be southeast or northeast and not exactly east. This meant that each camp could only be as wide as the center camp of the Levites, and the length of each camp would be determined by the number of people in it.

The numbers of each tribe are given in chapter 1. To get the total number per camp, add the totals of each tribe in that camp together. When this is done, we get the following totals: camp of Judah = 186,400; camp of Reuben = 151,450; camp of Ephraim = 108,100; and the camp of Dan = 157,600. The camp of Judah was east, the camp of Reuben was south, the camp of Ephraim was west, and the camp of Dan was north.

Missler[22] describes how an aerial view of the camp would look: the Levites in the center like a square, the four camps of Judah, Reuben, Ephraim, and Dan surrounding it, each only as wide as the Levites' camp. The length of each camp would therefore be proportional to the number of men in it. Look at the numbers in each camp (and therefore the length of the camp), the directions they extend in,

21 Ibid., 211.
22 Ibid., 211–213.

and try to draw the aerial view of the camp. It turns out that when you draw the aerial view it formed a giant cross.[23] This is from the Old Testament! Just another coincidence? Or is this one more evidence of the design of the whole Bible, a design that points to Jesus Christ? You may never look at all these lists of names and numbers in the Bible the same way again.

CONSISTENT USE OF IDIOMS AS EVIDENCE FOR DIVINE INSPIRATION

Another interesting finding in the Bible is the consistency of the use of certain idioms (which are words used as a symbol for something that may not be obvious in their literal meaning), across the whole Bible, even with its many writers over thousands of years. As we shall see in the next chapter, the Bible exhibits remarkable unity. These idioms can be subtle, but yet the consistency is remarkable. You can test this by taking a concordance, picking a word and seeing how it is used, that is, if it is consistently associated with a certain theme or idea. Let's look at several of these, including some that have to do with the tabernacle as described above.

The word "oil"

- The word "oil" in the Bible seems to be connected with the theme of the anointing from the Holy Spirit.

- In Exodus 29:7, Aaron the priest is anointed on his head with the anointing oil to consecrate him for his ministry.

- In Psalm 89:20, David is spoken of as being anointed with holy oil and consecrated. In this case, the oil is not literal but speaks of his being empowered and chosen.

- In Psalm 92:10, the writer speaks of himself as being exalted and anointed with "fresh oil."

- Then, in the New Testament, in Hebrews 1:9, Jesus is spoken of as being anointed with the "oil of gladness" above His fellows and being exalted.

Throughout the New Testament believers anointed with the Holy Spirit are said to be empowered, renewed, consecrated, and prepared for ministry. So there is a consistency in the usage and the idea of being anointed with oil.

---

23 Ibid., see 208–213 for a complete description.

Now one caution is in order here. If you use a concordance you will of course sometimes find simply the literal usage of the word also, such as the usage in **Ezekiel 32:14: "cause their rivers to run like oil."** In this passage judgment is being described, as well as a comparison of water to oil. What we are looking for is when oil is used as an idiom, or word picture/symbol, for something else, even sometimes when literal oil is meant. **Oil is used in connection with anointing and very consistently over the whole Bible.** In the same book, in Ezekiel 16:9, Jerusalem itself is spoken of as being "anointed with oil" meaning "consecrated" after cleansing. In **2 Corinthians 1:21–22**, there is a clear connection between the idea of anointing and the Holy Spirit: **"Now he which stablisheth us with you in Christ, and hath anointed us, is God. Who hath also sealed us, and given the earnest of the Spirit in our hearts."**

"Rock"

How about the word "rock"?

- Exodus 17:6 speaks of the rock in Horeb, which Moses struck, and water came forth from the rock, so the people could drink.

- In Deuteronomy 32:4 God is called the "Rock," and again in 1 Samuel 2:2 and Psalm 18:2 and in Isaiah 17:10, where He is called "the rock of my strength."

- Going over to the New Testament (Matthew 7:24) Jesus commends the wise man who builds his house upon a rock, which in this illustration represents someone who listens to God and obeys Him, building on God and His Word, not on the world.

- In Romans 9:33 the Lord is referred to as a "rock of offense" for those who tried to be saved by the law rather than through faith in Him.

- In **1 Corinthians 10:4** Paul writes, talking about the people of Israel at the time of Moses: **"And did all drink the same spiritual drink; for they drank of that spiritual Rock that followed them: and that Rock was Christ."** So Jesus is spoken of as the Rock they drank from in a spiritual way, just as they drank physically of the literal rock. This makes spiritual sense when we think of things Jesus said such as **"If any man thirst, let him come unto me, and drink" (John 7:37),** or **"Whosoever will, let him**

take the water of life freely" (Revelation 22:17). And in 1 Peter 2:7-8 Jesus is spoken of as a "rock of offence" again.

We can see that the word "rock" consistently refers to the Lord, all across the Bible with its many writers over thousands of years. This speaks of a design of one mind, rather than many minds writing different books which more than likely would vary tremendously on how this word was used as a symbol. The same can be said for the use of the word "oil" and for some others we will look at now.

"Leaven"

- Leaven, as in baking bread, seems to be a type for sin as it is used idiomatically in the Bible. Let's see if its usage bears that out.

- In Exodus 12:15, at Passover, the leaven is to be "put away out of your houses." In Leviticus 2:11, leaven is to be left out of any meat (grain) offering unto the Lord.

- In Matthew 16:6, 11, leaven is used to symbolize the false teachings of the Pharisees, being portrayed as something that contaminates.

- It is also spoken of this way in **1 Corinthians 5:6**, where it is said of sin permitted in the church: **"Your glorying is not good. Know ye not that a little leaven leaveneth the whole lump?"**

- And **Matthew 13:33 says: "The kingdom of heaven is like unto leaven, which a woman took, and hid in three measures of meal, till the whole was leavened."** This parable, like the one before it in the same chapter, is often interpreted as being a good thing happening to the church as it grows, like the mustard seed growing into a giant tree, with the "birds of the air" nesting in its branches. But many scholars, studying the way the "birds of the air" and "leaven" are used in the rest of Scripture to indicate a bad influence, see these parables as referring to the contamination of the church with sin and false doctrine. The parable of the tares in Matthew 13:24–30 also continues the same theme of contamination of the church.

So we see the consistency in the usage of "leaven" as a contaminating influence, in different ways, by different writers from different cultures over many centuries, just as we would expect if the Bible was inspired by

one mind. **Would we expect this at all from different human writers from different walks of life and different eras? Would we expect this from a disjointed collection of books that just happened to be thrown together?**

"Wells" (as in water well)

Sometimes places are used as significant symbols by what takes place there.

- In John 4, when Jesus meets the Samaritan woman at Jacob's well, He tells her about how He will give her **"living waters" (John 4:13–15).**

- **Proverbs 10:11 says: "The mouth of a righteous man is a well of life."**

- And Isaac, whom we have already seen is used as a type for Christ, meets his bride by a well, the well of Lahairoi. This means the well of **"living waters" (Genesis 24:62).**

[?] What do these consistent idioms show?

Some of these symbols and idioms are clearer and easier to see than others. Yet we definitely notice a consistency in their usage. **This doesn't just happen with one word or symbol, but with word after word as you trace each one through the Bible.** Remember that when you do this you are not necessarily looking for the times when the word is used in a literal sense only (although sometimes these fit the pattern too) but when the word is used symbolically or idiomatically. We know that in our American culture an English word used today may not carry the same meaning as it did even one hundred years ago. **All language is like a living organism, constantly changing and growing. Yet the Bible writers were writing over thousands of years, from all walks of life, in very different cultures. Would we expect to find this consistency with so many words without any common outside influence on the writers?**

Rhetorical devices in the Bible-consistent usage

Another similar phenomenon is the rhetorical devices used in the Bible. These are literary devices such as puns, similes, metaphors, etc. We have looked at examples of these already. One example is called "enigma," where truth is expressed in mysterious language or "riddles." We see this in **Genesis 49:10, "The sceptre shall not depart from Judah, nor a lawgiver from between his feet, until Shiloh come,"** and also in Judges 14:14, where Samson uses a riddle. Another rhetorical device is called "Epanodos" or "inversion," where words are repeated in inverse order with the same sense. We see this in Genesis 10: 1–31, in the genealogy given there, and also in **Isaiah 6:10: "Make the heart of this people fat, and make their ears heavy, and shut their eyes; lest they see with their eyes, and hear with their ears, and understand with their heart, and convert, and be healed."** These are just two examples of these; there are many more like them, as Missler describes in *Cosimc Codes*.[24]

The Principle of First Mention

[?] How does the principle of first mention point to divine inspiration?

Another feature in the Bible that speaks of its design is called the principle of first mention. A good definition of this principle is given by Henry Morris in his book : "The very first time an important word or concept of Scripture is mentioned in the Bible (usually, though not always in the book of Genesis), its usage in that passage provides the foundation for its full development in later parts of the Bible."[25] Morris goes on to mention some examples.

"Light"

The word "light" is first spoken by God in **Genesis 1:3 ("Let there be light").** So light came into the universe. When Jesus came to earth, **John 3:19 says, "Light is come into the world."** And **Revelation 22:5 says, "The Lord God giveth them light."** We see that as light came into the universe, so Jesus is spoken of as light entering our world, and the Lord himself is the provider of light.

"Faith"

The word for "faith" (believed) is first used in **Genesis 15:6: "Abraham believed God, and it was counted unto him as righteousness."** In Romans 4, the whole theme of justification by faith in Jesus Christ alone, which is the essence of the gospel, is spoken of and developed using this verse about Abraham as a starting point.

---

24 Ibid., 377–393.

25 Morris, *Many Infallible Proofs*, 210.

"Hope"

The first occurrence of the word "hope" is in the book of Joshua. Joshua had come across the Jordan River to destroy Jericho; but one woman there, Rahab, had heard of what God had done for Israel and had risked her life to protect two Israelite spies who had been sent to Jericho, and Rahab put her faith in the true God. She had asked in return to have her and her family spared when Israel came to conquer Jericho. The two men told her to **"bind this line of scarlet thread in the window" (Joshua 2:18),** and as long as Rahab and her family remained in the house they would be safe. This sounds much like the blood on the doorpost at Passover causing those inside the house to be spared, and the scarlet color is important, signifying blood. The word "line" in verse 18 is the same word that is translated "hope" in every other instance in the Old Testament, and it occurs for the first time here. So this blood-colored "hope in the window"[26] was what caused her to be spared.

"Blood"

The word "blood" first appears in Genesis 4:10, where it is said that the innocent blood of Abel who was killed by Cain cries out from the ground. Abel was the first righteous man to shed his blood (see Matthew 23:35), and all the prophets who succeeded Abel who were killed unjustly were a testimony against their murderers. **Hebrews 12:24** says that the blood of Jesus **"speaketh better things than that of Abel,"** not only as a testimony of condemnation for those who reject Him, but also forgiveness and salvation for those who trust in Him as Lord and Savior:[27] **"For this is my blood of the new testament, which is shed for many for the remission of sins" (Matthew 26:28).**

"Grace"

The first use of the word "grace" is found in **Genesis 6:8**, where it is said of Noah that he **"found grace in the eyes of the Lord." Ephesians 2:8** states that **"by grace are ye saved"** and that this grace is a "gift." Yet by this grace we are **"made the righteousness of God in him" (2 Corinthians 5:21),** and we **"receive abundance of grace and of the gift of righteousness"** through Jesus Christ **(Romans 5:17).** Noah was only made just in the eyes of God by receiving

---

26   Ibid., 212.

27   Ibid., 213.

His gift of grace through faith. Likewise, we are "justified by faith," and we therefore have **"peace with God through our Lord Jesus Christ; by whom also we have access by faith into this grace wherein we stand" (Romans 5:1, 2).**

This principle of first mention is just another evidence that the entire Bible is a product of design, across many writers and time periods, rather than by chance or human arrangement alone.[28]

THE LAST BOOK OF THE BIBLE TIES IT ALL TOGETHER

? How does the book of Revelation point to divine inspiration of the Bible?

Finally, we look at the last book of the Bible, the book of Revelation. There is, of course, much symbolism in the book of Revelation, as anyone knows who has read it. What many may not realize is that this same symbolism is represented across the entire Old Testament. There are several hundred Old Testament allusions and symbols in the book of Revelation, in each of its twenty-two chapters—almost one for every verse! What we will see is that this effectively ties the whole Bible together as one supernaturally designed book. Let's look at a representative sample of these from each chapter and then ask some questions and come to some conclusions.

The "Son of Man" description

In **Revelation 1:13–16** there is a description of the Lord Jesus: **"Like unto the Son of man, clothed with a garment down to the foot, and girt about the paps with a golden girdle. His head and his hairs were white like wool, as white as snow; and his eyes were as a flame of fire; and his feet like unto fine brass, as if they burned in a furnace; and his voice as the sound of many waters."** Now notice **Daniel 7:9: "The Ancient of Days did sit, whose garment was white as snow, and the hair of his head like the pure wool; his throne was like the fiery flame, and his wheels as burning fire."** And also **Daniel 10:5–6: "A certain man clothed in linen, whose loins were girded with fine gold of Uphaz: his body also was like the beryl, and his face as the appearance of lightning, and his eyes as lamps of fire, and his arms and**

---

28 Ibid., see 210–215 for a complete discussion of this first-mention principle.

his feet like in color to polished brass, and the voice of his words like the voice of a multitude."

Notice the many striking similarities in symbolism. They are not a word-for-word match as might be the case for a copier; yet they sound as if they came from the same author. Yet these two authors lived more than five hundred years apart.

The "First and the Last"

And this is only one verse. In **Revelation 1:17** Jesus says He is **"the first and the last."** This is the same thing God says about Himself in Isaiah 41:4, 44:6 and other places.

The "Tree of Life"

In Revelation 2:7 the "tree of life" is mentioned; it is also mentioned in Genesis 2:9, Genesis 3:22, 24, and Proverbs 11:30.

The "seven spirits of God"

In Revelation 4:5 the "seven spirits of God" are mentioned. **Isaiah 11:2** describes seven attributes of the Spirit of God: **"And the spirit of the Lord (1) shall rest upon Him, the spirit of wisdom (2) and understanding (3), the spirit of counsel (4) and might (5), the spirit of knowledge (6) and of the fear of the Lord (7)."** So the seven spirits are explained in Isaiah 11, where they are really seen to be seven attributes of one Spirit. And in Exodus 25:37, the lampstand (which is fed by the oil, which we have already seen symbolizes the Spirit) has seven lights. Here we see the consistency of the symbol of seven being the complete number of God and in connection with the Spirit of God, yet not word-for-word copying and too subtle to say that John the writer of the book of Revelation just lifted this idea out of the referenced Old Testament texts.

Symbols of judgment tie the Old Testament together as one book

Next look at **Revelation 6:12–13: "And I beheld when he had opened the sixth seal, and lo, there was a great earthquake, and the sun became black as sackcloth of hair, and the moon became as blood. And the stars of heaven fell unto the earth, even as a fig tree casteth her untimely figs, when she is shaken of a mighty wind."** Now look at **Isaiah 50:3: "I clothe the** heavens with blackness, and I make sackcloth their covering." Isaiah 34:4 states: "And all the host of heaven shall be dissolved, and the heavens shall be rolled together as a scroll: and all their host shall fall down, as the leaf falleth off from the vine, and as a falling fig from the fig tree." And finally **Joel 2:10**: "The earth shall quake before them; the heavens shall tremble: the sun and the moon shall be dark, and the stars shall withdraw their shining."

These passages use common language and symbols associated with the Lord's judgment and also may point to a future time when there may be a more literal fulfillment, such as meteors falling from the sky or a great cloud cover or the heavens themselves being changed. The point here is not to try to figure out how much is literal and how much is figurative. **The main thing to see in these examples is how so many of these Old Testament symbols are incorporated into one book, the book of Revelation, and to see how they not only show the unity of symbology of the Old Testament, but how the whole Old Testament with all its symbols can be amazingly tied together in the final book of the Bible, Revelation.**

The book of Revelation demonstrates one mind behind the Scriptures

Would a human author, uninspired, just happen to use these symbols so consistently the way the Old Testament uses them? Would he bother using so many, with such variety, and would he be able to write something that made sense and used Old Testament symbols, some of which are very subtle, to predict future events? Is this what the evidence points to?

Or is it easier to believe the same mind inspired all the writers, and so this is why the same basic symbology was used, despite there being so many Old Testament writers from different cultures over many centuries, and the writer of Revelation was also so inspired to take these hundreds of symbols used in the Bible and put them together in a powerful, majestic revelation? Could the evidence lead to this conclusion?

TYPES AND FORESHADOWINGS-CONCLUSION

The divine inspiration and design of the Bible can be believed and seen from the evidence; the view that the Bible was solely a human product can also be believed but must be believed in spite of the evidence. Last, we will look at some other unique features of the Bible.

CONCLUSION

THE BIBLE HAS BEEN PROVEN!

If one does not want to believe the Bible is a God-inspired book, but rather a human product alone, then he or she needs to be able to explain away an extremely large number of unique qualities of the Bible. If a person does want to believe it is the Word of God, then the question is: do the features of the Bible we have observed fit this belief? Is the Bible what you would expect from a divinely inspired text?

Unique book, precise transmission, and reliable history

We observe the following features: a remarkable unity despite diversity in authorship, culture and time period; unprecedented wide circulation and translation; the survival of the Bible despite its being persecuted as no other book; its uniquely powerful impact and teachings all these setting it apart from other books.

No evidence of invention or deception

Furthermore, we would expect that such a book from God would contain no invention or deception. What we find is that the theory the biblical writers invented history does not hold up to critical examination and even exposes poor scholarship by some so-called scholars. We would expect there would be some on-the-surface discrepancies because of having independent writers who did not collaborate with one another to invent material. But if this is a book of God these discrepancies should be able to be resolved and explained satisfactorily. This is in fact what we do find, that in many cases a very simple explanation neatly clears up a "contradiction" that had some scholars denying the authenticity of the text without adequate investigation.

Prophetic proof

God Himself challenges us to examine what He predicts and also what comes to pass and, by doing so, see that only He has the unique ability to know the future perfectly. This sets Him apart from all other "gods" or idols. And we see that when this claim is tested it is proven, whether we are talking about the life of Jesus, Jewish history, or specific places and nations. What we see is proven prediction and fulfillment, unlike any other book or prophet. We see a qualitative difference between the vague "prophecies" of New Age "prophets" and the precise, 100 percent accurate predictions of the biblical prophets.

Scientific foreknowledge as proof of divine inspiration

We would expect no proven scientific errors in a book from God and would also expect many scientific insights which had not been discovered at the time of writing that people would not likely have gotten from the contemporary culture. And, sure enough, we find so much advanced scientific insight from many fields of science, that was not discovered in many cases until modern times that we have to either conclude the Bible writers were given "inside information" from their Creator or they were all just lucky guesses. And we find that the so-called "scientific mistakes" in the Bible put forth by critics turn out to come from either misinterpretations of the text, translation errors or superimposing the surrounding culture's beliefs onto the Bible's text. And other "holy books" contain proven scientific errors, unlike the Bible.

Numerical design of text of Bible as proof of divine inspiration

Since God has created a universe that is highly structured and mathematically precise, if the Bible is His Word, we would not be shocked to find the same type of precision in its text. We would definitely be impressed if we found features that were either unlikely or impossible for humans alone to put into the text. This is exactly what we find, and in many cases it takes modern computer technology to dig them out. We find complex interlocking patterns involving the number seven and other numbers as well, some of which are beyond the ability of the human writers to contrive.

"Bible codes" provide evidence for divine inspiration

Another mathematical phenomenon in the Bible, the "codes," or "equidistant letter sequences" (ELS), although sometimes misused and subject to criticism from unsound methodology used by some popularizers, are another feature that is actually consistent with a God who is both the Master Mathematician and the one who knows the "end from the beginning." Encoded words and phrases found in the biblical text seem to defy all attempts of critics to show they could have arisen by chance or by human design alone. In the author's opinion no convincing disproof of the code phenomena has been brought forth. This evidence would seem to be uniquely targeted to our skeptical, computer-literate generation and fits perfectly with God's methodology.

Subtle types and foreshadowings point to one mind behind the Scriptures

The more we dig into the text, the more we see that even small details fit into a large design, and that design points to the grand theme of Jesus Christ and His redemption of humankind. This is just what we would expect of the book of God. There are so many subtle types and foreshadowings: in a person such as Joseph or Moses; or events such as the account of Abraham and Isaac in Genesis 22; or in dates given such as the date of the landing of the ark; or the numbers in each camp of Israel; or the details of the practices in the feasts of Israel; and many others. Furthermore, all of these are all pointing in some way to Jesus Christ and are prophetic of His life. This leads to two conclusions. One is that it is extremely unlikely someone would even perceive these subtle types and shadows to fabricate a story to fit them, since they would not be discerned until after the fulfillments happened. The second is that the Old Testament writers could not have just happened to include these types and allusions by chance and have them be so precisely fulfilled, especially in the life of Christ.

Consistent use of symbols and idioms point to one mind behind Scripture

Finally, we find the consistent use of symbols, idioms, and rhetorical devices across the entire Bible further cementing its unity and the evidence for its design. The way words are used for the first time and then developed thematically is a consistent pattern also fitting with inspiration by one mind. The last book of the Bible, Revelation, not surprisingly illustrates the unity of symbols used in the Old Testament and also combines and summarizes these into a final message pointing, of course, to Jesus Christ. Most important, all these features are there simultaneously and interlock with all the codes, mathematical features of sevens, prophecies and so on.

Conclusion: The Bible is truly a miraculous book!

What are the possibilities? The Bible has properties that cannot be explained by chance. So many different things are contained therein that are like wheels within wheels, each one with astronomical odds of random occurrence. How could they all interlock by chance and much less have a coherent, powerful book come out?

Fabrication theories fail completely

Would a fabricated or contrived text demonstrate the properties we observe? It would have to maintain unity and power to impact, be consistent across many manuscripts, and stand up unfailingly to archaeological investigation. It must show no evidence of collusion and yet have all seeming discrepancies able to be resolved. It must also contain hundreds of successful predictions of events, places, and people, with no proven false predictions. It must also somehow have correct scientific insights thousands of years in advance, intricate patterns of sevens and other numbers that are beyond the reach of chance occurrence or human contrivance, and it must contain many complex encoded words, including those that predict future events, interwoven into the text. Finally it must also contain a great variety of detailed but subtle types and foreshadowings that all nevertheless point consistently to one Person and message. Again such a contrivance would be a greater miracle, especially without an adequate cause to explain it, than a divinely inspired Bible.

A final challenge to you, the reader

We need to ask: "What else could God have done to show it was Him giving us the message of the Bible?" An even more important question is: "What will you do about it?" What we have reviewed over all these pages has not just been for the purpose of an intellectual exercise. The whole of the book, as we have seen, points to Jesus Christ.

Our predicament

God is holy, all-knowing, and pure. To be in His presence therefore requires perfect purity and sinlessness (Matthew 5:48), because His very presence would destroy anything less, much as the bright sun can't help eliminating darkness. This means the best of us, based on our own imperfect merits and record of deeds, would not be allowed to live in His presence for eternity (Romans 3:23).

God's solution and our response

But the whole Bible demonstrates how God solved our dilemma for us. God solved our sin problem in the person of Jesus Christ by His dying on the cross, and rising from the dead to pay the penalty for our sins and to purchase a place in heaven for us (Isaiah 53:6). We can be completely forgiven and made blameless and fit for heaven by trusting in the finished work of Jesus Christ (Acts 16:30). We don't get to heaven by trying to perfect ourselves by our own efforts which we cannot do but by our trusting solely in the redemption provided by Jesus Christ, who is both God and perfect man. He offered himself on the cross as the atoning sacrifice for our sins (1 John 2:2). Therefore, our subsequent good deeds are done not to earn heaven, but in gratitude for what God has already done for us (Ephesians 2:8–10).

The Bible is complex, but the message is simple

We are in need of God's forgiveness, and we need to acknowledge our unworthiness. We have broken God's laws and fallen short of His perfect standard. We need to be willing to turn from whatever God shows us is wrong in our lives (this is called *repentance*) and put our trust in the finished work of Christ on the cross to save us (Romans 3:20–28). It is praying a prayer, confessing to Him that we are sinners, transferring our trust from ourselves and our own works to Jesus Christ alone and His finished work of atonement on the cross for us. It is inviting Him into our hearts and lives, in our own words (Romans 10:8–10). There is no other way to be able to live in the presence of a loving, just, holy God. To be away from His presence for eternity is called hell, the only state of existence left for those who choose to exclude God from their lives. God will give each of us our choice.

The Bible points to a personal relationship with God

The Bible itself is not to be worshipped. Rather it points you to a personal walk with its Author, by His design, a walk of obedience, trust, and love. The Bible is the only book where the Author, the Holy Spirit, can live inside of you as you read it and shine His light on every word. The Bible is a Living Word that points to a Living God. It does not point to a dead idol, ritual, or religion, but a vibrant love relationship with the Living Word, who became flesh and died and rose again, nailing our sins to His cross (Colossians 2:13–15), that we might not live apart from Him, but rather walk in perfect joy and holiness with Him forever.

Trusting in Christ and inviting Him to live in your heart is just the beginning of growth. His Word has intrinsic power and is engrafted into our very souls. Meditate on each verse. The promises God gives in the Bible are exceedingly great and precious and are meant to be meditated on, recited back to oneself, memorized, taken into your heart, and believed on. They will have a supernatural effect on your life, and **this fact is the greatest evidence of all that the Bible is indeed God's inspired Word.** God has given us proof that this is His authentic Word, able to provide us with all the comfort, peace, guidance, and hope we need to walk with Him throughout our whole life and on into eternity.

BIBLIOGRAPHY

Archer, Gleason L. *A Survey of Old Testament Introduction.* Chicago, IL: Moody Press, revised and expanded edition, 1994.

Anderson, Sir Robert. *The Coming Prince.* Grand Rapids, MI: Kregel Classics, reprinted 1957.

Barnett, Paul. *Is the New Testament Reliable? A Look at the Historical Evidence.* Downers Grove, IL: Intervarsity Press, 1986.

Blanchard, John. *Does God Believe in Atheists?* Auburn, MA: Evangelical Press, 2000.

Bruce, F. F. *The Books and the Parchments.* London, England.: Pickering & Inglis, revised edition, 1971.

—. *The Canon of Scripture.* Downers Grove, IL.: Intervarsity Press, 1988.

—. *The New Testament Documents: Are They Reliable?* Leicester, England: Intervarsity Press, fifth edition, 1943, reprinted 1997.

Caner, Ergun Mehmet & Caner, Emir Fethi. *Unveiling Islam.* Grand Rapids, Mich.: Kregel Publications, 2002.

Cornuke, Robert. *The Lost Shipwreck of Paul.* Bend, OR: Global Publishing Services, 2003.

Decker, Ed & Hunt, Dave. *The God Makers, A Shocking Exposé of What the Mormon Church Really Believes.* Eugene, OR: Harvest House Publishers, updated and expanded edition, 1997.

Decker, Ed & Matrisciana, Caryl. *The God Makers II, Startling New Revelations About Modern Day Mormonism.* Eugene, OR: Harvest House Publishers, 1993.

Eastman, Mark, and Chuck Missler. *The Creator Beyond Time and Space.* Costa Mesa, CA: The Word for Today, 1996.

Eastman, Mark, and Chuck Smith. *The Search for Messiah.* Fountain Valley, CA: Joy Publishing, 1996.

Freedman, David Noel & Grant, Robert M. *The Secret Sayings of Jesus, A Modern Translation of the Gospel of Thomas with Commentary.* New York, NY: Barnes & Noble Books by arrangement with Doubleday & Co., Inc., 1993.

Guthrie, Donald. *New Testament Introduction.* Downers Grove, IL: Intervarsity Press, revised edition, 1990.

Habermas, Gary. *The Historical Jesus: Ancient Evidence for the Life of Christ.* Joplin, MO: College Press Publishing Co., 1996.

Habermas, Gary & Licona, Michael. *The Case for the Resurrection of Jesus.* Grand Rapids, MI: Kregel Publications, 2004.

Haley, John W. *Alleged Discrepancies of the Bible.* New Kensington, PA: Whitaker House, 1992.

A Cup of Trembling: Jerusalem and Bible Prophecy. Eugene, OR: Harvest House Publishers, 1995.

Hunt, Dave. *Cosmos, Creator, and Human Destiny, Answering Darwin, Dawkins, and the New Atheists.* Bend, OR: The Berean Call, 2010.

—. *In Defense of the Faith: Biblical Answers to Challenging Questions.* Eugene, OR: Harvest House Publishers, 1996.

Jeffrey, Grant. *Armageddon: Appointment with Destiny.* Toronto, Ont.: Frontier Research Publications Inc., 1997.

—. *The Handwriting of God: Sacred Mysteries of the Bible.* Toronto, Ont.: Frontier Research Publications Inc., 1997.

—. *The Mysterious Bible Codes.* Nashville: Word Publishing, 1998.

—. *The Signature of God: Astonishing Biblical Discoveries.* Toronto, Ont.: Frontier Research Publications, 1996.

Kitchen, K. A. *On The Reliability of the Old Testament.* Grand Rapids, Mich.: William B. Eerdmans Publishing Co., 2003.

Lightfoot, Neil R. *How We Got the Bible.* Abilene, TX: Abilene Christian University Press, 1986.

Lutzer, Erwin W. *Seven Reasons Why You Can Trust the Bible.* Chicago: Moody Press, 1998.

McDowell, Josh, *Evidence That Demands a Verdict*, San Bernardino, Calif.: Here's Life Publishers Inc., 1979.

—. *More Evidence That Demands A Verdict (Evidence That Demands A Verdict Vol. II)*, Nashville, TN: Thomas Nelson Publishers, 1993.

—. *New Evidence That Demands a Verdict*, Nashville: Thomas Nelson Publishers, 1999.

—. *A Ready Defense.* Nashville: Thomas Nelson Publishers, 1993.

McDowell, Josh, and Bill Wilson. *He Walked Among Us: Evidence for the Historical Jesus.* San Bernardino, CA: Here's Life Publishers Inc., 1988.

Missler, Chuck. *Cosmic Codes: Hidden Messages from the Edge of Eternity.* Coeur D'Alene, ID: Koinonia House, 1999.

—. "The Christmas Story," audiotapes and notes, Coeur D'Alene, ID: Koinonia House, 1994.

—. "Daniel's 70 Weeks," audiotapes and notes, Coeur D'Alene, ID: Koinonia House, 1991.

—. "Footprints of the Messiah," audiotapes and notes, Coeur D'Alene, ID: Koinonia House, 1992.

—. "How We Got Our Bible," audiotapes and notes, Coeur D'Alene, ID: Koinonia House, 2000.

—. "Learn the Bible in 24 Hours," CD ROM, Coeur D'Alene, ID: Koinonia House, 2000.

—. *Personal Update* magazine, Coeur D'Alene, ID: Koinonia House; the following editions: June 1999, February 2000, April 2000, July 2000, June 2001, July 2001, March 2002.

Moller, Dr. Lennart. *The Exodus Case: New Discoveries Confirm the Historical Exodus.* Copenhagen NV, Denmark: Scandinavia Publishing House, 2002.

Morey, Robert A. *Horoscopes and the Christian.* Minneapolis, MN: Bethany House Publishers, 1981.

Morris, Henry. *Many Infallible Proofs: Evidences for the Christian Faith.* Green Forest, AK: Master Books, 1974, updated edition 1996.

—. *The Remarkable Record of Job.* Green Forest, AK: Master Books, 1988.

Moshay, G. J. O. *Who Is This Allah?* Gerrards Cross Bucks, United Kingdom: Dorchester House Publications, 1994.

Oakland, Roger, Chuck Missler and Dave Hunt. "Countdown to Eternity" video, produced by Eternal Productions in cooperation with Calvary Chapel, 1997.

Price, Randall. *Searching for the Original Bible.* Eugene, OR: Harvest House, 2007.

—. *The Stones Cry Out.* Eugene, OR: Harvest House, 1997.

Schafi, Abd El. *Behind the Veil: Unmasking Islam*, Caney, KS: Pioneer Book Company, 2002.

Snelling, Andrew A. *Earth's Catastrophic Past, Vol. I and II, Geology, Creation & The Flood.* Dallas, TX: Institute For Creation Research, 2009.

Strobel, Lee. *The Case for Christ.* Grand Rapids, MI: Zondervan Publishing House, 1998.

—. *The Case for Faith.* Grand Rapids, MI: Zondervan Publishing House, 2000.

—. *The Case for the Real Jesus.* Grand Rapids, MI: Zondervan Publishing House, 2007.

Weldon, John, with Clifford and Barbara Wilson. *Decoding the Bible Code: Can We Trust the Message?* Eugene, OR: Harvest House Publishers, 1998.

CHAPTER SUBJECT OUTLINE

IF YOU'RE A FAN OF THIS BOOK, PLEASE TELL OTHERS...

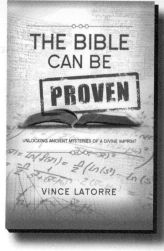

- Write about *The Bible Can Be Proven* on your blog, Twitter, MySpace, and Facebook page.

- Suggest *The Bible Can Be Proven* to friends.

- When you're in a bookstore, ask them if they carry the book. The book is available through all major distributors, so any bookstore that does not have *The Bible Can Be Proven* in stock can easily order it.

- Write a positive review of *The Bible Can Be Proven* on www.amazon.com.

- Send my publisher, HigherLife Publishing, suggestions on websites, conferences, and events you know of where this book could be offered at media@ahigherlife.com.

- Purchase additional copies to give away as gifts.

CONNECT WITH ME...

To learn more about *The Bible Can Be Proven*, please contact me at:

Vincent Latorre

Latorreq@aol.com

You may also contact my publisher directly:

HigherLife Publishing

400 Fontana Circle

Building 1 – Suite 105

Oviedo, Florida 32765

Phone: (407) 563-4806

Email: media@ahigherlife.com

ABOUT THE AUTHOR

Vince Latorre's search to reconcile the Bible with science and history led to many hours in libraries and bookstores sifting through several hundred books and articles on science, textual criticism, and theology. Through his exhaustive research, the author came face to face with the powerful scientific evidence for creation as well as the evidence for the historical reliability of the Bible. In his latest book, *The Bible Can Be Proven*, Vince Latorre shares the results of his research to strengthen believers and inform honest seekers.

Vince Latorre is a professional accountant and certified lay speaker in the United Methodist Church.